Phineas Camp Headley

The Hero Boy; or , the Life and Deeds of Lieut.-Gen. Grant

Phineas Camp Headley

The Hero Boy; or , the Life and Deeds of Lieut.-Gen. Grant

ISBN/EAN: 9783337189723

Printed in Europe, USA, Canada, Australia, Japan

Cover: Foto ©ninafisch / pixelio.de

More available books at **www.hansebooks.com**

OR,

THE LIFE AND DEEDS

OF

LIEUT.-GEN. GRANT:

BY

REV. P. C. HEADLEY,

AUTHOR OF "NAPOLEON," "JOSEPHINE," "WOMEN OF THE BIBLE," ETC

NEW YORK:
WILLIAM H. APPLETON, 92 GRAND STREET.
1865.

TO

JESSE R. GRANT,

THE FATHER OF THE BOY;

WHOSE EARLY HISTORY, LIKE THAT OF HIS

ILLUSTRIOUS SON,

AND WHOSE SERENE OLD AGE

BRIGHT WITH THE LIGHT OF CHRISTIAN HOPE,

PRESENTS A BEAUTIFUL EXAMPLE

OF SUCCESS IN LIFE,

This Volume

IS GRATEFULLY DEDICATED

BY

THE AUTHOR.

PREFACE.

The author of this volume acceded the more readily to the desire of others, in preparing it, because it was for *boys*. To interest and instruct them, who are to bear the burdens of the church and state in the peaceful future which must ere long succeed the stormy period, has been the inspiring hope. The materials were from immediate friends of the subject of biography, or other reliable sources, so far as the years previous to the Great Rebellion are concerned. The incidents of his early life are, for the most part, from data furnished by General Grant's father. He stated that the published stories of purchasing a horse of Farmer Ralston, and the quarrel with his Canada cousin—also letters purporting to be his early correspondence—are fictions entirely; they are therefore omitted. He made the pencil sketch from which the view of Point Pleasant, and the humble home of General Grant's infancy, were engraved. Larke's compilation, and Carleton's "Days and Nights on the Battle Field," have been valuable books of reference.

The deeds of the Lieutenant-General since the conflict opened, are spread abroad in official and unofficial records, so that no serious error is possible, unless by singular oversight, or misprint of the pages. It is believed to be a correct outline of a hero's life.

And, to give a more distinct impression of the war field over which General Grant moved, outline maps are added. A glossary of military terms is also given. The pages were not written to glorify a military chieftain, and add to the ephemeral productions of the day, but to present to our youth a record reliable as the sources of information could make it, of an unostentatious, earnest, brave, and successful man. It is offered to the homes of the people with the prayer that the memorial of a distinguished general who sprang from a humble dwelling in the wilderness of the West, may aid in moulding character for the country's need, and for the "Better Land."

NOTE.

This volume is the first of a series for boys, entitled "The Young American's Library of Modern Heroes." The biography of the brilliant astronomer, patriot, and commander, General O. M. Mitchel, is in press; to be followed by "The Life of Captain John Ericsson; or, The Miner Boy and his Monitor"—a biography of rare interest, from authentic sources. Other volumes will be added to the series.

CONTENTS.

CHAPTER I.

The Grant Family—The Orphan Boy—Home and Birth of Ulysses—How he got his Name—His School Days—Don't know what Can't means, ... 1

CHAPTER II.

The "Log Hauling"—The Young Patriot wants an Education—His Opportunities—How he becomes Cadet—West Point Military Academy—Where and What is it?—Young Grant as Cadet—His Classmates—He Graduates—Never quarrels, ... 8

CHAPTER III.

The Young Lieutenant—He joins his Regiment—Goes to Louisiana—Is in the Mexican War—The First Battle—The Long March—Vera Cruz—Returns to the States—Is Married—Ordered to Oregon—Resigns, ... 17

CHAPTER IV.

The Captain turns Farmer—He is not Afraid of Work—In the Leather Trade—The Call to Arms again—Captain offers his Service—His First Post of Duty—Is appointed Colonel, ... 27

CHAPTER V.

Three Months Men—Colonel Grant joins his Regiment—In Camp—Off for the Field of Action—A Rapid March—Promotion—Grant loses no Time—He is Commissioned Brigadier-General—A Good Story—Headquarters at Cairo—A True American—He seizes Paducah—Secession Flags—A Noble Proclamation—The "Stove-pipe General," 30

CHAPTER VI.

Columbus—Exchange of Prisoners—Battles—General Grant writes to his Father—Cares for the Wounded—A New Department of Command—Prepares for a Grand Movement upon the Enemy—His Strategy—Issues Orders—The Advance, ... 47

CHAPTER VII.

The Gunboats Move up the Tennessee—Delay—Open Fire upon Fort Henry—The Fort Surrenders—Right on to Fort Donelson—The Fleet Disabled—Foote Wounded—The Forces of Grant close on the Fortress—The Terrific Contest—The Victory—Promotion—Striking Contrasts, ... 61

CHAPTER VIII.

The more the Hero does, the more is he expected to do—His Kingdom Enlarged—Anecdote about his Habits—Major-General Grant's First Work—Congratulations—Martial Movements—No Plundering allowed—Up the River—Sword presented—Scours the Country—Moves toward Corinth—Preparations for Battle, ... 87

CHAPTER IX.

Saturday Night—General Grant a Scout—The Signals of Battle—The Combat Opens—The Scenes of Carnage—The Critical Hour—The Heroic Onset—The Victory—General Grant's Bravery—The Good News in New York and Washington—A Speech in favor of Grant, who is assailed—Scenes on the Battle Field of Shiloh, .. 103

CONTENTS.

CHAPTER X.

Corinth the next Goal of the Army—Getting ready to March—The "Grand Army of the Tennessee"—The Advance—The Siege—The Surrender—The Pursuit—The captured Sheep—General Halleck's Farewell—Grant at Memphis—How he deals with Traitors, 119

CHAPTER XI.

The Position of our Army—The Grand Programme—Armies in Motion—Bragg tries to Deceive Grant—The Advance toward Iuka—The Fight—The Victory—The Stampede—General Grant's Words of Cheer—Despatch from the President—A Curiosity, ... 134

CHAPTER XII.

A larger Field, and bolder Plans—Getting Ready—Skirmishes—Cotton—Negroes—Jews—Speculators—Grant's Sense of Honor—Vicksburg and the Mississippi—Farragut's Fleet—The Bombardment—Failure—A worthless Canal—The Noble Logan—Holly Springs Surrenders to the Rebels—Amusing Scenes, ... 145

CHAPTER XIII.

The Grand Plan Deranged—Sherman's Flotilla—His Assault on Vicksburg—Defeat— Fatal Ambition—Disloyalty— President's Proclamation of Freedom, and General Grant—Vicksburg again—Canals around the City a Failure—The Copperhead and the Bush, . . 156

CHAPTER XIV.

A New Plan—Admiral Farragut's Ship—Porter's Fleet—Hot Work—Thrilling Scene—Grierson's Raid — Ludicrous Scenes — Banks and Grant—Passing Grand Gulf Batteries—The Grand Advance—The Night March—The Night Battle—Port Gibson Taken—Governor Yates and the Victory, ... 164

CHAPTER XV.

Sherman—Deceiving the Enemy—General Grant's Wisdom, and humane Care of the Men—Ready to move again—Governor Pettus frightened—Grant's Despatch—A Battle—The Capital taken—News—Crossing the River—The Investment and Assault—The Attack repeated—The Siege—The Messenger deserts—The Prison Fortress—Amusing Incidents, ... 180

CHAPTER XVI.

The captured Courier—Grant and the Letters—The Sappers and Miners—How they do their strange Work—All is ready—The Explosion—The Advance—The Flag of Truce—The Message, and General Grant's Answer—The Capitulation—The Fourth of July in Vicksburg—The Glad Tidings—The Loss and Gain—The President and General Grant—Scenes after the Fall of the Fortress—Bill of Fare—The Dead—Hurrah! 195

CHAPTER XVII.

The Eastern Army—Port Hudson falls—The "Father of Waters" open—Joe Johnston pursued—Jeff. Davis's Library found—Jackson surrenders—General Grant's care of his Soldiers—His Politics—Anecdotes—Looks after his Department—Mrs. Grant visits him—General Grant goes to Memphis—A splendid Reception, . 219

CHAPTER XVIII.

General Grant at New Orleans—His Simplicity in Dress—Reviews the Thirteenth Army Corps—Sad Accident—Recovers from the serious Injuries—He cares for the Soldier in little things—A new and larger Command—Chickamauga and Chattanooga—An amusing Incident—The Feelings of the Rebels—General Grant at Chattanooga—Clearing the Track—Jeff. Davis on Lookout, ... 233

CHAPTER XIX.

Preparations for Battle again—The successful Trap—The brave Advance of General Wood—The Contest opened—The Three Days' Fight—General Hooker above the Clouds—General Grant's Despatch — General Bragg's—General Meigs's Despatch — General Grant at the Coffin of Colonel O'Meara, ... 245

CHAPTER XX.

General Sherman at Knoxville—The President and the Victories—Major-General Grant's Congratulations—Colonel Ely, the Indian Sachem's Tribute—Excitement in Washington—A Medal—Other Honors—Hon. Mr. Washburn's Speech—Grant's untiring Activity—Visits a sick Child—He is invited to a Banquet—Accepts the Honor—The brilliant Festival, ... 273

CHAPTER XXI.

The Spring Campaign—General Grant at Washington—Scenes in the Hotel—The Levee—The Presentation of the Commission of Lieutenant-Generalship—General Grant's Reply—The summit of Honor—He visits the Potomac Army—The Fancy Soldier—The Crisis, ... 291

CHAPTER XXII.

The Advance—Richmond—The path to the Rebel Capital—The "Wilderness"—The opening of Battle—The Days of Carnage—The Death of Sedgwick—Of General Rice—General Grant's Strategy—General Butler—Sheridan—Sherman—The grand flanking March to North Anna—Chickahominy—James River—What the Rebels think, ... 209

Definition of Military Words, ... 337

CHAPTER I.

The Grant Family—The Orphan Boy—Home and Birth of Ulysses—How he got his Name—His School Days—Don't know what Can't means.

ABOUT two hundred and fifty years ago, two brothers, by the name of Grant, came from Scotland to the wilderness of the New World. The grandfather of Ulysses settled in Pennsylvania. His son, Jesse R. Grant, was born in Westmoreland County, January, 1794. With his father's family he went to the great and distant valley of the West, in the spring of 1799,—sixteen years after the war of the Revolution closed. There were no canals or railroads then. The usual mode of emigration was to carry the family and household goods in the canvas-covered wagon. The toilsome journey was made along rough roads, through dark forests, and across rapid streams. At length the bruised and soiled vehicle which carried his earthly possessions stopped in Ohio. Not a single State had been formed out of the extensive region called the Northwestern Territory, lying between the Alleghany and Rocky Mountains. It was at one time claimed by the

French under the name of Louisiana. A large portion of this rich country was the wide hunting ground of the Indians. Often, while the white settler was chopping in the woods to clear his land, the bullet or tomahawk of the savage, from a thicket or behind a tree, would strike him; and, falling dead, his body would be found, sometimes a great while after, by the dear ones he left in his cabin. The celebrated Tecumseh was the mighty chief and warrior there. Bloody battles had been fought not far from Mr. Grant's humble dwelling.

In 1804, when the Reserve became partially settled, Mr. Grant removed to Deerfield. Here he died, leaving Jesse fatherless. To use his own words:

"I was left a poor orphan boy at eleven years of age, with none to guide my way through the world. I saw that I was destined to get my living by the sweat of my brow, and that it was necessary to select some calling that promised to pay the best; so I learned the tanning business. I followed that until I was sixty, and then retired."

Thus did young Jesse, from the earliest childhood inured to pioneer life, with God's blessing, carve his way alone, to an honorable position in society, and to wealth.

When the last war with England threw the country into excitement, and unsettled to some extent its business, the family removed to Maysville, Ky. In 1815, when hostilities ceased, Jesse returned to Portage County, Ohio, and commenced the business of tanning in Ravenna. Fever and ague, once the scourge of the West, compelled

BIRTHPLACE OF GENERAL GRANT.—Page 3.

young Grant to go South again in 1820. A few months later he returned to Ohio. This charming region had already attracted enterprising people from the colonies East. An interesting peculiarity in the climate is alluded to by early residents in their accounts of the country; and that is, the *cool* evenings. So much of the land was shaded by forests, that the ground did not get warm during the day; and soon as the sun dropped behind the green ocean of verdure, the air was cold at midsummer there, as in our autumn here. This made the shining bosom of the wide rivers especially cheering to those whose humble dwellings stood on the banks. Among these was the house of an emigrant from Pennsylvania, who came two years before. His daughter, Hannah Simpson, who was born only twenty-five miles from Philadelphia, in Montgomery County, a woman of character and prudent economy, won the heart of Jesse. In June, 1821, they were married. Their first home was at Point Pleasant on the Ohio River, in Clermont County, Ohio. It is a beautiful spot, below the mouth of Indian Creek. You will see by the map, that the Little Miami River separates Clermont County from Hamilton, whose principal town is Cincinnati, justly called the "Queen City" of the West.

In this new home by the Ohio a son was born, April 27th, 1822. The humble dwelling is still standing. It is "a small one-story frame cottage." It was not worth more than two or three hundred dollars before the war.

But every victory gained by the general, or a promotion, adds in the owner's estimate another hundred dollars to the price of the cottage." Strangers not unfrequently stop, on their way down the river, to see the recently unknown and unnoticed home.

The first question about him, was one which has been asked over every child: "What shall we name him?" I knew a little girl ten years of age, for whom it was not answered. The parents could not agree upon a name, so they called her "Tommy," leaving her to select a name whenever she could suit herself. I have often wondered how she succeeded in making a choice among all the names she had heard and seen.

I will give you the origin of our Western boy's name, in the language of his father, who wrote me about it:

"The maternal grandmother was quite a reader of history, and had taken a great fancy to Ulysses, the great Grecian general, who defeated the Trojans by his strategy of the wooden horse. She wished the child named Ulysses. His grandfather wanted to have him named Hiram. So both were gratified by naming him Hiram Ulysses. When I wrote to Mr. Hamer, then a member of Congress from our district, to procure the appointment of cadet, he wrote to the War Department, and gave his name 'Ulysses S. Grant.' And we could not get it altered. Simpson was his mother's maiden name. We had a son named Simpson, and Mr Hamer confounded the two names.

We regarded it a matter of but little consequence, and so let it stand."

The absence of *fear* was always a characteristic of Ulysses. When two years of age, while Mr. Grant was carrying Ulysses in his arms on a public occasion through the village, a young man wished to try the effect of a pistol report on the child. Mr. Grant consented, saying, "The child has never seen a pistol or gun in his life." The baby hand was put on the lock and pressed quietly there, till it snapped, and off went the charge with a loud report. Ulysses scarcely stirred; but in a moment pushed away the pistol, saying, "*Fick it again! fick it again!*" A bystander remarked: "That boy will make a general; for he neither winked nor dodged." It is true such acts in childhood, which attracted no particular attention at the time, are related of distinguished men, as very remarkable, after they have become famous. Still, boys usually show talent or genius if they possess it, for any high achievement in after life.

At the village school, Ulysses was a faithful and diligent boy. He made excellent progress; and if not as brilliant as others of his age, what is better, he was "slow and sure."

Though he gave no striking evidences of genius— neither did Washington in early life—there was a beautiful resemblance to the Revolutionary leader's boyhood, in a peculiarity well expressed by one who ought to know · "*There was certainly a manly, dignified modesty* in his deportment which made him at least an uncommon lad."

He patiently committed to memory the dry, hard lessons, sure that, when older, he would understand them better and find them useful; unwilling to give up, when he came to a difficult question or problem. This was evidently the leading characteristic of the boy. It is related of him, that once he seemed to be fairly bewildered with his task; and a schoolmate, who saw his perplexity, said to him, "You can't master that."

Ulysses replied: "Can't! What does it *mean?*"

"Why, it means that—that you can't. *There!*"

This answer was not satisfactory. The young student thought he would find out the exact definition. He took the dictionary and began the search. He readily got to *can*, but there was no "*can't.*" As usual, when beyond his own knowledge, he went to his teacher, and inquired: "What is the meaning of can't? The word is not in the dictionary." The explanation of the abbreviation was soon given. But this was not all, nor the best of it. The affair afforded an opportunity to impress the great truth upon the minds of the school, that *perseverance* in well doing is the secret of success. Added the instructor: "If in the struggles of life any person should assert that 'you can't' do a thing you had determined to accomplish, let your answer be, 'The word can't is not in the dictionary.'" It was the same lesson learned by Robert Bruce from the spider which repeatedly failed to fasten its web, but at last succeeded. The desponding aspirant for the throne of Scotland put on new strength and fresh courage, thankful for the silent lesson which a kind Providence sent to him while he was ready to give up in despair. Not many boys learn so early and well the lesson as did the youthful Grant.

His father has given me another amusing little incident:

"I will relate another circumstance, which I have never mentioned before, which you may use as you think proper. He was always regarded as extremely apt in figures. When he was about ten years old, a distinguished phrenologist came along, and stayed several days in the place. He was frequently asked to examine heads, blindfolded. Among others, Ulysses was placed in the chair. The phrenologist felt his head for several minutes, without saying anything; at length, a distinguished doctor asked him if the boy had a capacity for mathematics. The phrenologist, after some further examinations, said: 'You need not be surprised if you see this boy fill the Presidential chair some time.'"

CHAPTER II.

The "Log Hauling"—The Young Patriot wants an Education—His Opportunities—How he becomes Cadet—West Point Military Academy—Where and What is it?—Young Grant as Cadet—His Classmates—He Graduates—Never quarrels.

ULYSSES early showed his Scotch blood. That is to say, he had the substantial, strong qualities of character for which the well-trained families of Scotland are remarkable. No people are calmer in action and more reverent in religious feeling, or surpass them in intelligence and integrity. When twelve years of age, he gave a fine illustration of self-reliance and manliness, along with the ability to manage difficult undertakings, which have marked his whole career.

His father wanted several sticks of hewn timber brought from the forest. The boy had learned already to drive "the team," and liked nothing better than to take the reins. Mr. Grant told Ulysses that he might harness, and go for the timber; men would be there with handspikes to assist in "loading up."

Soon Ulysses was on the way, whip and "lines" in

his hands, with the manly pride felt only in a higher degree by the king, or president, or general, in his position of honor and authority.

When he reached the forest, no men were there; for some reason they had failed to appear. He looked around him a few moments in surprise, thinking what to do.

The natural and indeed entirely proper course would have been, to wait a sufficient time, and then return home if assistance did not come. But the tanner boy, accustomed to all sorts of labor, and inclined to take responsibility from which others of his age would expect to be excused, resolved not to go without the timber. How to get the heavy logs on the wagon was the serious question. Just then his eye rested on a tree fallen over, and leaning against another. This made the trunk an inclined plane, rising gradually upward from the ground. Ulysses saw at a glance, how to make the horses do the work intended for the workmen with their handspikes. He hitched the team to each of the logs, and drew one at a time near the tree, and lying parallel with it; *i. e.*, in the same direction, lengthwise. The next thing was to swing the end round upon the inclined plane, and slide it along, till the timbers were at right angles with it, and projecting over it, far enough to admit the wagon under them. Then fastening the horses to these ends hanging over the back of the wagon, he dragged them in turn along into it; just as with your hand you could pull the "see-saw" board, with one extremity resting on the ground, over the fence or fulcrum supporting it, into a vehicle of any kind which stood beneath the end raised from the earth.

Having secured his load, the young teamster mounted it and drove homeward in triumph; again proving clearly that *can't* was not in *his* dictionary. When he reined up his team before the door of Mr. Grant, we can imagine the pleasing surprise with which he heard the story of Ulysses.

But the young woodman's prospects were not encouraging. His father's means were limited, and, excepting three months each winter in the common school, he had to assist in the work of the tannery and the home. Besides, books and newspapers for reading were very scarce.

At seventeen, Ulysses began to feel, as did his father, that decisive steps must be taken toward an education. It was often talked over at the fireside, and various plans suggested. The young man's taste for military life, the thorough instruction and economy of the Academy at West Point, suggested the possibility of getting an appointment there. The congressmen usually controlled the selection of the candidates for admission in their several districts. Political influence and position necessarily have much to do with the choice among the applicants. But Mr. Grant was hopeful. He wrote a letter to the Hon. Thomas Morris, member of the United States Senate from Ohio, requesting his influence to secure a place for his son in the Military Academy at West Point. Mr. Morris had another applicant, and wrote accordingly to the father of Ulysses; but informed him of a vacancy in the district of Hon. Thomas L. Hamer. It seems that a young man who had been appointed there, failed, for some reason, to enter the institution. This was the only chance for Ulysses. At the suggestion of Mr. Morris, Mr. Grant immediately corresponded with Mr. Hamer, who cheerfully proposed the tanner's son to the Government.

Young Grant was appointed. And now he must go before the examiners, who would either send him home again, or open to him the doors of the Academy. The trial included, with certain preparatory branches of study, a physical ordeal, to ascertain whether the body were perfectly sound. He passed safely through it all, and entered the school July 1st, 1839.

West Point is a romantic and beautiful spot on the west bank of the Hudson River, in Cornwall, Orange county, New York, fifty-two miles above New York city. The plain, or *plateau*, as it is termed, is one hundred and eighty-eight feet from the water; with an abrupt bank to protect it, and on the south and southwest, lofty summits to shut it in. Fort Putnam is more than four hundred feet higher, and looks down upon it. One beautiful plat of land is known as Kosciusko's Garden, in which stands the fine monument of this Polish refugee and patriot, who commanded the post at one time during the Revolution. Here a massive chain was stretched across the river to keep the enemy's boats from passing.

The Academy was established by act of Congress, in 1780; and is allowed to have only two hundred and fifty cadets, from fourteen to twenty-one years of age. Each of them is paid enough per month to defray all his expenses. By this method, instead of paying the bills for them, a manly independence is cultivated, while at the same time the education is gratuitous. They, in return, are to serve at least eight years in the army, unless allowed to resign or are dismissed.

The scenery is charming, and the school has every facility for a thorough preparation to enter any part of the military service. You recollect it was the scene of Arnold's treachery in 1780, which cost the accomplished spy, Major André, his life. Here Ulysses found just the means of culture he wanted. With a fondness for mathematics, he could enjoy the class drill, which is not surpassed in the country, and also have the finest apparatus for the demonstration of difficult problems, and all the science of war.

Grant, unlike a large number of the cadets, had no previous academic or collegiate course. But his studious habits, his close attention to the stringent rules of the institution, soon gave him a high position. Whether in the recitation room, in the military exercise, or in the annual encampment of the cadets, he attended to his *own business;* willing to "bide his time" in the career of honorable success.

And, my young reader, I must show you, in his own words, which I quote again from a letter, how Mr. Jesse R. Grant, Ulysses's father, spoiled a story of the Cadet's life. I intended to close this chapter with the narrative, which was already printed, purporting to be a fact, of a quarrel with his comrades, because, in accordance with the foolish custom, in literary institutions, of playing off practical jokes upon the freshman class, they made him the target of fun. The father says:

"The story about his 'flogging' the captain is untrue. He is said *to have never had a personal controversy in his life.* The nearest approach to it was with General H——, at the siege of Corinth. He says he desired *moving on the enemy's works* ten days before General H—— was ready, and saw that, by delay, they would lose the chance of bagging the rebel army, then completely in their power. He is sure he used stronger language to General H—— than he had ever used before to any person, and expected to be arrested and tried. But the General said to him : 'If I had let you take your own course, you would have taken the rebel army. Hereafter I will not dictate to you about the management of an army.' It was a common remark among the boys, when Ulysses got his appointment, that 'Lis' would make a good cadet in every respect but one ; that was, if he ever was engaged in war, he was too goodnatured to be *kicked* into a fight. In addition to freedom from personal controversy, it is believed he never used a profane word, nor told a deliberate falsehood—at least, under the parental roof. He was brought up in a Methodist family."

The allusion to Corinth you will understand better when you read the account of its siege. What an interesting glimpse is here given of "Lis," as his playmates called him! He was modest, kind, reverent, and true, in the bosom of that religious family, the parents little dreaming what a hero and nation's benefactor was trained under the humble roof, for his unrivaled field of action.

The freshman year passed away, and the annual trial of scholarship, dreaded by pupils who feel unprepared for it, came. Not a few failed in the examination of 1840, and left the institution, or fell back to a lower position; but Grant advanced to the third or next class, receiving also the appointment of corporal in the battalion of cadets. His progress was steady but not brilliant, in mathematics, French, drawing, and cavalry exercises. Quiet, sure of what he learned, and confident he could accomplish the thing he *proposed* to do, he was a fine example of the modest, reliable, and really successful student.

When the examination of 1841 again thinned the number of those with whom he started, he took no backward step, advancing to his place in the second class. The office of sergeant of the battalion, was a compliment given him by the cadets, for the summer encampment.

The hour of recitation, whether in philosophy, chemistry, or drawing, found him ready for the unsparing professor. He acquitted himself well in horsemanship, in infantry tactics, which relate to the use of small arms, and in artillery, or the handling of heavy guns. The next year, in a class of less than half the original number, he entered upon the last and crowning course of studies. He was honored with a commission as officer of cadets, who could command either a section, troop, or company. Few young persons bear, with propriety, authority. It often creates self-conceit or petty tyranny. But Cadet Grant won respect by doing just what belonged to his office, and no more. Faithful to his position, he was kind and respectful to all. He made the most of this last year at the academy.

Engineering, which is the science of building fortifications, bridges, &c., with the dry rules of law in its application to the country, military affairs, and the conduct of nations toward each other, he mastered by careful and hard study. Meanwhile, he perfected himself in horsemanship, and became one of the finest riders in the institution.

June 30th, 1843, only thirty young men of the hundred who put on the gray suit of the cadet four years before graduated. The Ohio boy was No. 21, or nearly in the middle of the class. The country youth of seventeen, who came from a district school, left behind him along his academic career seventy-nine of his classmates, among whom were sons of senators and of professional men. Many of them had been to college. Such was the reward of industry and a good character; a determination to do well, with a patient, honest straightforward course to secure his object. Without such qualities and exertion, Ulysses would have only been a poor tanner, or a very common farmer in the West.

Among those who finished the regular course with Cadet Grant at the Academy, were many distinguished officers in the Mexican war, and others who became conspicuous commanders in the great civil conflict of the Republic. The first in the class was Major-General W. B. Franklin, who led the Nineteenth Army Corps under General Banks. Generals Ingalls, Steele, and Judah, were of the same company of graduates. It is sad to know that several of them fought under the flag of secession,—brave officers in a bad cause. They little dreamed, while under the "star-spangled-banner" at West Point, enjoying its protection in the walks of science, and among the glorious scenery of the Hudson, with the warning example of Arnold suggested by it, that they should stand in battle array against each other. But such has been the result of *home education* in the hostile principles of freedom and oppression. The harvest of death and ruin on the field of war, followed the moral seed-sowing of many years, in the hearts of the people. A cultivated mind with wrong principles, is like a splendid engine off the track—it will do only harm.

CHAPTER III.

The Young Lieutenant—He joins his Regiment—Goes to Louisiana—Is in the Mexican War—The First Battle—The Long March—Vera Cruz—Returns to the States—Is Married—Ordered to Oregon—Resigns.

FOUR long years of study and drill were now over. Nobly proud and happy cadet! The educated young man looks out upon a life of service and honor. What shall be the first step? The army of the United States was scattered through the land, doing little besides occupying forts as garrisons, guarding the frontier wherever threatened by troublesome Indians, and superintending the opening of military roads through the wilderness. Vacancies in command did not often occur, and the new graduates must be content with the honorary titles of command. Grant was therefore breveted second lieutenant of the Fourth Regular Infantry, performing the duties of a private soldier. He joined his regiment, stationed at Jefferson Barracks, near St. Louis, and, with it, went on the occasional expeditions into the wild country lying back of the settlements scattered along the great rivers, to protect the defenceless inhabitants from the incursions of their savage neighbors. In the spring of 1844 he removed with his regiment up the Red River, in Louisiana.

While alluding to the aborigines, I must tell you that our Government, and the Indian agents and traders, have been far more guilty than the red men in regard to deeds of violence these have committed. This all our best military officers who have been among them will tell you. Scarcely an instance of massacre or war is recorded, which cannot be traced directly to some outrage upon them—such as breaking treaty, defrauding them of money due them—or robbing them of property. We have treated the poor Indian as if he were under no government, human or divine, but lawful plunder for the white man. No Christian person, certainly, can doubt that Providence, in the civil war, chastised the nation on account of such oppressive and treacherous treatment of the red race, along with the enslavement and cruel abuse of the African.

Months passed away without any striking events in this frontier-life of Lieutenant Grant. But a war-cloud was now gathering on the Southern horizon. Mexico and the United States had been disputing about the boundary line of Texas, which became about this time a State. Texas claimed more territory than Mexico said was hers. There was apparently no very strong desire on our part to settle the quarrel on righteous principles. Southern feeling and interests, which at last brought on the great Rebellion, led ambitious politicians to urge the claims of the Texans. The more territory given to slavery, the stronger would the aristocratic owners of the multiplying victims of their mercenary, aspiring desire, and lust, become. Mexico refused to yield to our demands. Both parties were willing to enter the field of deadly conflict. The Government determined to send to the border an "army of occupation;" that is, a force to secure the observance of the prescribed limit of Texas lands. General Zachary Taylor was the commander; a very heroic officer, and afterward President of the United States. This was in 1845. Lieutenant Grant was in the expedition, and marched with his regiment to Corpus Christi, where the troops were concentrating. The town is in Nueces County, and very important because situated on the southern shore of the Gulf of Mexico, and near the disputed territory. Vessels could bring supplies, and the troops move from it over the country.

Meanwhile young Grant was promoted to the rank of first lieutenant in the Seventh Regiment of the United States Infantry. But he was anxious to stay with his old comrades and the officers under whom he served, and requested the Government to let him remain. He was gratified in his choice; and the brevet or complimentary appointment was exchanged for the substantial honor of a regular commission as Second Lieutenant of the Fourth Infantry. The winter passed away with nothing decisive in military movements, till May 23d.

1846, when Mexico declared war, on the ground that we had invaded her territory.

General Taylor occupied the banks of the Rio Grande, opposite Matamoros, where the Mexicans were in force. Here he heard that the enemy were between him and Point Isabel, at the mouth of the river, and also threatening Fort Brown further up the stream. He at once resolved to reinforce the troops at the former place, and relieve the imperilled garrison at Fort Brown.

When the forces left the headquarters opposite Matamoros, whose guns were pointed toward our earthworks, the bells rang merrily; the people supposing the American troops were evacuating their position. The case was far otherwise, to the joy of Lieutenant Grant. The blooming, glorious spring of the South was inspiring; the grand old mountains in the distance were sublimely suggestive; but he felt, with a quiet enthusiasm peculiar to his nature, more deeply still, the stirring prospect of his first battle on the plains of national conflict. It is painful to recollect, that Generals Lee and Beauregard, of the rebel army, were among the most patriotic and able officers in the opening war. A glance at the map will show you that Point Isabel, Palo Alto, and Resaca de la Palma, lie on the Rio Grande, which separates Texas from Mexico, between the Gulf and Fort Brown. The army were marching on this line of towns toward the fort, when they met the Mexicans at Palo Alto. The engagement was sharp and bloody. Lieutenant Grant fought bravely, winning the admiration of the men and superior officers.

The next day the battle opened again at Resaca de la Palma, with fatal fury. The Mexican ranks were thinned, and reeled before our fire, leaving the field strewn with the slain, but under the "Stars and Stripes." Grant escaped unhurt, and with a growing reputation for gallantry in the fight. He was modest as he was brave, caring more for the character of a true soldier and patriot, than for the honors others less deserving might receive. The victorious battalions advanced up the Rio Grande, clearing the Texan frontier of the Mexicans; the lieutenant sharing the hardships and perils with the delight of a warrior who became one from taste and deliberate choice. The army then swept down the river into the enemy's country, toward Monterey, a strongly fortified position. A terribly severe but successful engagement resulted in the surrender of the place. Lieutenant Grant, in the desperate contest, was fearless and courageous, in the cheerful, faithful discharge of duty.

The time had come for a great and decisive struggle for victory and peace. The magnificent Mexican capital was to be the goal of the augmented forces under the command of General Scott, who was at the head of the United States army. His fleet came up the bay March 9th, 1847, bringing twelve thousand troops, with streamers flying and bands playing. It was a splendid sight. He landed the men safely at Sacrificios, three miles from Vera

Cruz, through the surf rolling high with crested breakers on the beach. General Taylor's forces were ready to join him in the siege of Vera Cruz, a strong and well-defended city, with its celebrated castle San Juan de Ulloa. Days of fearful warfare followed; but the Mexicans were compelled, at length, to yield to the valor of our troops.

In April, 1847, with our colors waving over the battlements of Vera Cruz, the army prepared to advance into the heart of the hostile territory. Lieutenant Grant was appointed quartermaster of his regiment. It was a post of responsibility, which required good judgment, honesty, and business ability. The officer had in charge the subsistence of troops and horses, and the general care of whatever had to do with the material interests of the forces in his department. Besides, this mark of confidence in his superior capacity gave him a place on the commander's staff, the group of officers who act as his escort and aid him in the execution of orders. The quartermaster, unless especially needed and called to the service on the staff, could remain in his own department in time of battle. But Grant preferred to mingle in the fray; and when the shot and shell began to fly, he was on his steed and on the plains of death.

The autumn of 1847 brought the terrible struggle of Molino del Rey. So prompt and reckless of danger was the calm, heroic lieutenant, riding coolly through the leaden hail, that he was appointed first lieutenant on the spot. Congress, which often is slow to recognize true merit, and confers undeserved honors, did not confirm the commission; and he refused to accept an empty brevet. The crimson field of Molino del Rey was won September 8th. Five days later, Chapultepec, a frowning, formidable stronghold, was stormed. Up to the battlements, raining destruction upon the assailants, the ranks of brave men sternly moved. None among them all was more daring and gallant than Grant. I will furnish the interesting proof of his splendid conduct, from the official reports of the officers of the day. Captain Brooks, of the Second Artillery, writes:

"I succeeded in reaching the fort with a few men. Here Lieutenant U. S. Grant, and a few more men of the Fourth Infantry, found me, and, by a joint movement, after an obstinate resistance, a strong field work was carried, and the enemy's right was completely turned."

Major Lee, in his report, says of the young soldier's conduct at Chapultepec:

"At the first barrier the enemy was in strong force, which rendered it necessary to advance with caution. This was done; and when the head of the battalion was within short musket range of the barrier, Lieutenant Grant, Fourth Infantry, and Captain Brooks, Second Artillery, with a few men of their respective regiments, by a handsome movement to the left, turned the right flank of the enemy, and the barrier was carried. Lieutenant Grant behaved with distinguished gallantry on the 13th and 14th."

The rising commander thus early learned the art of *outflanking* the enemy; displaying a cool, unyielding valor, rather than a dashing and ambitious warfare.

Colonel Garland, of the First Brigade, speaks very highly of Grant in the same action:

"The rear of the enemy had made a stand behind a breastwork, from which they were driven by detachments of the Second Artillery, under Captain Brooks, and the Fourth Infantry, under Lieutenant Grant, supported by other regiments of the division, after a short, sharp conflict. I recognized the command as it came up, mounted a howitzer on the top of a convent, which, under the direction of Lieutenant Grant, quartermaster of the Fourth Infantry, and Lieutenant Lendrum, Third Artillery, annoyed the enemy considerably. I must not omit to call attention to Lieutenant Grant, who acquitted himself most nobly upon several occasions under my observation."

There was an additional evidence of the hero's steady progress in the career of fame. He was brevetted captain in the United States Army, his rank to date from the great battle of Chapultepec, September 13th, 1847.

When, not long after, the victorious army entered Mexico, the splendid capital, Grant participated in the magnificent parade, and enjoyed the glory of the final achievement, to which all previous battles had been opening the way. Lieutenant Grant was in fourteen battles.

The treaty of peace was signed in February, 1848, on

the 22d of which, the noble and venerable J. Q. Adams was struck down in death on the floor of the Capitol, exclaiming, at the close of a long and blameless life of usefulness, "This is the last of earth." On July 4th, President Polk issued the formal proclamation of peace between the United States and Mexico. A large extent of territory was ceded to us, and we paid, on our part, several millions of dollars to the Mexican Government. The war cost us twenty-five thousand men, and seventy-five millions of dollars.

The disbanded army was again distributed among the forts in the States, and along the frontier. The hero of Chapultepec now made a new conquest. He won the hand of a Miss Dent, a sensible and excellent young lady, near St. Louis, Mo., and was married in August of that year. His military home was first at Detroit, Mich., and then at Sackett's Harbor, a post on Lake Ontario, in Northern New York. There was little to do in time of peace in these quiet barracks near a small and pleasant village. He is remembered by the people in Watertown, a handsome place several miles distant, as having a passion for playing checkers,—a game which, perhaps, my young readers have played, and is among the most harmless pastimes of the kind, because not often carried to excess, or associated with dangerous games of chance. The quartermaster (for in this position he continued), with characteristic perseverance and patience, would contest the advantage to be gained by the moves, and was hard to beat.

At this time, many of the settlers on the plains of California were without law and order; they were gold seekers, and reckless men. It becoming necessary to send a military force to restrain their passions, and prevent Indian depredations and massacre, the Fourth Infantry were selected to visit the Pacific coast. Lieutenant Grant went with a portion of it to Oregon. This wild and romantic life was very similar to that in the South, soon after he left West Point. The solitary marches in the grand old woods, the ancient rocks and rivers, with perils from the savages, had attractions for the young and adventurous spirit. While here, his regular commission as captain in the infantry came—another step in the career of honor.

After two years' service in the far and almost uninhabited West, Captain Grant saw so little prospect of activity and promotion, that he resigned his place in the army, and returned to his family near the city of St. Louis, to try his fortune in civil life. We shall see how he succeeded.

CHAPTER IV.

The Captain turns Farmer—He is not Afraid of Work—In the Leather Trade—The Call to Arms again—Captain offers his Service—His First Post of Duty—Is appointed Colonel.

FOR fifteen years the heroic Captain had handled books, firearms, and sword, instead of logs, leather, and horsewhip. What shall he do now, without office and employment? It did not cost him a tear nor take him long to put off the "regimentals," and appear in an old felt hat, blouse coat, and pants tucked into his boots, on a small farm in the neighborhood of Mr. Dent, his father-in-law, south-west of St. Louis. He had early learned to "rough it" in the woods of the West, and among the vats of the tannery. Had you been in St. Louis, you might have seen him in the winter, mounted on his wagon, in which a cord of wood was well packed, and driving the team into the city. Citizens of St. Louis recollect the plainly-dressed man who came with his load, delivered it to the purchaser, and returned to his country retreat.

With the hot Southern summer came leisure from

the woodman's traffic, and our hero must look for lighter work. His fine education qualified him for any business, and his character attracted the confidence of all. His neighbors were glad to employ and aid a stranger who was so generous and true as Captain Grant. He was just the collector some of them wanted to "dun" negligent debtors. They therefore put into his hands their debts. Like all the truly noble men of the world, he was honest and sincere in his dealings; and, trusting too readily to the apologies and promises of delinquent debtors, he had but small success. His failure reminds one of the forcible proverb: "It takes a rogue to catch a rogue." That is to say, a pure-minded person, unused to business contact with the unprincipled and vicious, makes a poor detective of rogues.

The Captain found that he was not made for a tax-gatherer or an auctioneer, or even a farmer. He was neither a talker, schooled to hard, suspicious dealings with his fellows, nor in the economical management of a farm. Military culture and habits were exactly the opposite in their fruits of character. Law, order, promptness, and manly bearing, were the lessons which had followed those of a virtuous and humble home.

The year 1859 brought, therefore, a change again in the plans of Grant. His tannery education now served him well. From his father in the West came a proposition to go into the leather and saddlery trade with him. What a singular and pleasant fact! The hero of Chapultepee again called by parental love to handle the tanned skins of cattle and sheep, and even horses, instead of the burnished sword and the military cap.

He removed to the city of Galena, on the banks of Fevre river, in Jo Daviess county, Illinois. The broad stream pours its waters into the Mississippi only six miles below the town. Along the river the shores rise to highlands or bluffs, sometimes very steep and grand. Galena is built on one of these. The streets consequently rise one above the other, like paths on a hillside, with steps between them. It was not only, as you see, a curious and picturesque city, but, being near the Mississippi and having a good harbor, was a centre of commercial life, of trade and resort, for a large region lying back of it. Soon the new sign of "Grant & Son" began to attract customers. The soldier recalls his early knowledge of the business, and quietly talks over the qualities and prices of his piles and rolls of leather.

The trade prospers; far and near the establishment becomes known. A great many shoemakers work up Captain Grant's goods, and the feet of his customers wear the contribution to "the arts of peace" made by him. It would really seem as if the Captain had settled down into a nice, permanent business, and his name would become famous as a successful, wealthy leather merchant. But it was the lull before a stormy life. An Illinois lawyer, in the autumn of 1860, was elected President of the

United States. The Southern politicians, who had for nearly half a century controlled the councils of the nation with a sleepless regard to the continuance of slavery, all the time desiring and hoping that the time of separation from the laboring North would come, were angry at the election of Mr. Lincoln. Then came, you will recollect, secession at Charleston, South Carolina, and, a few months later, the attack on Fort Sumter. This was a declaration of war by the South. That is to say, the thunder of the cannon around this fortress, named after the brave Gen. Thomas Sumter, of the Revolutionary War, who was called, on account of his successful bravery, "the Carolina Game Cock," revealed the dark plot of disunion, and the purpose to fight for it. The President, who is the commander-in-chief of all the forces of the United States, asked for volunteers to meet the terrible necessity of bloody war. Captain Grant was a loyal soldier, and his patriotism shone the more brightly because he did not belong to the Republican party, but had to some extent the feelings of a citizen of the South.

One morning, on reaching the store, and reading in the morning paper the account of the bombardment of Sumter, he walked round the counter, drew on his coat, and remarked: "Uncle Sam educated me for the army, and, although I have served faithfully through one war, I feel that I am still a little in debt for my education, and I am ready and willing to discharge the obligation." He then said: "I am for the war, to put down this wicked rebellion

Noble and high resolve! The true-hearted wife would not, had it been possible, dissuade him from it. The store was deserted. Captain Grant went into the street, consulted with a few men, and soon succeeded in raising a company, with which he went to Springfield, and tendered it to the Governor.

An Illinois representative also called upon Governor Yates, to recommend to him Mr. Grant as a fit person for some military position. The Governor, having received applications from men over six feet in height and of muscular frames, curiously eyed the small man, attired in homespun, who stood before him as an applicant.

President, governors, and people were like men awaking from sleep when the civil strife began. They hardly knew how to meet the new and alarming crisis. And, as the story goes, Governor Yates had no appointment for Grant, and he therefore left.

A short time after this occurrence, the Governor was very much distressed in regard to the raising of the quota of the State. He had plenty of offers for officers' positions, but he personally did not know the minutiae of regimental organizations,—how many privates composed a company, or how many subordinate officers there should be in a regiment. In his embarrassment he asked the representative if that plain little man to whom he had been introduced knew anything of those matters. The representative replied by bringing Grant into the Governor's presence.

"Do you understand the organization of troops?" inquired the Governor.

The reply was in the affirmative.

"Will you accept a desk in my office for that purpose?" was the next question.

"Anything to serve my country," was his reply.

And to work he at once went; and but for this, Captain Grant might still be unknown to the world.

To show you the spirit of the loyal Governor, and that he was just the man to appreciate Grant, soon as he knew him, here is a part of the letter he wrote to a citizen of Oskaloosa, who complained that traitors had cut down his flag, and inquired what he should do. The patriotic Yates replied as follows: "You say that the pole which floated the Stars and Stripes on the Fourth of July was cut down by secessionists, and that, at a picnic which you are to have, it is threatened that the flag shall be taken down, and you ask me whether you would be justifiable in defending the flag with firearms. I am astonished at this question, as much as if you were to ask me whether you would have a right to defend your property against robbers, or your life against murderers! You ask me what you shall do? I reply, Do not raise the American flag *merely to provoke* your secession neighbors; do not be on the aggressive; but whenever you raise it on your own soil, or on the public property of the States or county, or at any public celebration, from honest love to the flag and patriotic devotion to the country which it symbolizes, and any traitor dares to lay his unhallowed hand upon it to tear it down, *shoot him as you would a dog, and I will pardon you for the offence.*"

The volunteers poured in from the magnificent prairies of Illinois. Captain Grant had shown the Governor that he knew how to raise and manage men; his State taking the first place in the great West in the noble and priceless offering of her sons. I recollect one of these prairie farmers, of whom I must tell you. He was a youthful and devoted son, living with his parents on beautiful land, whose rising harvest seemed to say to the volunteer, "Don't go away." The tearful, parental eyes, while the lips by silence gave consent to his departure, added, "How can we spare you?" But treason was abroad, and *his* language was, "I *must* go. I freely give my life to my country. My farm is worthless unless rebellion is crushed, and life itself of no account." In one of the first battles he was wounded. When the wound healed, and his arm hung useless by his side, with a ragged bullet hole in his military coat, he said: "I only ask to go again, *and see it through*, even if I fall in battle. But war is a perfect despotism. The soldier is nothing but a machine. When told to go, he must march; when commanded to stand still, he must stop. Yet *it is right;* unquestioned authority is necessary over such masses of men."

This style of hero was just what Grant admired, for he was of the same type. And he longed for the field of conflict. His untiring and earnest work in the mustering deparment, did not satisfy his martial spirit. The Governor knew this.

In two weeks, the Governor told him he was called upon by the President to send two names for the office of brigadier-general; and proposed his name for one of them. The Captain, now Adjutant, declined the honor because he was *a stranger*. He never sought promotion, but *earned* it.

After the great work of meeting the call upon his State was finished, about the middle of June, 1861, Captain Grant repaired to his father's house in Covington, Ky.; a dutiful son, who knew that it might be his last visit there. We shall never read a record of the tender words from the now venerable father, nor of filial affection from the worthy son.

While under the paternal roof, a commission was issued by Governor Yates, making the late adjutant-general, colonel of the Twenty-first Regiment of Illinois Volunteers, dated June 15, 1861. At first, a fine-looking man was chosen colonel; but, having no military capacity, the regiment fell into disorder, and became the terror of the neighborhood where it was encamped. The Governor refused to commission the nominee of the regiment, and, by telegraph, inquired if Grant would take the troops, and bring the turbulent mass to order. His reply was like him,—he was ready, and sure of success.

A full regiment numbers about one thousand soldiers. But the term sometimes indicates more, and often less;

as when, after disease and bullets have done their work, not more than half or a third of the original number remain. Not far from this very time, a splendid regiment crowded in long and glittering lines Washington street, Boston, from one curb-stone to the other. A year afterward I saw only one hundred and twenty-five left, able to march, with blackened and torn banners, and their apparel and faces nearly as dark with exposure and powder-smoke. They still bore their proud name, as when the multitude admired and cheered their full and manly ranks.

CHAPTER V.

Three Months Men—Colonel Grant joins his Regiment—In Camp—Off for the Field of Action—A Rapid March—Promotion—Grant loses no Time —He is Commissioned Brigadier-General—A Good Story—Headquarters at Cairo—A True American—He seizes Paducah—Secession Flags—A Noble Proclamation—The "Stove-pipe General."

WHEN the first call for volunteers was issued, it was believed that the secessionists would be confined almost entirely to South Carolina, and a few in others of the cotton-growing States, where the slaves were most valuable to their owners. For this reason only seventy-five thousand soldiers, to serve three months, were asked for in all the Northern States. The Twenty-first Illinois belonged to the number; but they said if Grant commanded, and they were needed longer, they would reënlist. The brave fellows were as good as their word. Colonel Grant hastened to his own State, and joined his regiment at Mattoon, where it was organized. He then removed the troops to Casseyville for encampment. As if by magic, the gathering volunteers were transferred to the little canvas city, with its guards and sentinels, its frequent drill, and all the means of preparation for the field of deadly conflict. Without display of authority or noise, the Colonel kindly enforced the severest discipline, setting the example of obedience to superiors, and of simplicity in style of living. For a month this training continued, relieved by the presence of citizens to look upon the novel scene in our hitherto peaceful land, and the more welcome visits to the soldiers from so many Western homes, of sister, wife, and mother.

An application was made to the Governor to send a regiment to Quincy, one hundred and twenty miles distant. The trouble with the Governor was not the want of men, but the lack of transportation.

"Send my regiment," said Grant, "and I will find the transportation."

The command was given, and before night the regiment was under orders to march. On foot it was transported to Quincy; and when the men were there encamped, they were reported as belonging to one of the best disciplined regiments of Illinois volunteers.

At length the welcome order to the men came, to strike tents and be ready to march away to the field of conflict, turning their backs upon the scenes and friends of former days, perhaps forever.

The soldiers get very tired of the camp life. There is such monotony; no excitement of any importance, and but little to do. They prefer the toils of warfare and the storm of bullets, to the dull security of encampment.

Oh, it was a stirring scene on the morning of the

march! The boys packed the knapsacks, rolled up the blankets, and down with the tents in a hurry. Colonel Grant rode at the head of the columns, which formed in glad haste at the word of command. His calm face was lit up with rational delight. The natural *bent* of his genius, his years of experience in military affairs, and, more than all else, the sacred cause which led him away to the enemy's lines, inspired him with hope and courage. Reaching the Mississippi River, the troops embarked, and in fine style crossed the Father of Waters into Missouri. Then they swept along the war-path with rapid marches, leaving behind them, in six days, a distance of one hundred miles. The cars then bore them on as much further in a few hours, toward Northern Missouri. Their first duty was to guard the Hannibal and St. Joseph's Railroad, lying nearly west of Springfield, Illinois, as will be seen by reference to the map, and connecting the Missouri and Mississippi rivers. It is one of the railways which forms a link in the great chain of iron tracks connecting the vast and growing West with the older and enterprising East. The indispensable army work assigned to Colonel Grant's troop, was very forcibly apparent in a recent visit to the Potomac "front." For more than sixty miles from Washington, through the Old Dominion, which was one wide desert, with graves and carcasses of horses and mules, over which the crows were flying in myriads, the military road was protected by encampments of troops, looking in the distance like villages of white tents and log cabins, a few miles apart. At some points "block houses" were built, from whose second story the road could be seen in both directions, and the deadly bullet fired.

Several regiments had been ordered on this service, having their headquarters in Northern Missouri, and wanted a general. Who shall have this honor, from associates equally willing to accept it, till a regular appointment is made? Although the youngest colonel on the ground, Colonel Grant was selected, and became acting brigadier-general—another step in the line of promotion.

He took this command on the 31st of July, 1861, at a place called Mexico, on the North Missouri Railroad, south of the Hannibal and St. Joseph's. It was in the "District of North Missouri," and in the department of General Pope. The whole field of military operations is divided into distinct territories, each under the command of a general who has the direction of its martial movements.

August 9th, Grant was commissioned brigadier-general, and ordered to Southern Missouri, when General Jeff. Thompson was ready to advance upon us. He went to Ironton, and then to Marble Creek, where he built fortifications and placed a garrison to defend it. Jefferson City was threatened, too, and he hurried on to that town. For ten days his forces protected the place.

A member of the hero's staff relates an amusing and characteristic story of him during his Missouri campaigns:

"The hero and veteran, who was citizen, captain, colonel, brigadier and major-general within a space of nine months, though a rigid disciplinarian, and a perfect Iron-sides in the discharge of his official duties, could enjoy a good joke, and is always ready to perpetrate one when an opportunity presents. Indeed, among his acquaintances he is as much renowned for his eccentric humor as he is for his skill and bravery as a commander.

"When Grant was a brigadier in Southeast Missouri, he commanded an expedition against the rebels under Jeff. Thompson, in Northeast Arkansas. The distance from the starting point of the expedition to the supposed rendezvous of the rebels was about one hundred and ten miles, and the greater portion of the route lay through a howling wilderness. The imaginary suffering that our soldiers endured during the first two days of their march was enormous. It was impossible to steal or "confiscate" uncultivated real estate, and not a hog, or a chicken, or an ear of corn was anywhere to be seen. On the third day, however, affairs looked more hopeful, for a few small specks of ground, in a state of partial cultivation, were here and there visible. On that day, Lieutenant Wickfield, of an Indiana cavalry regiment, commanded the advance guard, consisting of eight mounted men. About noon he came up to a small farmhouse, from the outward appearance of which he judged that there might be something fit to eat inside. He halted his company, dismounted, and with two second lieutenants entered the dwelling. He knew that Grant's incipient fame had already gone out through all that country, and it occurred to him that by representing himself to be the general he might obtain the best the house afforded. So, assuming a very imperative demeanor, he accosted the inmates of the house, and told them he must have something for himself and staff to eat. They desired to know who he was, and he told them that he was Brigadier-General Grant. At the sound of that name they flew around with alarming alacrity, and served up about all they had in the house, taking great pains all the while to make loud professions of loyalty. The lieutenants ate as much as they could of the not over-sumptuous meal, but which was, nevertheless, good for that country, and demanded what was to pay. 'Nothing.' And they went on their way rejoicing.

"In the mean time General Grant, who had halted his army a few miles further back for a brief resting spell, came in sight of, and was rather favorably impressed with the appearance of this same house. Riding up to the fence in front of the door, he desired to know if they would cook him a meal.

"'No,' said a female, in a gruff voice; 'General Grant and his staff have just been here, and eaten everything in the house except one pumpkin pie.'

"'Humph,' murmured Grant; 'what is your name?'

"'Selvidge,' replied the woman.

"Casting a half dollar in at the door, he asked if she would keep that pie till he sent an officer for it; to which she replied that she would.

"That evening, after the camping ground had been

selected, the various regiments were notified that there would be a grand parade at half past six, for orders. Officers would see that their men all turned out, &c.

"In five minutes the camp was in a perfect uproar, and filled with all sorts of rumors. Some thought the enemy were upon them, it being so unusual to have parades when on a march.

"At half past six the parade was formed, ten columns deep, and nearly a quarter of a mile in length.

"After the usual routine of ceremonies the acting assistant adjutant-general read the following order:

"'HEADQUARTERS, ARMY IN THE FIELD.
"'SPECIAL ORDER, No. ——.

"'Lieutenant Wickfield, of the —— Indiana cavalry, having on this day eaten everything in Mrs. Selvidge's house, at the crossing of the Ironton and Pocahontas and Black River and Cape Girardeau roads, except one pumpkin pie, Lieutenant Wickfield is hereby ordered to return with an escort of one hundred cavalry, and eat that pie also.

"'U. S. GRANT,
"'Brigadier-General Commanding.'"

Grant's orders were law, and no soldier ever attempted to evade them. At 7 o'clock the lieutenant filed out of camp with his hundred men, amid the cheers of the entire army. The escort concurred in stating that he devoured the whole of the pie, and seemed to relish it.

The next mark of confidence in him by the Government, and of advancing greatness, was his appointment to the important post of Cairo. This town, you will notice, lies upon a point of low land on the Mississippi shore, in the State of Illinois. The country around it is called "Egypt." Its position gave it great value to the Union cause. It guarded the mouth of the Ohio River, and was the key to the waters above. Here supplies, and all the means of carrying on the war in that vast region, could be received. When General Grant made his headquarters at Cairo, with General McClernand's brigade added to his troops, his department of command extended along the shores of the Mississippi as far as Cape Girardeau. He now had a field of action large enough to reveal his strength, and develop his fine qualities of generalship. At this early stage of the rebellion, Kentucky tried to stand alone—*i. e.*, to be *neutral;* neither loyal to the Stars and Stripes, nor under the flag of secession. It seems ridiculous as well as shamefully wrong, when we think of so absurd a position. The rebels were the first to make it impossible. They did not care nor try to find and keep the boundary between Tennessee and Kentucky; but, whenever convenient, crossed over and helped themselves to whatever would aid their cause.

The towns of Columbus and Hickman, situated on the Mississippi River, within the limits of Kentucky, were entered and fortified. Bowling Green, on the Big Barren River, a tributary of Green River, and at the head of navigation, one hundred and forty-five miles from Frankfort, was also seized.

General Grant heard of these aggressions, and concluded it was his turn and time to play at the same game. September 6, 1861, he sent a body of troops in steamers, quietly down the river to Paducah, a town at the mouth of the Tennessee, which, from the very location, was a post highly valued. Nineteen days later, he repeated the bold action, by despatching a force to Smithland, at the mouth of the Cumberland. Thus you will readily perceive, that he not only followed up closely the policy of the rebels, but gained power by blockading the rivers which opened channels of trade into their confederacy. Bread, arms, and other supplies were cut off, which hitherto had floated over those streams undisturbed. These points also became tributary to his army operations, and aided materially in driving out the guerillas on the Ohio River below them.

The real insincerity of Kentucky then, and the wickedness of betraying her high trust, was seen in the flaunting flags of secession flying in the breeze over Paducah, when the Union forces marched into its streets. These banners were designed to welcome the troops of treason, who were advancing four thousand strong, and expected soon, instead of our own, by the inhabitants.

When we speak of Kentucky, we mean the State in its relation to the Government, and not of all the people living in it. For, from the beginning of the terrible rebellion, very many citizens were loyal to the old flag; and soon as it was borne along the streets, upheld by gleaming bayonets and followed by cannon, they rose, like Roderick Dhu's men, in Sir Walter Scott's beautiful story, "The Lady of the Lake," out of the forest brakes, from their concealment, and with shouts of joy hailed the "Star-spangled Banner." General Grant, soon as he had gained complete possession, leaving open no communication with the enemy, issued a proclamation, remarkable for calm and prudent tone, designed to encourage the true-hearted people, and disarm the excited and misguided subjects of Jeff. Davis—the great defender and bloody advocate of rebellion, secession, and American slavery. Here is the famous proclamation:

PADUCAH, KY., September 6, 1861.

To the Citizens of Paducah: I am come among you, not as an enemy, but as your fellow citizen. Not to maltreat you, nor annoy you, but to respect and enforce the rights of all loyal citizens. An enemy in rebellion against our common Government has taken possession of, and planted his guns upon the soil of Kentucky, and fired upon you. Columbus and Hickman are in his hands. He is moving upon your city. I am here to defend you against this enemy, to assist the authority and sovereignty of your Government. *I have nothing to do with opinions*, and shall deal only with armed rebellion, and its aiders and abettors. You can pursue your usual avocations without fear. The strong arm of the Government is here to protect its friends and punish its enemies. Whenever it is manifest that you are able to defend yourselves, and maintain the authority of the Government, and protect the rights of loyal citizens, I shall withdraw the forces under my command. U. S. GRANT,

Brigadier-General Commanding

In keeping with the plain, noble words of the commander, was his appearance at headquarters in camp at Cairo. Had you been sent to look for him, you might have believed that officer with dashing uniform, whose gilt buttons and shoulderstraps shone in the sunlight, and whose air was that of conscious power, to be our hero. But you would have to look again; and, passing by all the *showy* generals, colonels, and captains, fix the eye on that still, plain man, whose clothes are scarcely better than those of a common soldier, with an unadorned black and bruised felt hat on his head, smoking, with a thoughtfully careless air, a cigar. I wish we could leave out the cigar; smoking, and chewing tobacco is condemned by all sensible persons, even those who have the habit, as nearly always useless, if not injurious. Still, good men in early life acquire a taste for the weed, and then it is hard to give it up. General Grant belongs to this class, we must allow. Some allusion was made, one day, to General Grant's "stove-pipe" hat, and his constant companion, a cigar, in a sarcastic tone; when an enthusiastic friend wittily replied: "Such a bright stove-pipe as Grant should be excused for *smoking*."

CHAPTER VI.

Columbus—Exchange of Prisoners—Battles—General Grant writes to his Father—Cares for the Wounded—A New Department of Command—Prepares for a Grand Movement upon the Enemy—His Strategy—Issues Orders—The Advance.

COLUMBUS, eighteen miles below, was an important position, from which the movement on Paducah was made by the rebels. So the General thought he would pay the enemy a visit there. But just as he was getting ready with troops to do so, the Government demanded five regiments; which left him too weak to seek, with hope of success, for headquarters in Columbus. Major-General Bishop Polk was in command there, with twenty thousand men. A number of prisoners of war had been taken in the skirmishes of the armies; and, about the middle of October, General Polk and General Grant had correspondence on the subject of an exchange. General Polk, in his note, referred to the "Confederate States;" to which Grant replied: "I recognize no 'Southern Confederacy' myself, but will communicate with higher authorities for their views." The hero, in a patriotic way, was decidedly "spunky" in the affair. Whatever became of the prisoners, trusting that loyal hearts among them felt as he did, he would have nothing to do with a proposition which called on him to recognize a government founded on treason. While this was transpiring, Brigadier-General Jeff. Thompson was advancing northward in Missouri. General Grant had not given him permission to do so, and immediately determined to apprise him of the fact. He ordered a part of his forces under Colonel Plummer, stationed at Cape Girardeau, Mo., to march forward to Fredericktown, and, joined by Colonel Carlin, advancing from another direction, cross the rebel chieftain's path.

The mild, soft morning of October 21st brought the time of meeting in battle. Thompson had three thousand five hundred men, who fought bravely; but they were compelled to yield to Yankee bullets and steel. It is true, our force was superior by a few hundred troops. For two hours the contest lasted, followed the next day with a pursuit of the enemy twenty-two miles. General Grant's reply to Colonel Plummer's despatch, conveying tidings of victory, reveals his kind and noble nature. After congratulating the brave troops on the courage and cheerful submission to hardships with which they were willing "to meet their rebellious brethren, even at great odds," he adds: "Our loss, small as it was, is to be regretted; but the friends and relations of those who fell can congratulate themselves in the midst of their affliction, that they fell in maintaining the cause of constitutional freedom, and the integrity of a flag erected in the first instance, at a sacrifice of many of the noblest lives that ever graced a nation."

Colonel Plummer took forty-two prisoners, an iron twelve-pounder, and other arms, with a number of horses. It was also discovered that Confederate forces sent from Columbus to cut off Colonel Oglesby, who had gone to prevent a junction of General Price with General Thompson, were concentrating at Belmont. General Grant resolved to go himself and see what they were trying to do. He gave General McClernand command of a brigade, and led another himself. The troops marched from Cairo November 6th, 1861, and were soon crowding the river steamers. The sun was high when they landed, the next day, at Belmont. Forming immediately into line of battle, they moved on the rebel works, commanded by General Cheatham. The dauntless Union forces marched forward toward the camp. Between it and them was an abatis of twenty acres of fallen timber; *i. e.*, the trees so laid and pointed as to make it difficult as possible to get over or through them. Onward pressed the troops into the formidable defence, under a deadly storm of bullets and enormous shells, which came shrieking from the guns at Columbus, over their heads. Down went General Grant's horse under him, while a rifle ball struck General McClernand, but was turned from its fatal mission by the pistol in his holster. Winding among stumps and creeping through boughs, the brave three thousand reached the camp, and, with a wild, exultant shout, they charged home, and sent the seven thousand rebels, or more, staggering toward Columbus. The Union forces swept into the enemy's camp, and through it; and, taking the battery of twelve guns, burned the baggage, leaving only smoking ruins behind. But just when victory seemed folding its wings on their banners, reënforcements came over from Columbus and Hickman, and turned the tide of battle. Our troops retired to the transports, under the protecting fire of the gunboats.

General Fremont, then at the head of the department in which the field of conflict lay, about this time was superseded by General Hunter.

It was a brilliant affair. When General Halleck scanned the battle with his fine military appreciation, he said: "Grant will do to trust an army with."

While the rebels lost, in killed and wounded, two thousand eight hundred, General Grant lost, in all, less than six hundred. Of the cannon taken, two were captured from us at Bull Run.

Extracts from a letter General Grant wrote to his father, whom he did not forget in his absorbing work on the war plains, will interest the reader. It bears the date of October 8th, 1862:

"I can say, with great gratification, that every colonel, without a single exception, set an example to their commands that inspired a confidence that will always insure victory when there is the slightest possibility of gaining one. I feel truly proud to command such men.

"From here we fought our way from tree to tree through the woods to Belmont, about two and a half miles, the enemy contesting every foot of ground. Here the enemy had strengthened their position by felling the trees for two or three hundred yards, and sharpening their limbs, making a sort of abatis. Our men charged through, making the victory complete, giving us possession of their camp and garrison equipage, artillery, and everything else.

"We got a great many prisoners. The majority, however, succeeded in getting aboard their steamers and pushing across the river. We burned everything possible, and started back, having accomplished all that we went for, and even more. Belmont is entirely covered by the batteries from Columbus, and is worth nothing as a military position—cannot be held without Columbus.

"The object of the expedition was to prevent the enemy from sending a force into Missouri to cut off troops I had sent there for a special purpose, and to prevent reenforcing Price.

"Besides being well fortified at Columbus, their number far exceeded ours, and it would have been folly to have attacked them. We found the Confederates well armed, and brave. On our return, stragglers, that had been left in our rear (now front), fired into us, and more recrossed the river and gave us battle for a full mile, and afterward at the boats, when we were embarking.

"There was no hasty retreating or running away. Taking into account the object of the expedition, the victory was complete. It has given us confidence in the officers and men of this command, that will enable us to lead them in any future engagement without fear of the result. General McClernand (who, by the way, acted with great coolness and courage throughout, and proved that he is a soldier as well as a statesman) and myself each had our horses shot under us. Most of the field officers met with the same loss, besides nearly one third of them being themselves killed or wounded. As near as I can ascertain, our loss was about two hundred and fifty killed, wounded, and missing."

Soon as the brigades returned to Cairo, the General expressed to them his delight in their heroism, referring to his Mexican campaigns for the first and only time, so far as we know:

HEADQUARTERS, DISTRICT OF SOUTHEAST MISSOURI,
CAIRO, November 8, 1861.

The General commanding this military district returns his thanks to the troops under his command at the battle of Belmont on yesterday.

It has been his fortune to have been in all the battles fought in Mexico by Generals Scott and Taylor, save Buena Vista, and he never saw one more hotly contested, or where troops behaved with more gallantry.

Such courage will insure victory wherever our flag may be borne and protected by such a class of men. To the brave men who fell, the sympathy of the country is due, and will be manifested in a manner unmistakable.

U. S. GRANT, Brig.-Gen. Commanding.

But the noble leader in the strife did not forget that there was a third class of men, besides the living in the ranks and the dead which had left them—the wounded in the hands of the enemy. When, after the struggle, General Grant, under a flag of truce, sent a detachment to bury the dead and remove the wounded, they heard the song of "The Star-spangled Banner" rising on the still air. Following the sound, they discovered under a tree a warrior with both legs mangled, from whose feverish lips the national anthem rang out over the gory plain. Of such material was the chieftain's army made.

Another incident strikingly illustrated a mournful peculiarity of the war—near relatives and friends fighting against each other. Captain Brooks, of the Twenty-seventh Illinois, came against a corpse. Looking at the dead surgeon, he recognized his own brother, who, he knew, was in the rebel army, but had no intimation where he was serving the cause of treason.

The rebels had not the means then in our power to care for even their own suffering troops on the red and furrowed field. General Grant sent a message to General Polk, requesting permission to have all these helpless soldiers taken from the field, and provided with medical treatment and proper attention. General Polk, replied that they were provided for, and his Government required him to place all prisoners at the disposal of the Secretary of War.

Four days later—November 12th—General Grant

sent to the Government an account of the Belmont fight. In this he says:

"The balance of my forces, with the exception of the reserve, was then thrown forward—all as skirmishers—and the enemy driven foot by foot, and from tree to tree, back to their encampment on the river bank, a distance of two miles. Here they had strengthened their position by felling the timber for several hundred yards around their camp, and making a sort of abatis. Our men charged through this, driving the enemy over the bank into their transports in quick time, leaving us in possession of everything not exceedingly portable. Belmont is on low ground, and every foot of it is commanded by the guns on the opposite shore, and, of course, could not be held for a single hour after the enemy became aware of the withdrawal of their troops. Having no wagons, I could not move any of the captured property; consequently, I gave orders for its destruction. Their tents, blankets, &c., were set on fire, and we retired, taking their artillery with us, two pieces being drawn by hand; and one other, drawn by an inefficient team, we spiked and left in the woods, bringing the two only to this place. Before getting fairly under way, the enemy made his appearance again, and attempted to surround us. Our troops were not in the least discouraged, but charged on the enemy again, and defeated him. Our loss was about eighty-four killed, one hundred and fifty wounded—many of them slightly—and about an equal number missing. Nearly all the missing were from the Iowa regiment, who behaved with great gallantry, and suffered more severely than any other of the troops."

Early in the winter, a new order of things commenced in the Western army, under General Halleck, who had been called from California, made a major-general, and put in command of the Department of the West. The limits of the military districts were more clearly defined, and a more complete control given to the officer in command. General Grant had made his mark. General Halleck saw in him a splendid commander, and, after enlarging the district of Cairo to one of the first importance, he put it in charge of General Grant. Another good step was taken in the path of renown. The man, as the boy had been, was still "slow and sure" in his progress— noiseless and steady in his course, like the rising sun.

The first thing to be done by the General, in his larger field of action, was to assign to the commanders under him their positions, and organize the new troops under his authority. These recruits were fitted for service and sent to Paducah, Fort Jefferson, and other points, to be ready for combined movements on the enemy, while the plan of dividing the forces in this way, would make it quite impossible for the rebels to guess correctly the number of men in General Grant's department.

When, on the 10th of January, 1862, General McClernand landed at Fort Jefferson with his forces, the rebels were on hand with armed vessels. So, in the morning, after the troops had gone ashore under the cover of the cannon of two gunboats, these pushed out into the river opposite the fort, guarding, like two dark sentinels, the transports which conveyed the men. It was a brief watch. Suddenly three armed vessels appeared moving directly upon the gunboats. Then, what a stir of preparation for a naval engagement! "Boom! boom!" go the heavy guns of the enemy; and a quick reply of louder tone flies from the decks of the waiting antagonist.

Though the rebels had three vessels to our two, after a brief trial of strength, the prows of the foe were turned toward Columbus, and ours in hot pursuit. They escaped only by getting under the guns of that fortress. During these preparations for grander movements, the enemy's pickets had shot many of our own in the neighborhood of Cairo. My young readers know what the duty of these men is. They are sent out in advance of the armies, to watch the enemy, and give notice of an advance. It is contrary to the rules of honorable warfare, and inhuman, to designedly kill them. It often happens, that random shot and shell destroy them. A rebel picket was found in a garden of the Southwest, dead, and with a rose in his hand, which he was plucking when the fatal messenger of destruction came among the flowers.

General Grant was justly indignant at the murder of his soldiers, who in the cold winter time had to stand in the chilly air long hours, with nothing to amuse or cheer them but the consciousness of fidelity to the country, and faith in God. He issued, therefore, the following order, reflecting honor upon the head and heart of its author:

HEADQUARTERS, CAIRO, January 11, 1862.

BRIGADIER-GENERAL PAINE, *Bird's Point:* I understand that four of our pickets were shot this morning. If this is so, and appearances indicate that the assassins were citizens, not regularly organized in the rebel army, the whole country should be cleared out for six miles around, and word given that all citizens making their appearance within those limits are liable to be shot.

To execute this, patrols should be sent out in all directions, and bring into camp, at Bird's Point, all citizens, together with their subsistence, and require them to remain, under the penalty of death and destruction of their property, until properly relieved.

Let no harm befal these people, if they quietly submit; but bring them in and place them in camp below the breastwork, and have them properly guarded.

The intention is not to make political prisoners of these people, but to cut off a dangerous class of spies.

This applies to all classes and conditions, age and sex. If, however, women and children prefer other protection than we can afford them, they may be allowed to retire beyond the limits indicated—not to return until authorized.

By order of

U. S. GRANT, Brig.-Gen. Commanding.

A great expedition was in prospect, and perfect secresy was desirable, as intimated in the order. In three columns, led by Generals Paine, McClernand, and C. F Smith, under General Grant, the large army of nineteen regiments of infantry, six of cavalry, and seven batteries of artillery, were to move. Their destination you will learn in the narrative of the vast enterprise. When this magnificent war machine was on the track, awaiting the will of the competent engineer, he gave the troops another order, which equally displays wisdom and manly patriotism:

"Disgrace having been brought upon our brave fellows by the bad conduct of some of their members, showing on all occasions, when marching through territory occupied by sympathizers of the enemy, a total disregard of the rights of citizens, and being guilty of wanton destruction of private property, the General commanding *desires and intends to enforce a change in this respect.* * * *

"It is ordered that the severest punishment be inflicted upon every soldier who is guilty of taking or destroying private property; and any commissioned officer guilty of like conduct, or of countenancing it, shall be deprived of his sword and expelled from the camp, not to be permitted to return."

It was now just midwinter. The Western and Northern homes still retained the cheerful light left by the "holidays;" and the merry bells of sleighing rang along the streets familiar to many of the brave volunteers. In the moving host on the banks of the Mississippi, the largest proportion had no other experience than these pleasant pastimes amid the business labors of peaceful life.

They now look on the broad river, filled with floating ice, on which they are to embark, and along the dreary roads of frost and mire beyond, and *think of home*. But no faltering and no complaint from "the boys," all unused to hardships, is seen or heard in those ranks.

McClernand threatened Columbus, to make the enemy believe an attack was at hand; while Grant sent other divisions around in the rear, to ascertain the enemy's strength. In six days, one column marched more than seventy-five miles, and the cavalry force one hundred and forty, amid storms and through mud and water.

The very important discovery was made by the daring and perilous expedition, that, between Columbus and the Paducah and Maysfield Railroad lying east of it, the enemy's force was not large; that Columbus itself was weaker than had been supposed; and that there were indirect roads to that stronghold not upon any map, affording means of attack unknown before. Indeed, that entire portion of Western Kentucky was open to the invasion of Union troops. And now the genius of the hero, in comprehensive, daring plans of campaign, appears.

The Cumberland and Tennessee rivers, you notice, on the boundary of Kentucky, approach each other. The distance between them, there, is a dozen miles. On the eastern side of the Tennessee, the enemy had built the fortress, Fort Henry; and on the western shore of the Cumberland is the still more formidable stronghold, Fort Donelson. You will see the great importance of the ramparts guarding the waters, when you trace these to the Ohio, and remember that, were there no obstruction, a Union army could pass from that river to the very centre of the treasonable Confederacy.

Commander Foote, of the navy, had been sent in the autumn of 1861 to create and command a fleet of gunboats on the Mississippi. He personally superintended the naval enterprise, and had now ready for service seven gunboats, four of which were iron-clad. They were built at Cincinnati and St. Louis, then taken to Cairo to complete the outfit, and man them. General Grant issued orders, when the crews were called for, requesting the land officers not to interfere with the demand, if their men were among the volunteers.

All this time, the troops were holding and blockading the ports at the mouth of the Tennessee and Cumberland rivers. Other forces on land and water kept up the alarm at Columbus, by firing on the fort. The silent, determined Grant, was getting thoroughly ready to make a bold push into Kentucky.

To deceive the enemy, if possible, is regarded as lawful policy in war. I suppose, on the same ground that you would feel it right to defend yourself by deception from a maniac, a person frantic with passion or strong drink, or even a ferocious beast. To escape or conquer, by creating false impressions and searching out the designs, has always been a part of the strategy and management of warfare.

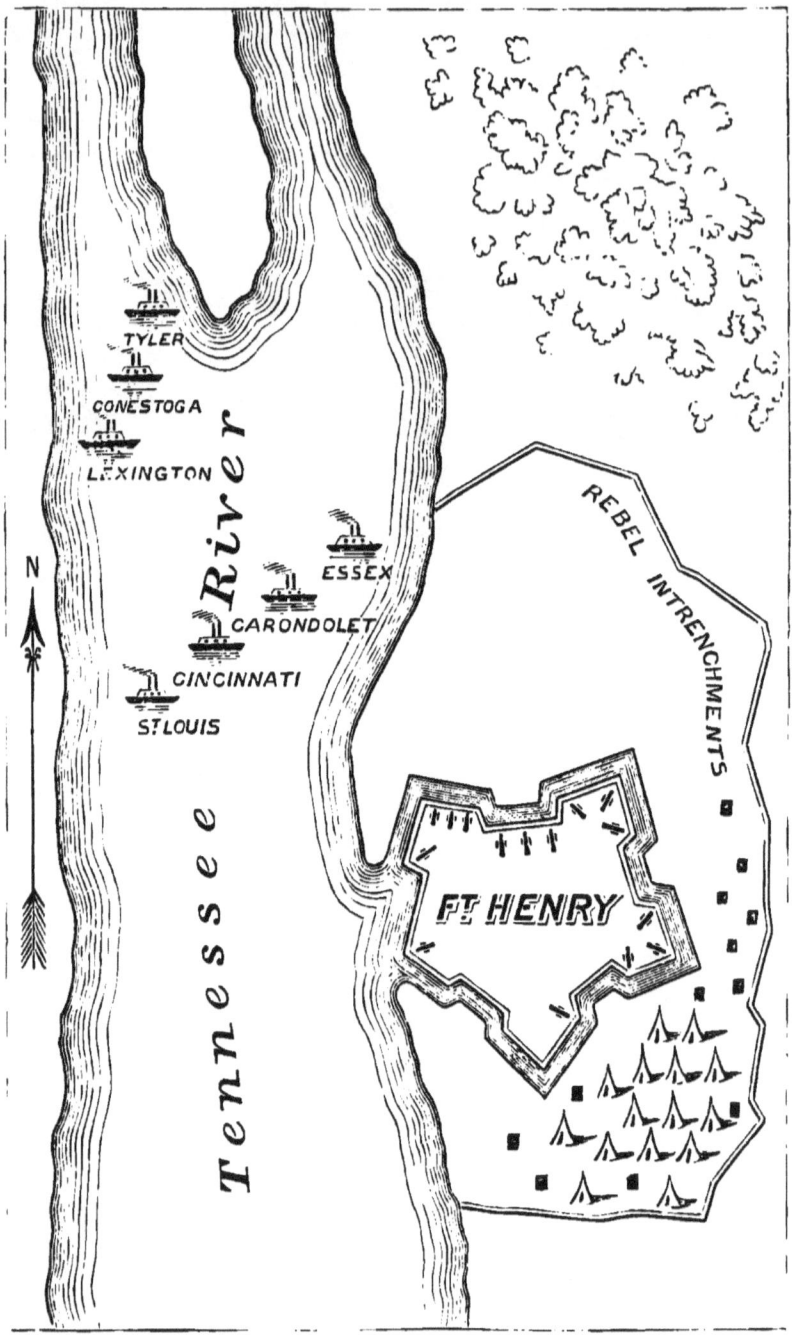

MAP OF FORT HENRY.—Page 81.

CHAPTER VII.

The Gunboats Move up the Tennessee—Delay—Open Fire upon Fort Henry—The Fort Surrenders—Right on to Fort Donelson—The Fleet Disabled—Foote Wounded—The Forces of Grant close on the Fortress—The Terrific Contest—The Victory—Promotion—Striking Contrasts.

FORT HENRY was to be the first goal of the grand advance. The first day of February was the Sabbath. In imagination you may go to Cairo, and glance at its scenes. In the streets it is *mud, mud, mud!* Dirty people, dogs, pigs, and carts are mingled in ludicrous confusion. Though a mild, sunny day, and birds are singing, nothing else, as you look, reminds you of the holy time. Steamers ascend with soldiers on the river, and all the sights of a port in time of war during the week, meet you in your walks about the town. But hark! the church bells toll the hour of worship. Sweet music amid the din and discord through which it floats! Enter this church, and, among the many soldiers, there is the nobly true and devout Commodore Foote. His fleet are ordered to keep the Sabbath, and maintain the worship of God in the ships.

With an army and navy led by such commanders, how sublime the spectacle, and how invincible the advance in a righteous cause! If you visit the flagship of the Commodore, he will show you, amid the fourteen heavy guns and all the strong machinery of those dark engines of destruction, the *Sacred Place*—a quiet spot, where those who desire may commune with God.

It is Monday. The strange fleet, unseen before upon the Western rivers, steams from Cairo with ten regiments of troops in accompanying steamers, and, at nightfall, wheels into the Tennessee. In the morning, approaching Fort Henry, the anchors are dropped and scouts sent ashore.

"You will never take Fort Henry!" said a woman in a farmhouse which they entered.

"Oh, yes, we shall. We have a fleet of iron-clad gunboats," said one.

"Your gunboats will be blown sky-high before they get into the fort."

"Ah! How so?"

The question reminded the talking woman that she was telling secrets, and she said no more. The scouts informed her that she must explain, or go with them a prisoner. She then said:

"Why, the river is full of torpedoes; and they will blow up your gunboats."

The intelligence was carried to the Commodore, and six infernal machines raked from the bottom. The plan was, to pour shot and shell upon the fort from the river in front, and drive with this storm of iron and fiery hail the rebels out, for General Grant to catch with his troops in the rear.

It seems that Admiral Foote had suggested to General Grant that the roads were so bad, it would be well for the land force to start an hour in advance. And when the General expressed his confidence in the ability of the troops to reach the field in time, the Admiral replied, good-naturedly: "I shall take the fort before your forces get there;" words that proved to be prophetic of the important result.

On the 5th, the fleet lay before the fortress, the dark-mouthed ordnance waiting the gunner's hand to pour forth fire and hail upon it. The first plan was to invest or surround the fort, before the attack, and to secure the garrison. But hearing that reënforcements were coming, at noon, it was decided not to wait for the troops, but that the Commodore should try the fight alone. The command flies over the fleet to open the battle. It is answered by a huzza, and in another moment the thunder of cannon shakes the decks, wrapped in smoke, and the massive iron hail and exploding shells falling in the fort give the garrison notice that the Yankee "tars" are knocking for admission within the walls. For two hours Fort Henry rained back her storm of heavy shot, striking the flagship Cincinnati thirty-one times. Suddenly the tempest ceases and the rebel flag comes down · the garrison begin to fly. General Tilghman, finding his retreat cut off by the advancing troops of General Grant, decides upon a surrender.

He was then rowed to the Admiral's ship, and, standing before him, inquires what terms would be granted. "Unconditional surrender!" was the brave and patriotic reply.

The rebel officer's answer were the words of a gentleman who appreciated high qualities of character in a foe:

"Well, sir, if I must surrender, it gives me pleasure to surrender to so brave an officer."

"You do perfectly right to surrender," added the heroic Foote; "but I should not have surrendered to you on any condition."

"Why so? I do not understand you," answered General Tilghman, with surprise.

"Because I was fully determined to capture the fort, or go to the bottom," was the satisfactory response of the gallant Admiral.

"I thought I had you, Commodore; but you were too much for me."

"How could you fight against the old flag, General?"

"Well, it did come hard at first; but if the North had let us alone, there would have been no trouble. They would not abide by the Constitution."

The Commodore assured him the opposite of that was the truth, and that the South was responsible for the blood shed that day.

Truly, "had more of this spirit been manifested in the early months of the war, the conflict would not have been so protracted." Thousands of lives would have been spared, and the bow of peace would now span the heavens, had half-hearted warfare and *unused* victories been confined to those "early months."

Soon after, General Grant arriving, the fruits of the conquest were handed over to him. The rebel account of the battle, given by General Tilghman in his despatches, bears fine testimony to the greatness of Grant's character, rising above the mean revenge and tyranny of baser minds when flushed with victory:

FORT HENRY, February 9, 1862.

Colonel W. W. MACKALL, A. A.-General, C. S. A., Bowling Green:

SIR: Through the courtesy of Brigadier-General U. S. Grant, commanding Federal forces, I am permitted to communicate with you in relation to the result of the action between the fort under my command at this place, and the Federal gunboats, on yesterday.

At eleven o'clock and forty minutes, on yesterday morning, the enemy engaged the fort with seven gunboats, mounting fifty-four guns. I promptly returned their fire, with the eleven guns from Fort Henry bearing on the river. The action was maintained with great bravery by the force under my command until ten minutes past two P. M., at which time I had but four guns fit for service. At five minutes before two, finding it impossible to maintain the fort, and wishing to spare the lives of the gallant men under my command, and on consultation with my officers, I surrendered the fort. Our casualties are small. The effect of our shot was severely felt by the enemy, whose superior and overwhelming force alone gave them the advantage. * * *

I communicate this result with deep regret, but feel that I performed my whole duty in the defence of my post.

I take occasion to bear testimony to the gallantry of the officers and men under my command. They maintained their position with consummate bravery, as long as there was any hope of success. I also take great pleasure in acknowledging the courtesies and consideration shown by Brigadier-General U. S. Grant and Commodore Foote, and the officers under their command.

I have the honor to remain, very respectfully,

Your obedient servant,

LLOYD TILGHMAN, Brig.-Gen. C. S. A.

Another interesting fact about this despatch is, the exhibition of Tilghman's character. Deluded with the attractive lie of secession, he speaks of duty with the earnestness of an honest man in a bad cause, and also displays the qualities of a gentleman. Doubtless there are many heroic, Christian officers and soldiers in the Confederate army, just as there were among the British troops when they attempted to force on us oppressive laws.

The prisoners were soon disposed of, and the fort garrisoned by Union troops. General Grant sent to his enthusiastic battalions an order, welcomed with a shout, to march the next morning toward Donelson. The occupation of Fort Henry was only "clearing the track" for that powerful defence. General Floyd, Buchanan's Secretary of War, was in command of the rebel forces. General Buckner commanded the men about the fort, while Generals Pillow and Johnson were at the head of other divisions. To the twenty thousand troops were added the fugitives from Fort Henry. General Grant's forces numbered about fifteen thousand. The enemy had the great advantage of a thoroughly fortified position. Again, there was some miscalculation in regard to the time required to march along the winding way, over sand hills, through ravines, and forests ancient and dark, lying between the forts. The first day, the column moved four miles into the woods, and there, tentless, lay down on the cold ground, around their crackling fires, to bivouac for the night.

The pickets silently watched for signs of a lurking enemy.

General Lewis Wallace was left at Fort Henry to keep the prize. Colonels Oglesby, Wallace, McArthur, and Morrison bravely led brigades of Western boys. Schwartz, Taylor, Dresser, and McAllister had with this division their fine batteries. In the second division, Colonel Lanman was at the head of the second brigade, Colonel Smith the third; Major Corender had a regiment of Missouri artillery. But there was a singular body of troops deserving special notice—Colonel Birges' sharpshooters. They were old hunters in the grand woods, and could pick a squirrel from a treetop far as he could be seen. A little tight cap covered their heads; a knapsack of buffalo skin, and a powder horn, hung upon the gray felt uniform. Each had a shrill whistle. They came and went, like unearthly messengers of death, through the dim forest, delighted with the wild excitement and hardships of their weird life. The cavalry swept the country to see what the enemy were about.

Such was Grant's cavalcade, moving forward in the light of the next morning, February 12th.

In the afternoon, the white tents of the enemy on the hills in the intrenchments came in sight. After surveying the field of impending battle, again the soldiers slept on the ground, a chilly wind fanning the fires of their camp. But the following day was bright and mild. While yet the rosy beams which herald the sun glowed in the east, the sudden scream of a rebel shell was heard over the heads of Colonel Oglesby's brigade. "Hurrah! hurrah!" is the response. Every brave fellow is at his gun, or standing ready to hear the order to answer the foe. There stood sombre Donelson, frowning defiance on the advancing host of the Republic, with flying banners wheeling around the citadel of treason and anarchy.

Soon McClernand's division defile away to the west and south of the fortifications, and Smith's to the north and west. Could you have looked from the battlements of Donelson, you would have beheld the Union army forming a great crescent, with its tips nearly to the river's bank above and below the fort; thus holding the massive defence *in the curve*. The centre of the curve was not complete. The transports on the waters were to furnish the troops for this important point. The boats were *not* "on time." But the hostile armies were too near not to fight. Sanguinary skirmishing, and occasionally a deadly

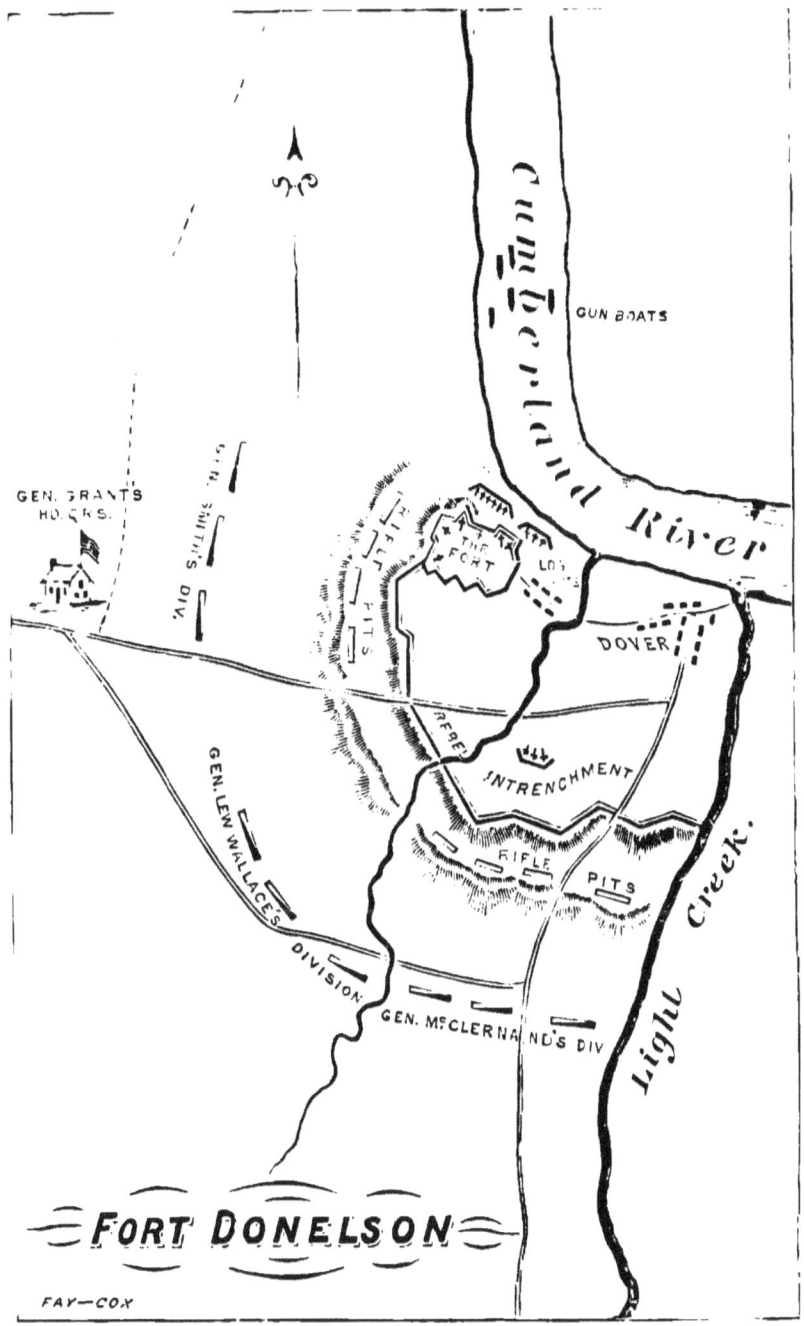

MAP OF FORT DONELSON.—Page 68.

contest for some position outside of the ramparts, became the order of the day—the prelude of the awful tragedy at hand.

Among the rifle pits and earthworks west of the town, was a redoubt, or walled defence, protecting rebel batteries. General McClernand decided to take it. The men from the prairies, whose field of action had been the furrowed plain and golden harvest land, went up without wavering to the volcanic centre. They reached the impassable abatis. Taylor's splendid battery dashed forward to the rescue, but the rifle bullets of the enemy dropped his gunners. Colonel Birges' hunters were sent for, and soon stole in ambush near the lines of fire. Away sped the balls. Soon the rebel guns were silenced. A head, apparently, rose above the breastworks; toward it whistled a bullet, piercing only *a hat.* A shout of laughter from the enemy followed. "Why don't you come out of your old fort?" shouted a concealed sharpshooter. "Why don't you come in?." was the reply. "Oh, you are cowards!" exclaimed another Union soldier. "When are you going to take the fort?" came back.

At three o'clock P. M. on the 14th, Commodore Foote brought up the already scarred leviathans of naval warfare, and opened the assault upon the fort. In another moment, fire, smoke, falling shot and bursting shells covered the fleet, and the lofty walls and grounds of Fort Donelson. It was a terrible scene.

While Commodore Foote's flagship, the St. Louis,

was under a tempest of the massive iron hail, he said to the pilot, kindly: "Be calm and firm. Everything depends upon coolness now." The next moment, a sixty-four pound shot came hissing along the decks; a stunning sound—a crash—and the pilot lay a mangled corpse at the Commodore's feet. The ball had crushed its way through the iron plating, and a fragment pierced the Admiral's ankle. Still, his courage and faith made him quite forgetful of the painful injury. Through the steering apparatus of this vessel and the Louisville, other heavy balls have been hurled, leaving them both at the mercy of the current; and they were compelled to drift from the scene of action. In one hour and a quarter it was all over, and Fort Donelson was wild with the hurrah of fancied victory.

It was now General Grant's turn to try on the land side, and see what he could do. He determined to invest the fort, watch and wait, till the disabled gunboats were ready to join in the onset again. But the rebels, after a council of war by the generals, unexpectedly decided his plan of operations. On the 15th, early in the morning, a large body of their troops was hurled suddenly upon the extreme right of General Grant's encircling army. It seemed an auspicious moment for the cause of treason. The prince of Government thieves, Floyd, was as sure of the Union army as he was of the public property, when in the Cabinet of a President who was willing to be the tool of such traitors. Generals Pillow and Johnson were to hurl half of the rebel army upon McClernand: General

Buckner was to dash on General Wallace from another point, and beat his forces back on McClernand, and so throw the whole into hopeless confusion.

The light of Saturday, February 15th, lay on the battlements of the fortress, and on the myriad tents within and around it. In the loyal North, but few were astir in the wintry air. The partially disciplined but brave volunteers were startled from their sleep on the cold ground, to meet the mighty tide of battle. With flying banners, and shouts, the hostile columns sweep down upon the extreme right of General Grant's encircling battalions.

The Union ranks stand up bravely; but there is a limit to the most heroic resistance, and they fall back before the overwhelming force, leaving two batteries of artillery in the enemy's hands. Reënforcements hasten to the relief of our men, and then the two lines close in deadly combat; both seem resolved to conquer, or be annihilated. The rebels yield, losing their batteries, excepting three of the guns; but, reënforced, they rush back with fiend-like yells, flanking our troops. The day looks dark for the Stars and Stripes.

The worst of all is, that at this moment other Union regiments brought into the field mistake their brethren in arms for the enemy, and open fire. Great confusion, of course, follows. Frightened troops fly to the rear, tossing their guns away as they go. Among these, see that officer, Gilpin-like, plunging down the road, looking pale and wild, crying: "We are cut to pieces! The day is lost!"

"Shut up your head, you scoundrel!" is the blunt and stern reply of General Wallace.

General Pillow telegraphed to Nashville: "On the honor of a soldier, the day is ours!"

Whoever thought this in the ranks of the rebels, or feared it in our own, General Grant did not. If it were true that the battle was lost, he felt, as did another chieftain, that "there was time to fight another."

Generals Buckner and Pillow united their brigades, and again moved upon our ranks, fancying they had not much more fighting to do to complete the victory. The dead and wounded on the conquered field have been robbed. Flushed with success and spoils, they opened the terrific storm of battle hail again. Over the bloody brook, the piled bodies, and the mangled living, rushed the angry masses of armed men. The rebel forces struck at length the First Nebraska, whose stalwart hunters neither feared nor wasted fire, and the "proud waves were stayed." They stood wild and raging a moment; and, failing where the hunters were most effective in their aim, then trembling, rolled back.

It was noon. The chagrined Pillow began to realize the sentiment of Dr. Young:

"Our morning's glory is our evening's sigh."

Lying before the breastworks, in ambush, were Birges' sharpshooters. A splendid rebel marksman, whose rifle had slain a number of our officers, and one of these hunt ers, had a singular, almost a comical duel. The former, raising his hat above the ramparts, deceived the sharpshooter, sending a loud laugh to the equally shrewd antagonist. Then a return shot passed over him. Turning on his back, he loaded his gun, and lay perfectly still. After waiting awhile, the rebel thought his ball had done the work. Up went his head, cap and all, that he might enjoy the view of his dead enemy. "Crack!" went the well-aimed rifle, and backward into the trenches fell the just now laughing rebel.

Now look into that tent at headquarters, where our hero of the "timber-hauling" memory sits, without any shadow of despondency on his face; whose lips, well surrounded by short, sandy hair, are compressed with his native inflexibility of purpose. One after another the subordinate officers bring in reports from the commanders. His lighted eye glances over the pages scarcely dry, and with triumph he exclaims to a member of his staff: "We have them now just where we want them." His plan is formed. The rifle pits on the northwest angle of the fort must be carried, and make an approach for the batteries to shell it. General Smith's division, stationed there, had been in reserve, and could start fresh on the daring and awful venture. General Wallace is ordered to drive the rebels, before whom he had retired, back, and assault the works there.

Colonel M. L. Smith led the brigade. Right there on the bloody field, with a desperate attack before them, and certain death to many, the Eighth and Eleventh Missouri fairly quarreled for the honor of taking the front, the most exposed position in the assault. What patriotic and martial enthusiasm! And that is the way the Western "boys" go into any great enterprise. Half-hearted ways of doing, they know nothing about. To the announcement of the work before them, the reply was, "Hurrah! hurrah!" and then "Forward!" to the storming of the ramparts. But away in the mellow glory of the setting sun, in solid masses, General Smith's division advances over the meadow, toward the bristling rows of rifle pits. Along the dauntless lines of "citizen soldiery," like an incarnation of the daring and gallantry of the high occasion, rides the veteran, his long locks whitening to the "almond blossom," streaming back upon the electric air of that eventful evening. Another moment, the crater of destruction opens. Heavy shot and bursting shell make clean avenues through the unflinching columns. They close again for another harvest of death. Up and down that front, lifting high his cap, amid the hissing missiles that rend the air, gallops General Smith. "Steady! steady!" and it is steady—steady advance and steady slaughter. Wallace is doing his work on the right, and Cook upon the left. Against fallen trees, into the thunder-cloud ablaze, and raining bolts, the unshrinking battalions dash, as though they were leaping into the spray of a summer sea.

Watch a moment, my young friend, that apparent

chaos of confusion, wrapped in flame and smoke. "Hurrah! hurrah!" Look! the Stars and Stripes are waving in the farewell smile of the terrible yet glorious day. The blackened remnant of the assaulting columns stand on the heights; while all along the Union lines ring the glad shouts of restored confidence and of exultation.

The sun goes down on a gory scene, but with the clear promise of victory upon his return to light the fortress piled within and around with bodies of the slain.

The morning dawned; and when the brave men looked toward the unconquered battlements, behold, a flag of truce was flying there! The foe has decided to negotiate for a surrender.

We must let "Carleton," who was there, tell, from the lips of a captured officer, what transpired in the fort during that night of repose to our wearied warriors:

"I cannot hold my position a half hour. The Yankees can turn my flank or advance directly upon the breastworks," said General Buckner.

"If you had advanced at the time agreed upon, and made a more vigorous attack, we should have routed the enemy," said General Floyd.

"I advanced as soon as I could, and my troops fought as bravely as others," was the response from General Buckner, a middle-aged, medium-sized man. His hair is iron gray. He has thin whiskers and a moustache, and wears a gray kersey overcoat with a great cape, and gold lace on the sleeves, and a black hat with a nodding black plume.

"Well, here we are, and it is useless to renew the attack with any hope of success. The men are exhausted," said General Floyd, a stout, heavy man, with thick lips, a large nose, evil eyes, and coarse features.

"We can cut our way out," said Major Brown, commanding the Twentieth Mississippi, a tall, black-haired, impetuous, fiery man.

"Some of us might escape in that way, but the attempt would be attended with great slaughter," responded General Floyd.

"My troops are so worn out and cut to pieces and demoralized, that I can't make another fight," said Buckner.

"My troops will fight till they die!" answered Major Brown, setting his teeth together.

"It will cost the command three quarters of its present number to cut its way through; and it is wrong to sacrifice three quarters of a command to save the other quarter," Buckner continued.

"No officer has a right to cause such a sacrifice," said Major Gilmer, of General Pillow's staff.

"But we can hold out another day, and by that time we can get steamboats here to take us across the river," said General Pillow.

"No, I can't hold my position a half hour; and the Yankees will renew the attack at daybreak," Buckner replied.

"Then we have got to surrender, for aught I see," said an officer.

"I won't surrender the command, neither will I be taken prisoner," said Floyd. He doubtless remembered how he had stolen public property while in office under Buchanan, and would rather die than to fall into the hands of those whom he knew would be likely to bring him to an account for his villany.

"I don't intend to be taken prisoner," said Pillow.

"What will you do, gentlemen?" Buckner asked.

"I mean to escape, and take my Virginia brigade with me, if I can. I shall turn over the command to General Pillow. I have a right to escape if I can, but I haven't any right to order the entire army to make a hopeless fight," said Floyd.

"If you surrender it to me, I shall turn it over to General Buckner," said General Pillow, who was also disposed to shirk responsibility and desert the men whom he had induced to vote to secede from the Union and take up arms against their country.

"If the command comes into my hands, I shall deem it my duty to surrender it. I shall not call upon the troops to make a useless sacrifice of life, and I will not desert the men who have fought so nobly," Buckner replied, with a bitterness which made Floyd and Pillow wince.

It was past midnight. The council broke up. The brigade and regimental officers were astonished at the result. Some of them broke out into horrid cursing and swearing at Floyd and Pillow.

"It is mean!" "It is cowardly!" "Floyd always was a rascal."

"We are betrayed!" "There is treachery!" said they

"It is a mean trick for an officer to desert his men. If my troops are to be surrendered, I shall stick by them," said Major Brown.

"I denounce Pillow as a coward; and if I ever meet him, I'll shoot him as quick as I would a dog," said Major McLain, red with rage.

Floyd gave out that he was going to join Colonel Forrest, who commanded the cavalry, and thus cut his way out; but there were two or three small steamboats at the Dover landing. He and General Pillow jumped on board one of them, and then secretly marched a portion of the Virginia brigade on board. Other soldiers saw what was going on—that they were being deserted. They became frantic with terror and rage. They rushed on board, crowding every part of the boat.

"Cut loose!" shouted Floyd to the captain.

The boats swung into the stream and moved up the river, leaving thousands of infuriated soldiers on the landing. So, the man who had stolen the public property, and who did all he could to bring on the war, who induced thousands of poor, ignorant men to take up arms, deserted his post, stole away in the darkness, and left them to their fate.

It is not strange that a messenger appeared, bringing this message:

> HEADQUARTERS, FORT DONELSON, February 16, 1862.
>
> SIR: In consideration of all the circumstances governing the present situation of affairs at this station, I propose to the commanding officer of the Federal forces the appointment of commissioners to agree upon terms of capitulation of the forces and fort under my command, and, in that view, suggest an armistice till twelve o'clock to-day.
>
> I am, sir, respectfully, your obedient servant,
>
> S. B. BUCKNER, Brig.-Gen. C. S. A.
>
> To Brigadier-General GRANT, commanding United States forces near Fort Donelson.

Had the rebel General known his conqueror, he would never have sent such a line. Grant did not want many minutes to consider his reply. In place of any such proposal, the bearer's hand had the subjoined brief and comprehensive note:

> HEADQUARTERS, ARMY IN THE FIELD,
> CAMP NEAR DONELSON, Feb. 16, 1862.
>
> To GENERAL S. B. BUCKNER, Confederate Army:
>
> Yours of this date, proposing an armistice, and appointment of commissioners to settle terms of capitulation, is just received. *No terms other than unconditional and immediate surrender can be accepted. I propose to move immediately upon your works.*
>
> I am, respectfully, your obedient servant,
>
> U. S. GRANT, Brig.-Gen. U. S. A. Commanding.

Buckner knew, what Grant did not, that Pillow and Floyd had fled the night before, leaving him alone. The proud, helpless, and chagrined Buckner was obliged to make the best of a very unpleasant affair. So he wrote this answer:

HEADQUARTERS, DOVER, TENNESSEE, Feb. 16, 1862.

To Brigadier-General U. S. GRANT, U. S. A.:

SIR: The distribution of the forces under my command, incident to an unexpected change of commanders, and the overwhelming force under your command, compel me, notwithstanding the brilliant success of the Confederate arms yesterday, to accept the ungenerous and unchivalrous terms which you propose.

I am, sir, your very obedient servant,

S. B. BUCKNER, Brig.-Gen. C. S. A.

And thus fell into the hands of General Grant and his army, the whole of the forces that garrisoned the works of Forts Henry and Donelson, with the exception of one small brigade of rebel troops, which escaped during the night with Generals Floyd and Pillow.

No pen can describe the delirium of joy, when the shattered columns of freedom marched with music and banners into the abandoned fortress. Men torn with fragments of iron forgot their pain, and hurrahed for the flag over them.

The rebel loss in the surrender of Fort Henry, was the commander, General Tilghman, his staff, and about sixty men, the rest of the garrison having moved to support the troops at Fort Donelson. At Fort Donelson, the rebels lost General Buckner, over thirteen thousand prisoners, three thousand horses, forty-eight field pieces, seventeen heavy guns, twenty thousand stand of arms, and a large quantity of commissary stores. The rebels killed in the last engagement were two hundred and thirty-one, and wounded, one thousand and seven, some of whom were prisoners. The Union loss was four hundred and forty-six killed, one thousand seven hundred and thirty-five wounded, and one hundred and fifty prisoners. The Union troops having to fight in an open field, against the works of the rebels, accounts for the disparity of numbers in killed and wounded.

Two regiments of rebel Tennesseeans, who had been ordered to reënforce the garrison at Fort Donelson, marched into that work on the day after the capitulation, being unaware of its capture. They went along, with their colors flying and their bands playing, and were allowed to enter the camp without any warning as to the character and nationality of those who held it in possession. The whole force (one thousand four hundred and seventy-five men and officers) were at once captured.

The result of this campaign was far more valuable than would at the first sight appear. The rebel line, at this particular part of the country, may be said to have extended from Columbus to Bowling Green, Ky., a distance of one hundred and twenty miles, with the extreme points of each wing resting on those two places, which had been strongly fortified. The reduction of Forts Henry and Donelson, and the opening of the rivers at this point, broke the centre or backbone of this whole line, and, as a natural consequence, the wings had to fall. In a few days after, both Bowling Green and Columbus were in the possession of the Union troops, the rebels having evacuated those defences.

The victory was telegraphed to Washington in the following words:

CAIRO, February 17, 1862.

To Major-General McCLELLAN:

The Union flag floats over Fort Donelson. The Carondelet, Captain Walke, brings the glorious intelligence.

The fort surrendered at nine o'clock yesterday (Sunday) morning. General Buckner and about fifteen thousand prisoners, and a large amount of materiel of war, are the trophies of the victory. Loss heavy on both sides.

Floyd, the thief, stole away during the night previous, with five thousand men, and is denounced by the rebels as a traitor. I am happy to inform you that Flag-Officer Foote, though suffering with his foot, with the noble characteristic of our navy, notwithstanding his disability, will take up immediately two gunboats, and, with the eight mortar boats which he will overtake, will make an immediate attack on Clarksville, if the state of the weather will permit. We are now firing a national salute from Fort Cairo, General Grant's late post, in honor of the glorious achievement.

[Signed]   GEO. W. CULLUM,
Brig.-Gen. Vols. and U. S. A. and Chief of Staff and Engineers

To the dispatch was added these patriotic words:

"The United States flag now waves over Tennessee It shall never be removed."

The victory was attended with displays of valor unrivalled in the war fields of the world. Oh, how those volunteers of the West breasted the wasting fire, and went down in ranks, hailing, with dying shout and glance, the starry flag! In the Ninth Illinois regiment, a soldier received a shot through his arm. The wound was dressed, and again he hastened to his place in the ranks. Soon after, a ball entered his thigh, and he fell. His brave associates offered him help. "No," he replied; "I think I can get along alone." Away he staggered, leaning on his gun, through the iron and leaden hail, found a surgeon, who did *his* work, and gave the brave refreshment. He rose, and saying, "I feel pretty well; I must go into the fight again," he joined his comrades. He stooped to point his gun; a bullet pierced his neck, and went downward into his body. The next moment, balls riddled his head, and the mangled hero fell in death. Such were the warriors, who, thinking not of fame or life, lay down under the dear old flag waving on the battered walls of Donelson.

The magnificent conquest sent a thrill of joy over the nation. Thousands of cannon in the peaceful towns of the North thundered forth the rejoicing, and banners floated over almost every loyal house.

Our modest victor, in the successful performance of a great duty to the country he loved better than life, took another stride in the rapid march of fame. He was made Major-General of Volunteers, dating from the day of the fort's surrender, February 16, 1862.

No one would suspect, from the manner of General Grant, amid these exciting events and clustering honors, the echoing salutes and hurrahs of the soldiery and the people, that he was the hero and object of them all. Unostentatious, "calm as a clock," he kept time to the "drum-beat of duty," unheeding the storm of conflict, or the sunshine of triumph around him.

Let us take a glimpse of scenes apart from the hero and the strife. A friend, who went to the fort after the victory, in behalf of the Christian Commission—one of the noblest enterprises called out by the war, blessing the embattled hosts in its care for them physically and spiritually—related two striking incidents. He visited a hospital steamer, and found, not far apart, fatally wounded, a religious and a profane young man. The former was ready to die under the old flag, with a banner seen only by faith, bearing the "Star of Bethlehem," and the "stripes by which we are healed" flying over him. The other said: "I have never prayed. And do you think, after such a life, I will now ask for mercy? Never! I will face the music." And soon he also died.

Going to the plains of death, he saw a soldier half buried in the snowy mud, lying on his back, with a Testament, which had fallen from the side pocket of his coat, on the breast. Farther on, he came against a corpse, from the pocket of whose coat a pack of cards had dropped, and were scattered over it, and on the ground. What instructive contrasts along the track of unpitying war!

In the *Atlantic Monthly* appeared the following fine little poem, commemorative of the costly yet magnificent victory:

"O gales, that dash the Atlantic's swell
    Along our rocky shores,
Whose thunders diapason well
    New England's glad hurrahs;

"Bear to the prairies of the West
    The echoes of our joy,
The prayer that springs in every breast—
    'God bless thee, Illinois!'

"Oh, awful hours, when grape and shell
    Tore through the unflinching line!
'Stand firm! Remove the men who fell!
    Close up, and wait the sign!'

"It came at last: 'Now, lads, the steel!'
    The rushing hosts deploy;
'Charge, boys!' The broken traitors reel;
    Hurrah for Illinois!

'In vain thy rampart, Donelson,
    The living torrent bars;
It leaps the wall—the fort is won—
    Up go the Stripes and Stars.

"Thy proudest mother's eyelids fill,
 As dares her gallant boy,
And Plymouth Rock and Bunker Hill
 Yearn to thee, Illinois."

CHAPTER VIII.

The more the Hero does, the more is he expected to do—His Kingdom Enlarged—Anecdote about his Habits—Major-General Grant's First Work—Congratulations—Martial Movements—No Plundering allowed—Up the River—Sword presented—Scours the Country—Moves toward Corinth—Preparations for Battle.

HE fighting yet prudent chief had brought under the Union flag so much territory from the mad rule of treason, the Government presumed he could go on "conquering and to conquer."

And, accordingly, the field was laid out for vaster and more difficult operations. February 14th, General Halleck, who was at the head of military affairs, formed for Grant the new district of West Tennessee. Refer to the map once more, and you will observe its extent. It was bounded on the south by Tennessee River and State line of Mississippi, and on the northwest by Mississippi River, far north as Cairo. He could select his own headquarters. Over this large region he was military king. That is, he had the control of affairs in his own hands. And you must not forget, that no monarchy is more absolute than the power of martial command. The genius of its unquestioned sway is well expressed by the Roman centurion's words to Christ, nearly two thousand years ago: "For I am a man under authority, having soldiers under me; and I say to this man, Go, and he goeth; to another, Come, and he cometh; and to my servant, Do this, and he doeth it." This power *will* be abused by bad men. A poor sick soldier carried the certificate of his inability to serve, signed by the surgeons and all inferior officers, to the commander; who, half intoxicated, refused to read them, and ordered the man on duty. He had to obey; but, in the effort to do so, staggered a moment, and fell dead. Such facts are too many, and sad enough. Power is a dangerous trust.

It has proved to be safe in the rapidly-growing command of General Grant. Many of the officers of the regular army, pleading, as an apology, the change of climate and social scenes away from domestic life, have freely used stimulants. This is a deplorable habit, and never a protection against exposure.

Provost-General M. R. Patrick, of the Potomac army, a Christian patriot and hero, who had been in Mexico with "Bob Lee," as he called him familiarly, and went through the Seminole war, assured me that only those who, with himself, abstained entirely from strong drink, escaped Southern diseases, without fleeing, in hot weather, to the North.

Some amusing incidents have occurred in connection

with the stories about General Grant; who is a thoroughly correct, and, many Christian friends believe, a religious man. About this time, several gentlemen, acting as a delegation, called on General Halleck, and desired his removal, when the following scene occurred:

"You see, General," said the spokesman, "we have a number of Illinois volunteers under General Grant, and it is not safe that their lives should be intrusted to the care of a man who so constantly indulges in intoxicating liquors. Who knows what blunders he may commit!"

"Well, gentlemen," said General Halleck, "I am satisfied with General Grant, and I have no doubt you also soon will be."

While the deputation were staying at the hotel, the news arrived of the capture of Fort Donelson and thirteen thousand prisoners. General Halleck posted the intelligence himself on the hotel bulletin; and, as he did so, he remarked, loud enough for all to hear:

"If General Grant is such a drunkard as he is reported to be, and can win such victories as these, I think it is my duty to issue an order, that any man found sober in St. Louis to-night shall be punished with fine and imprisonment."

This was ironical pleasantry, designed to silence the complaining gentlemen, who were evidently not as much afraid of *intemperance*, as they were of General Grant.

"Do you know what the personal habits of General Grant are?" was the interrogation addressed to one who had fought long under him. He answered:

"I know that he is one of the most moderate of men in his desires. His purity is equal to his modesty. His personal character, to my certain knowledge, is without a blot. He is tenderly devoted to his wife and family."

The first official act in the wider field of his wise administration, was a congratulatory order. He had not been in haste, as an inferior, inflated mind would have been; but when the calm of a new order of things came, he addressed his brave troops:

HEADQUARTERS, DISTRICT OF WEST TENNESSEE,
FORT DONELSON, February 17, 1862.

The General commanding, takes great pleasure in congratulating the troops of this command for the triumph over rebellion gained by their valor, on the 13th, 14th, and 15th instant.

For four successive nights, without shelter, during the most inclement weather known in this latitude, they faced an enemy in large force, in a position chosen by himself. Though strongly fortified by nature, all the additional safeguards suggested by science were added. Without a murmur this was borne, prepared at all times to receive an attack, and, with continuous skirmishing by day, resulting ultimately in forcing the enemy to surrender without condition.

The victory achieved is not only great in the effect it will have in breaking down rebellion, but has secured the greatest number of prisoners of war ever taken in any battle on this continent.

Fort Donelson will hereafter be marked in capitals on the map of our united country, and the men who fought the battle will live in the memory of a grateful people.

By order,

U. S. GRANT, Brig.-Gen. Commanding.

The day before this order was issued, February 16th, he was made Major-General. He did not pause to enjoy victories, or simple authority. He followed up, with tireless activity, every advantage gained. This is the only royal road to success anywhere in life.

Commodore Foote's fleet was sent toward the headwaters of the Cumberland, and a land force to act with it, along the western shore.

Three days later, Clarksville, a depot of supplies sufficient for Grant's use nearly a month, surrendered without a shot; resistance was so utterly hopeless. He ordered the destruction of the Tennessee Iron Works, which furnished iron plates for rebel ships; and the torch was applied to the extensive buildings, making one of the many bonfires that blaze along the track of war.

War is only *waste*, from beginning to end. The object of the ruin to property, is to weaken the strength of the foe. With all the attending loss and horrors, as the world is, an appeal to arms is sometimes unavoidable, if justice and truth are maintained.

Leaving a sufficient force there to hold and use the place, February 20th the gunboats pushed onward toward Nashville, anticipating its conquest by the Union army. Martial law was declared; in other words, *army rule*, till the number of loyal citizens was large enough to maintain civil law in West Tennessee.

Major-General Grant was fully committed, in feeling and action, to the righteous cause of crushing the excuse-less rebellion. But he hoped the South would see the folly and ruin of her course; he therefore avoided all occasions for unjust and ungenerous complaint, whatever the inhumanity of his foes. How considerate and magnanimous the tone of the proclamation, "published for the information of the command":

Headquarters, Department of Missouri,
St. Louis, February 23.

The Major-General commanding this department desires to impress upon all officers the importance of preserving good order and discipline among these troops, and the armies of the West, during their advance into Tennessee and the Southern States.

Let us show to our fellow citizens of these States, that we come merely to crush out this rebellion, and to restore to them peace and the benefits of the Constitution and the Union, of which they have been deprived by selfish and unprincipled leaders. They have been told that we come to oppress and plunder. By our acts we will undeceive them. We will prove to them that we come to restore, not violate, the Constitution and the laws. In restoring to them the glorious flag of the Union, we will assure them that they shall enjoy, under its folds, the same protection of life and property as in former days.

Soldiers! let no excesses on your part tarnish the glory of our arms! The orders heretofore issued from this department in regard to pillaging, marauding, and the destruction of private property, and the stealing and concealment of slaves, must be strictly enforced. It does not belong to the military to decide upon the relation of master and slave. Such questions must be settled by the civil courts. No fugitive slave will, therefore, be admitted within our lines or camps, except when especially ordered by the General commanding. Women and children, merchants, farmers, and all persons not in arms, are to be regarded as non-combatants, and are not to be molested, either in their persons or property. If, however, they assist and aid the enemy, they become belligerents, and will be treated as such. As they violate the laws of war, they will be made to suffer the penalties of such violation.

Military stores and public property of the enemy must be surrendered; and any attempt to conceal such property by fraudulent transfer, or otherwise, will be punished. But no private property will be touched, unless by order of the General commanding.

Whenever it becomes necessary, forced contributions for supplies and subsistence for our troops will be made. Such levies will be made as light as possible, and be so distributed as to produce no distress among the people. All property so taken must be receipted fully and accepted for as heretofore directed.

These orders will be read at the head of every regiment, and all officers are commanded strictly to enforce them.

By command of   Major-General HALLECK.
W. H. MCLEAN, Adjutant-General.
   By order of   Major-General U. S. GRANT.
J. A. RAWLINS, A. A. G.

Then came the evacuation of Nashville by the enemy, and its occupation by our troops under General Buell, of whom a rebel officer remarked:

"We can leave our homes, and General Buell will protect our slave property more vigilantly than we can do it ourselves."

February 23d, General Grant accompanied Admiral Foote up the river to Nashville. The sail was all unlike bloody war! The banks were green, the birds singing in the fragrant air, and bloom and verdure lay in the background to the horizon's rim. A week had passed since the dead of Donelson were buried; and the wounded were lying without such sights to gladden the filmy eye of the wasted warriors. When the troops still in the ranks walked the streets of Nashville, no rebels were so insulting as *females*. General Buell could not endure it, even from *Southern women*. Look up to that handsome piazza, under whose shadow he is passing. The fair and proud owner waves a secession flag, shouting: "Hurrah for Jeff. Davis and the Southern Confederacy!" The General's horse makes "right about face," and the rider lifts his hat, quietly saying: "An excellent house for a hospital." Before the sun went down, the *ambulances* stood before the door of the mansion, and the stretchers passed through it.

General Grant called on Mrs. James K. Polk, the widow of the former President, under whose administration was opened the Mexican war, and the cadet commenced his military career. He little dreamed then, he should ever call upon the widow, a rebel in a conquered city.

The interview was cold and formal. She merely expressed the hope that her husband's *tomb* would be the protection of her home and property. The United States, which so elevated her before almost unknown husband, she despised.

The work on the Cumberland was now well done; and the fleet of Commodore Foote, who, since the terrible scenes at Donelson, on crutches had been dragging his swollen, aching ankle around the ship's deck, with cheerful devotion to the dear flag, started up the Tennessee River.

The voyage was often very exciting. The Union citizens, who from fear had been silent, came out openly, and, lining the banks, hailed with shouts of welcome the starry banner of their country. Others muttered words of scorn and hate, and acted more like growling demons than Americans.

Finding there were not large bodies of the hostile troops in the region, General Grant removed his headquarters from St. Louis to Fort Henry, resolved to push the war ships a hundred miles or more up the Tennessee.

It is a singular fact, showing how much mean rivalry and disloyalty there has been in the army and at the North, that, soon as a general became successful, the slanderous report went abroad, and efforts were made for his removal. But in some instances, the cause of disaffection, if known, would have justly awakened public indignation.

When General Grant was appointed to his command, he was approached by certain reporters of the press, to secure a place, and the compensation of it, on his staff. Generals Halleck, Sherman, and C. F. Smith agreed with the upright Grant, that no Government funds should be applied to such a purpose. The "cut" made a wound, whose irritation was aimed at the offenders. General Sherman was called crazy, and General Smith a traitor

It was only at the special request of General Grant, that the Senate confirmed the nomination of General Smith, and he was able to retain General Sherman; he assuring the Government that both were true men.

Much of the abuse of General Grant, from time to time, is traceable to the same source. It is easy to give offence, by stern integrity, to the "hangers-on" and followers of an army. It is easier still, after a paper, however obscure, has boldly assailed an officer, to send the evil report over the world. Good people often aid in the circulation of a falsehood undesignedly, because they saw not its beginning, and believe the periodical which started, or gave it currency.

At this juncture, the clamor against General Grant was renewed, and there was some appearance of success in the shameful assault upon his character and ability. But again the attack proved a failure.

On the spring day of March 11th, 1862—a season which, in the Southern States, is crowned with flowers and celebrated with sweetest song birds, at this early date—there was a pleasant and animating affair in Fort Henry. At the commander-in-chief's tent, a company of officers were gathered. Calling out "the hero," they presented him with an elegant sword, to express their high regard and confidence. General Grant modestly accepted the gift, thanking the donors for their esteem and trust. The blade was fine burnished steel; the handle of ivory, mounted with gold; two scabbards accompanied it—one of richest gilt, for parade, the plainer one for service. A beautiful rosewood case enclosed the elegant gift; and a simple inscription told the story of its presentation:

"Presented to General U. S. Grant, by G. U. Graham, C. B. Lagon, C. C. Marsh, and John Cook, 1862."

His mind was absorbed with the great interests at stake, and by the plans of a campaign; and it is doubtful whether he thought of the merited compliment again, unless he happened to glance at the splendid weapon.

Forces were immediately sent to scour the country, and learn the number and strength of the enemy. Not far from Paris, Ky., a severe fight occurred, resulting in the loss of more than a hundred men to the rebels, and of the position. To understand the exact posture of the Western warfare, you will recollect that General Grant had, in respect to important positions, cleared Kentucky and Tennessee of rebel occupation; and the attention of the army and the country was turned toward the Mississippi River to its mouth. At Corinth, the enemy was strongly intrenched, to guard the route southward, and seize any opportunity that might offer for regaining lost territory.

Turn to the map, and you will see at once the importance of the place; situated, as it is, at the junction cf the Memphis and Charleston, and Mobile and Ohio Railroads, and lying between the Mississippi and Tennessee Rivers. Besides, below, on the "Father of Waters," Island No 10, a formidable position in the broad current, and Vicksburg, a strongly fortified city, not only on the banks of the stream, but at a great railroad junction, were across the path of the Northern battalions, and in the way of the gunboats. The rebels, therefore, did not seriously fear any trouble on the river, but prepared to meet the victorious foe at Corinth, and dispute his advance on the Tennessee. To cover the vast area of operations with proper authority, a new division of the battle field was made. "The Department of Mississippi" was created, including the valley from the western part of Tennessee and Kentucky to Kansas. At its head was General Halleck. General Grant had transported his troops in steamers down the Cumberland and up the Tennessee to Pittsburg Landing, which is nearly south of Paducah and Paris, twenty miles from Corinth.

Jeff. Davis had sent the popular Beauregard to the Western field, to meet the struggle, and arouse the friends of the Confederacy to aid in the crisis at hand. General Albert Sidney Johnston was the senior in command, but the former planned the battles in his own department. They were at Corinth. General Grant held an important command under General Halleck, and had his headquarters at Savannah, a little town ten miles from below Pittsburg Landing. General Buell, after pursuing, with the Army of the Ohio, General Johnston, who retreated from Fort Donelson through Nashville, leisurely crossed the country to unite his forces with those of General Grant.

March 15th, the troops at Savannah made a dash into Tennessee between Corinth and Jackson, on the road to

Columbus, burned a bridge, and tore up the track. The effect of the raid was to stop a long train of rebel soldiers, and delay the concentration at the stronghold, Corinth.

The generals of the Confederate troops matured a bold and shrewd plan of attack. It was, to anticipate both Corinth and General Buell, and steal the march on General Grant, falling on him unexpectedly and unprepared, "bagging" his army and munitions of war, and seizing the steamers on the river. Three miles from the river is Shiloh church, an old log house, with rough rafters, spaces between the logs once filled with clay, windows without glass, and plain boards for seats. It stands on one of the roads diverging from the main highway, leading from Pittsburg Landing to Corinth, where more than forty thousand rebels were organizing their grand advance on General Grant.

General Van Dorn was expected from Arkansas with thirty thousand more. The petted generals of the Confederacy were ready to strike. The Union troops were thinking only of the expected struggle at Corinth. The former had fifteen thousand more men than we had. The organization of these splendid armies may interest you:

Commanding General, General Albert Sidney Johnston. Second in command, General P. G. T. Beauregard. First Army Corps, Lieutenant-General L. Polk. Second Army Corps, Lieutenant-General Braxton Bragg. Third Army Corps, Lieutenant-General W. J. Hardee. Reserves, Major-General B. Crittenden.

Confronting this host were the Union troops, under Commanding General, Major-General U. S. Grant. First Division, Major-General J. A. McClernand. Second Division, Brigadier-General W. H. L. Wallace. Third Division, Major-General Lewis Wallace. Fourth Division, Brigadier-General S. A. Hurlbut. Fifth Division, Brigadier-General W. T. Sherman.

The enemy intended to surprise them by a rapid march, at early dawn on Saturday. General Grant passed daily between his headquarters and the Landing.

On the mild evening of April 2d, 1862, pickets were fired upon on the Corinth road, and a dash was made through a forest, capturing several of our men. Still, our officers thought the enemy were only making a reconnoissance; just sending up a few troops to inquire after our condition.

But General Grant's fears were excited. He suspected an attack, and returned, after he had gone for the night to Savannah, and went out himself as a scout. But no signs of battle appearing, he again started for his headquarters, leaving an order to fire a signal gun if there were appearances of battle. Meanwhile, General Johnston issued a stirring address to his troops:

SOLDIERS OF THE ARMY OF THE MISSISSIPPI:

I have put you in motion to offer battle to the invaders of your country, with the resolution and discipline and valor becoming men, fighting, as you are, for all worth living or dying for. You can bu' march to a decisive victory over agrarian mercenaries, sent to subjugate and despoil you of your liberties, property, and honor.

Remember the precious stake involved; remember the dependence of your mothers, your wives, your sisters, and your children, on the result. Remember the fair, broad, abounding lands, the happy homes, that will be desolated by your defeat. The eyes and hopes of eight million people rest upon you. You are expected to show yourselves worthy of your valor and courage, worthy of the women of the South, whose noble devotion in this war has never been exceeded in any time. With such incentives to brave deeds, and with trust that God is with us, your general will lead you confidently to the combat, assured of success.

By order of   General A. S. JOHNSTON, Commanding.

Like Satan in Paradise, a traitor anywhere can be eloquent in his crime, if he have genius and culture; and more melancholy than insanity is such a spectacle of perverted powers.

CHAPTER IX.

Saturday Night—General Grant a Scout—The Signals of Battle—The Combat Opens—The Scenes of Carnage—The Critical Hour—The Heroic Onset—The Victory—General Grant's Bravery—The Good News in New York and Washington—A Speech in favor of Grant, who is assailed—Scenes on the Battle Field of Shiloh.

HE position of affairs, Saturday night, was unlike any other in the progress of the war. There was certainly the appearance of vigilance in our army. But the divisions were scattered; the Commanding General was at Savannah, ten miles from the threatened point, and Buell twenty miles away. Rebel sympathizers in the region had thoroughly posted the enemy, whose superior force had, it would seem, every possible advantage. And you must recollect, that nothing excepting the picket firing and light skirmishing changed at all the force of the many considerations which pointed to Corinth, the enemy's stronghold, as the battle field.

General Grant, we have seen, personally reconnoitred, to discover, if there were any, the indications that the rebels had advanced.

The beautiful Sabbath dawned. The foe, whose knowledge of our strength and position, and whose secrecy had favored the enthusiastic expectation of annihilating General Grant's forces, was in striking distance, moving like shadows through the twilight of the forest toward the dreaming battalions of the Republic. They had four lines, one behind the other; General Hardee led; next came General Bragg, then Bishop Polk, and, lastly, General Breckinridge's reserves. On they sweep. Sleeping soldiers in the tents die before the flying bullets. They bend in a semicircle round General Prentiss, whose shouts, "Don't give way! Stand firm!" are in vain.

But where is General Grant? "Boom! boom!" came the sound of the signal gun he had ordered if an attack occurred. He instantly ordered his horses, and the train ready. He sent a messenger to General Buell, ten miles away; and, in an hour and a quarter, was at the head of the army. The noble Sherman had already ridden with the speed of the wind over the field of chaotic strife, and stemmed the tide of disaster.

I shall not attempt to give you the exact aspect of the field, but the general result, especially General Grant's part in the fortunes of the day.

He found the fresh troops of Prentiss routed. Indeed, the entire front was broken in, and crushed back a mile. The mad, proud surges of rebellion, after carrying on their crest wrecks of Prentiss's, and then McClernand's command, dashed against that of Wallace. A shell cut open General Johnston's thigh, and he was borne to the rear to bleed to death, while the terrible blow was concealed from his troops.

All the while, General Grant was breasting the wild tumult of panic and invasion, causing the arrest of a dozen frightened field officers, who were flying, and crying, "We are whipped! Let every man who can, save himself!" With General Sherman to second every wisely-ordered movement, he held and reorganized the tumultuous masses of soldiery for ten long hours of bloody carnage.

At length there is a chance for the gunboats on the river, and their globes of iron and imprisoned fire go shrieking, bursting, up the ravine down which General Bragg's forces move, by order of Beauregard, to drive the broken columns of our army into the river. Destruction rides upon the awful storm of batteries protected by, and acting in concert with the boats. Said Colonel Fagan, of an Arkansas brigade:

"Three different times did we go into the 'Valley of Death,' and as often were forced back by overwhelming numbers, intrenched in a strong position. That all was done that possibly could be done, the heaps of killed and wounded left there give ample evidence."

About noon, General Buell reached the ground in advance of his columns He asked General Grant what preparations he had made for retreat in case of defeat.

"I am not going to be defeated," replied the iron man.

"Such an event is possible," added Buell; "and it is the duty of a prudent general to provide for such a contingency."

General Grant pointed to the transports, quietly asking:

"Don't you see those boats?"

"Yes; but they will not carry more than ten thousand, and we have thirty thousand."

"Well, ten thousand are more than I intend to retreat with," replied General Grant. General Buell evidently anticipated defeat.

When the sun hung low in the sky of that Sabbath day, he sent his beams aslant through the murky atmosphere, and along the ghastly heaps of the fallen. "We shall hold them yet," General Grant had said, even before any besides himself believed it. Yes, that fading sunlight has morning splendor in its farewell, to his eye. Whatever others may have thought then, or still believe, General Grant expected to come unconquered out of the dire confusion.

There is a commotion on the bank opposite, and then a shout. General Buell is in sight. "Hurrah! hurrah! hurrah!" The boats cross, and receive the timely reenforcement.

Oh, what a night was that, while we in our Northern homes were reposing peacefully after the undisturbed worship of the hallowed time! The shells went screaming through the sky, the terrible tokens of an unwilling pause in the combat. Tents and arms wore ruddy gleams from the forest fired by the burning fragments scattered among the dry leaves and branches. The transports steamed back and forth on the lurid waters, conveying the troops of General Buell, which ought to have been within available distance three days before.

Monday's sun streaked with herald beams the east, when General Grant, with General Buell's army of the Ohio added, anticipated Beauregard, whose intention it was to fall on the Union troops and gain the Landing, and ordered an attack. The fancied annihilator of General Grant was met by Nelson, on whose front the gunboats had driven back the rebels. For an hour the doubtful struggle raged, till Mendenhall's battery came up, and poured in the grape. Hazen also was ordered forward. "Into position there! Lively, men!" shouts Captain Tirrell to his battery, flying from one thundering tube of flame to another. "Grape and canister!" he said to the officers of the twelve-pounders, and away he rode again to another post of peril.

Crittenden, McCook, Rousseau, advance. A little later, the general and final engagement is opened. Then, what deeds of valor lend sanguinary glory to the awful plains of battle for a nation's life! The falling banner is seized, before it touches the dust, from the hand of the slain. Colonel Ammen, the first in the broken lines from General Buell's transports, husks corn and feeds his noble steed in the tempest of shells. The maddened host of treason fall like a descending avalanche on the right wing, left wing, and centre; and while our ranks go down in heaps, theirs also fall, but without any faltering or abatement of fiery valor. Major Taylor's Chicago artillery cuts a terrible swath through their heavy columns; and when the smoke lifts, no sign of havoc remains, save under their feet; the same compact front appears. The rebels, intoxicated with whiskey in which was dissolved gunpowder, and recklessly confident of driving our troops into the Tennessee, shout along the lines, "Bull Run! Bull Run!" And when our troops prevail, they shout back again, "Fort Donelson! Fort Donelson!"

Wrote an eyewitness of the terrific conflict:

"General Grant and staff, who had been recklessly riding along the lines during the entire day, amid the unceasing storm of bullets, grape, and shell, now rode from right to left, inciting the men to stand firm.

"About three o'clock in the afternoon, he rode to the left, where the fresh regiments had been ordered, and, finding the rebels wavering, sent a portion of his body guard to the head of each of five regiments, and then ordered a charge across the field, himself leading; and as he brandished his sword and waved them on to the crowning victory, the cannon balls were falling like hail around him.

"The men followed with a shout that sounded above the roar and din of the artillery, and the rebels fled in dismay as from a destroying avalanche, and never made another stand.

"General Buell followed the retreating rebels, driving them in splendid style, and by half-past five o'clock the whole rebel army was in full retreat to Corinth, with our cavalry in hot pursuit, with what further result is not known, not having returned up to this hour."

The die was cast—the victory won—the army saved! And the inspiring, resolute, heroic Grant, with the brave leaders about him, and General Buell's contribution of troops, had wrung the success from the jaws of destruction. He rode with his staff through the two days' carnage with majestic calmness, often within range of the enemy's guns, and the target of their fire. A cannon ball took off Captain Carson's head by his side.

The day after the victory, General Beauregard sent a despatch to General Grant, requesting permission to enter his lines and bury the dead. He replied, that, owing to the warmth of the weather, the slain had been at once interred, and there could be no occasion for a delegation to come across the boundary between the ravaged armies.

While the South was jubilant over the false report of Beauregard, that he "had a great and glorious victory," how sublime the Sabbath scenes which followed the battle! The chaplains of the noble army were leading thousands of devout soldiers in prayer and thanksgiving to God.

An amusing incident made a singular interlude to the

worship of one assembly. The chaplain was reading the lines,

"Show pity, Lord; O Lord, forgive!
Let a repenting rebel live;"

when a patriotic soldier, forgetting the exact meaning, exclaimed:

"No, sir; not unless they lay down their arms, every one of them."

Of the Union troops, one thousand six hundred and fourteen were slain, seven thousand seven hundred and twenty-one wounded, and three thousand nine hundred and sixty-three missing; making the entire loss more than thirteen thousand men. The enemy's loss was at least as great. Over twenty-five thousand husbands, fathers, and sons, killed, mangled, captured, and astray, is the cost of a single battle!

The gallant commander, who was himself slightly wounded in the ankle, commenced his despatches, giving the details of the conflict, in these words:

"It becomes my duty again to report another battle, fought by two great armies, one contending for the best government ever devised, and the other for its destruction. It is pleasant to record the success of the army contending for the former principle."

The tidings went like fire in a prairie over the great city of New York, until the wild joy rose from half a million of patriotic hearts. Thence it was telegraphed to the President, and both Houses of Congress. Mr. Colfax, since Speaker, asked leave to read the telegram. Amid cheers on every side rose the cry: "To the Clerk's desk! To the Clerk's desk!" Mr. Colfax obeyed; and, in a moment, all was still as the chamber of death. Full and clear the glad news floated through the halls of the Capitol. When the last word echoed on the air, the breathless silence of an instant was broken by the most enthusiastic demonstrations of delight. A salute of one hundred guns was fired; and the only faces shaded with gloom, were those of the mourners for "the unreturning brave," and of the disloyal parasites of the imperilled Government. The War Department, in behalf of the Government, thanked the hero.

But the poisoned arrows of jealousy and hate—in some instances, perhaps, misapprehension—were aimed afresh, and with more determined opposition, at the idol of the loyal people. The governors of several of the Western States waited on General Halleck, and asked for Grant's removal, urging the loss of life at Shiloh, and declaring him wanting in capacity and sobriety. General Halleck knew the hero too well to part with him, and placed him second in command to himself.

Hon. E. B. Washburne, of Illinois, defended General Grant from the detraction of his enemies, in an eloquent speech on the floor of Congress. My youthful reader will enjoy its perusal, and desire to preserve it. The following are its most striking passages:

WEST POINT IN 1840.—Page 111.

"I come before the House to do a great act of justice to a soldier in the field, and to vindicate him from the obloquy and misrepresentation so persistently and cruelly thrust before the country. I refer to a distinguished General, who has recently fought the bloodiest and hardest battle ever fought on this continent, and won one of the most brilliant victories. I mean the battle of Pittsburg Landing, and Major-General Ulysses S. Grant. Though but forty years old, he has been oftener under fire, and been in more battles, than any other man living on this continent, excepting that great chieftain now reposing on his laurels and on the affections of his countrymen, Lieutenant-General Scott. He was in every battle in Mexico that was possible for any one man to be in. He has received the baptismal of fire. No young officer came out of the Mexican war with more distinction than Grant, and the records of the War Department bear official testimony to his gallant and noble deeds. He resigned in 1855, and afterward settled in Galena, in the district I have the honor to represent on this floor.

"I came here to speak as an Illinoisian, proud of his noble and patriotic State; proud of its great history now being made up; proud, above all earthly things, of her brave soldiers, who are shedding their blood upon all the battle fields of the Republic. If the laurels of Grant shall ever be withered, it will not be done by the Illinois soldiers who have followed his victorious banner.

"But to the victory at Pittsburg Landing, which has

called forth such a flood of denunciation upon General. Grant. When we consider the charges of bad generalship, incompetency, and surprise, do we not feel that 'even the joy of the people is cruel'? As to the question whether there was, or not, what might be called a surprise, I will not argue it; but even if there had been, General Grant is nowise responsible for it, for *he* was not surprised. He was at his headquarters at Savannah when the fight commenced. Those headquarters were established there, as being the most convenient point for all parts of his command. Some of the troops were at Crump's Landing, between Savannah and Pittsburg, and all the new arrivals were coming to Savannah. That was the proper place for the headquarters of the Commanding General at that time. The General visited Pittsburg Landing and all the important points every day. The attack was made Sunday morning by a vastly superior force. In five minutes after the first firing was heard, General Grant and staff were on the way to the battle field; and, instead of not reaching the field till ten o'clock, or, as has been still more falsely represented, till noon, I have a letter before me from one of his aids who was with him, and who says he arrived there at eight o'clock in the morning, and immediately assumed command. There he directed the movements, and was always on that part of the field where his presence was most required, exposing his life, and evincing, in his dispositions, the genius of the greatest commanders

With what desperate bravery that battle of Sunday was fought! what display of prowess and courage! what prodigies of valor! Our troops, less than forty thousand, attacked by more than eighty thousand of the picked men of the rebels, led by their most distinguished generals!

"There is no more temperate man in the army than General Grant. He never indulges in the use of intoxicating liquors at all. He is an example of courage, honor, fortitude, activity, temperance, and modesty, for he is as modest as he is brave and incorruptible. To the bravery and fortitude of Lannes, he adds the stern republican simplicity of Guvion St. Cyr. It is almost vain to hope that full justice will ever be done to men who have been thus attacked. Truth is slow upon the heels of falsehood. It has been well said, that 'Falsehood will travel from Maine to Georgia while Truth is putting on its boots.'

"Let no gentleman have any fears of General Grant. He is no candidate for the Presidency. He is no politician. Inspired by the noblest patriotism, he only desires to do his whole duty to his country. When the war shall be over, he will return to his home, and sink the soldier in the simple citizen."

The tribute was just and appropriate. History gives no account of a war in which there was so much to learn by the combatants, and in regard to which. in the command of troops, so frequent changes were made as in the Union army. Washington held his position at the head of the Revolutionary forces through all the struggle, and his generals were seldom removed. Used to politics and unused to war, we have made great mistakes, but are also making great progress in real knowledge and strength. Universal freedom and well-being will be advanced through the nation's blood and tears.

It is interesting and useful to leave, occasionally, the storm of battle, the deeds of valor, the cruelty and unholy ambition, and look, as we have done, upon scenes which attend, and yet are apart from the contest. The bravest commanders often weep over these results of war, seldom found in the flaming bulletins of the strife.

It is Tuesday morning, and the wounded strewn over the field of Shiloh are borne away to hospitals. Among them is a brave, pious, and fatally wounded captain. He was shot through both thighs with a bullet. While carried from the ground covered with pools of water and blood, he gives the following narrative of the long night, whose shades had just departed, and uncovered its horrors to the calm, sweet light:

"While lying there, I suffered intense agony from thirst. I leaned my head upon my hand, and the rain from heaven was falling around me. In a little while a pool of water formed under my elbow, and I thought, if I could only get to that puddle, I might quench the burning thirst. I tried to get into a position to suck up a mouthful of muddy water, but was unable to reach within a foot of it. I never felt so much the loss of any earthly blessing. By and by, night fell, and the stars shone out clear and beautiful above the dark field, and I began to think of that great God who had given His Son to die a death of agony for me, and that He was up there—up above the scene of suffering, and above these glorious stars; and I felt that I was going home to meet Him, and praise Him there; and I felt that I ought to praise God, even wounded and on the battle field. I could not help singing that beautiful hymn :

> 'When I can read my title clear
> To mansions in the skies,
> I'll bid farewell to every fear,
> And wipe my weeping eyes.'

And there was a Christian brother in the brush near me. I could not see him, but I could hear him. He took up the strain, and beyond him another and another caught it up, all over the terrible battle field of Shiloh. That night the echo was resounding, and we made the field of battle ring with hymns of praise to God."

No commander before Grant, since time began, has recorded of his war plains such a scene—so sublime, so holy! General Rousseau, the Marshal Junot of our army, a dashing, gallant, splendid officer, in his correspondence gives this touching narrative :

"Two days after the battle of Shiloh, I walked into the hospital tent on the ground where the fiercest contest had taken place, and where many of our men, and those of the enemy, had fallen. The hospital was exclusively for the wounded rebels, and they were laid thickly around. Many of them were Kentuckians, of Breckinridge's command. As I stepped into the tent and spoke to some one, I was addressed by a voice, the childish tone of which arrested my attention.

"'That's General Rousseau! General, I knew your son Dickey. Where is Dick? I knew him very well.'

"Turning to him, I saw, stretched on the ground, a handsome boy, sixteen years of age. His face was a bright one, but the hectic glow and flush on the cheeks, his restless manner, and his gasping and catching his breath as he spoke, alarmed me. I knelt by his side, and pressed his fevered brow with my hand, and would have taken the child into my arms, if I could.

"'And who are you, my son?' said I.

"'Why, I am Eddy McFadden, from Smithville,' was the reply. 'I knew you, General, and I knew your son Dick. I've played with him. Where is Dick?'

"I thought of my own dear boy—of what might have befallen him; that he, too, deluded by villains, might, like this poor boy, have been mortally wounded, among strangers, and left to die. My heart bled for the poor child; my manhood gave way, and burning tears attested, in spite of me, my intense suffering. I asked him of his father. He had no father. 'Your mother?' He had no mother. 'Brothers and sisters?' 'I have a brother,' said he. 'I never knew what soldiering was. I was but a boy, and they got me off down here.'

"He was shot through the shoulder and lungs. I asked him what he needed. He said he was cold, and the ground was hard. I had no tent, nor blankets; our baggage was all in the rear, at Savannah. But I sent the poor boy my saddle blanket, and returned the next morning with lemons for him and the rest; but his brother, in the Second Kentucky Regiment, had taken him over to his regiment, to nurse him. I never saw the child again. He died in a day or two. Peace to his ashes!"

What a young and beautiful victim of treasonable men! What a terrible necessity is war!

CHAPTER X.

Corinth the next Goal of the Army—Getting ready to March—The "Grand Army of the Tennessee"—The Advance—The Siege—The Surrender—The Pursuit—The captured Sheep—General Halleck's Farewell—Grant at Memphis—How he deals with Traitors.

CORINTH is the ancient and scriptural name of a village, or small city, in Mississippi, near the boundary of Tennessee, which contained, before the war, twelve hundred inhabitants. The low lands in which it is situated, in wet weather are a swamp; in "a dry time," a plain of hard clay. In the background are ridges, affording elevated land for lines of defence. It has been already stated, that two grand railways have their junction at Corinth, which made it quite indispensable to the rebels. Here were Beauregard's fine headquarters, with telegraph wires running in every direction from his mansion.

A few days after the field of Shiloh was won, General Smith, chief of cavalry, was ordered to make a reconnoissance in that direction.

Toward Pea Ridge another survey was made. The

Mississippi had been opened below Island No. 10, which woke up the rebel chief to the possibility of danger to his cause in the great Southwest. To the planters he said: "Apply the torch to your cotton!" He thought, if the white heaps of the precious plunder were turned into bonfires, it would discourage the Union troops from fighting. How stupid such an idea in a shrewd general—when we had begun a fight on purpose to dethrone, *sack*, and make an ally to liberty of "King Cotton"!

Reconnoitring and skirmishing were all that was attempted till blooming May, the anniversary of General Grant's youthful soldiering in Mexico, when for the first time "under fire," sixteen years before. General Halleck was resolved to have an invincible army in the grand advance upon Corinth. He therefore gathered all the troops that could be spared in his extensive department to Pittsburg Landing, and called the combined forces the "Grand Army of the Tennessee." This title was a marked honor to Grant, who had been at the head of the army of the Tennessee. He had command of the right wing; General Buell of the centre, or Army of the Ohio; and General Pope of the left wing, or Army of the Mississippi. In the Army of the Tennessee, under General Grant, were twice the number of men included in either of the other armies.

Beauregard was prepared for the expected encounter at Corinth. After a council at General Halleck's headquarters, May 11th, the advance began. And now the vast host moved in all the grandeur of fully equipped and resolute legions, toward a foe prepared to dispute the onward march to their stronghold.

May 17th, the first shock came. The Fifth Division of General Grant's army, under Sherman, met the rebels in a severe conflict on the road to Corinth. They had to fall back before the human tide, crested with fire and steel, that beat in successive waves upon their opposing battle surges. This victory is inscribed on the banner of the splendid division who won it, "Russell's Court House"— a spot crimsoned with the blood with which it was purchased. This brief contest only opened the way to the fortress of rebel strength. And the question was, *How shall Corinth be taken?* It must either be by direct and bloody assault, or by siege; surrounding it, and compelling the imprisoned army to surrender.

Beauregard watched with sleepless vigilance his foe. He ordered troops to intrench on a ridge near Phillips's Creek, and oppose the Union forces. General T. Davis, of General Grant's army, approached the works; then, feigning a retreat, drew the garrison out, when a severe struggle routed the enemy completely. This occurred May 21st; and on the 27th, General Sherman also had a fight with the rebels.

Through all the days of skirmishing, pitched battle, and marching, the parallels, or long lines of our brave men, had pushed the front nearer and nearer to Corinth. May 28th, General Grant pressed up in force to within gunshot of the fortifications, to ascertain the posture and power of the enemy. He was resisted, but beat back the rebels.

The decisive hour has come; all is activity and excitement. We can give you a no more vivid description of the stirring and awfully sublime scenes of such a crisis in army operations, than one found in a letter from this field to the *Cincinnati Gazette:*

"Regiments and artillery are placed in position, and, generally, the cavalry is in advance; but when the opposing forces are in close proximity, the infantry does the work. The whole front is covered by a cloud of skirmishers, and then reserves formed, and then, in connection with the main line, they advance. For a moment, all is still as the grave to those in the background; as the line moves on, the eye is strained in vain to follow the skirmishers as they creep silently forward; then, from some point of the line, a single rifle rings through the forest, sharp and clear, and, as if in echo, another answers it. In a moment more the whole line resounds with the din of arms. Here the fire is slow and steady, there it rattles with fearful rapidity; and this, mingled with the great roar of the reserves as the skirmishers chance at any point to be driven in: and if, by reason of superior force, these reserves fall back to the main force, then every nook and corner seems full of sound. The batteries open their terrible voices, and their shells sing horribly while winging their flight, and their dull explosion speaks plainly of death; their canister and grape go crashing through the trees, rifles ring, the muskets roar, and the din is terrific. Then the slackening of the fire denotes the withdrawing of the one party, and the more distant picket firing that the work was accomplished. The silence becomes almost painful after such a scene as this, and no one can conceive of the effect who has not experienced it; it cannot be described. The occasional firing of the pickets, which shows that the new lines are established, actually occasions a sense of relief. The movements of the mind under such circumstances are sudden and strong. It awaits with intense anxiety the opening of the contest; it rises with the din of battle; it sinks with the lull which follows it, and finds itself in fit condition to sympathize most deeply with the torn and bleeding ones that are fast being borne to the rear.

"When the ground is clear, then the time for working parties has arrived; and, as this is the description of a real scene, let me premise that the works were to reach through the centre of a large open farm of at least three hundred acres, surrounded by woods, one side of it being occupied by rebel pickets. These had been driven back, as I have described.

"The line of the works was selected, and, at the word of command, three thousand men, with axes, spades, and picks, stepped out into the open field from their cover in the woods. In almost as short a time as it takes to tell it, the fence rails which surrounded and divided three hun dred acres into convenient farm lots were on the shoulders of the men, and on the way to the intended line of works. In a few moments more, a long line of crib work stretches over the slope of the hill, as if another anaconda fold had been twisted around the rebels. Then, as, for a time, the ditches deepen, the cribs fill up, the dirt is packed on the outer side, the bushes and all points of concealment are cleared from the front, and the centre divisions of our army had taken a long stride toward the rebel works. The siege guns are brought up and placed in commanding positions. A log house furnishes the hewn and seasoned timber for the platforms, and the plantation of a Southern lord has been thus speedily transformed into one of Uncle Sam's strongholds, where the Stars and Stripes float proudly. Thus had the whole army (under the immediate charge of General Grant, the commander in the field) worked itself up into the very teeth of the rebel works, and rested there on Thursday night, the 28th, expecting a general engagement at any moment.

"Soon after daylight, on Friday morning, the army was startled by rapid and long-continued explosions, similar to musketry, but much louder. The conviction flashed across my mind that the rebels were blowing up their loose ammunition, and leaving. The dense smoke arising in the direction of Corinth strengthened this belief, and soon the whole army was advancing on a grand reconnoissance. The distance through the woods was short, and in a few minutes shouts arose from the rebel lines, which told that our army was in the enemy's trenches. Regiment after regiment pressed on, and, passing through extensive camps just vacated, soon reached Corinth, and found half of it in flames. Beauregard and Bragg had left the afternoon before, and the rear guard had passed out of the town before daylight, leaving enough stragglers to commit many acts of vandalism, at the expense of private property. They burned churches and other public buildings, private goods, stores, and dwellings, and choked up half the wells in town. In the camps immediately around the town, there were few evidences of hasty retreat; but on the right flank, where Price and Van Dorn were encamped, the destruction of baggage and stores was very great, showing precipitate flight. Portions of our army were immediately put in pursuit.

"It seems that it was the slow and careful approach of General Halleck which caused the retreat. They would doubtless have remained, had we attacked their positions without first securing our rear; but they could not stand a siege. Their position was a most commanding one, and well protected."

General Grant's troops, under the brilliant chieftain Sherman, were first in the works. They had been conspicuous in the entire and triumphant progress from Shiloh, sustaining the heaviest blows, and bearing aloft, without wavering or failure, with a proud and immortal heroism, the banner of the Republic.

Near the "noon of night," May 29th, the last receding columns of treason disappear in the darkness from the walls of Corinth. Ten days before, General Grant had urged an advance upon the works, sure that the Union forces could "bag" the rebel army. After the foe had fled, General Halleck acknowledged the mistake, and assured General Grant he should, thereafter, *have his own way.* The work of besieging it began April 30th, and the morning sun of May 30th shone on the deserted fortress. What a change in a few brief hours has passed over the encampment! The day before, you might have seen, in all the shining pageantry of war, among the tents dotting the arena of stern defence, and under Confederate banners, the busy host of rebeldom. Rows of cannon and mortars grimly lining the embankments; shouts, laughter even, and dead men were there; now, the "white tents have disappeared, the heavy footsteps have ceased to sound, and no evidence, save the desolated, hard-trodden ground, and a few tent stakes, remain to tell the story." The victorious soldiers rush over the ground, searching everywhere for relics to commemorate the grand success of their arms; one picking up a broken sword, another a gun, and still another a fragment of a shell, or whatever could have interest as a memento of the struggle.

The mayor of the little and fallen city immediately asked protection for the property of the citizens; and, with prompt obedience to the orders of the commanding officer, guards stood at every door, safely keeping the homes of their enemies. So strangely does the work of demons and of angels blend in the sulphurous atmosphere of warfare!

But look beyond the silent battlements crowned with Union banners, and away farther than you can discern, down the railway toward Mobile—why, with rapid marches, sweep the lines of our heroes in saddle? Colonel Elliot's cavalry are on the wing, to reach Booneville in time to tear up the track, and cut off the enemy's retreat. 'Desolation! desolation!" was the exclamation on many lips, as the troopers dashed through the once fruitful fields. They suffered for food. See those few solitary, haggard sheep wandering over the scarred and desert-like land. 'Boys, after them!" says Colonel Elliot.

An odd interlude to the tragedy of war is that chase after the gaunt fugitives, whose masters have forsaken them. Jokes enliven the repast of the hungry men over the tough and juiceless mutton, taken in the vast slaughter-field of humanity—unlike the Divine abundance, and yet "without money and without price."

The horsemen destroyed the track, burned the depot, a train of cars, and a large quantity of arms, and, taking a different route back, reached Corinth again in safety. The rest of June was occupied in similar raids, till the enemy's power was broken in that region, and his lines were fifty miles from Corinth.

July 17th, General Halleck bade farewell to the troops of the Southwest, and went to Washington in the high office of General-in-Chief of all the United States forces.

The departure of General Halleck was followed by a new order of things. The "Department of West Tennessee" was created for General Grant—larger than his previous command. Take the map, and, beginning at Cairo, glance across to Donelson and Henry on the Tennessee River, and up its current to Northern Mississippi, and then to Memphis, of which possession had been taken after the surrender of Corinth, and you will have nearly the boundaries of his new military kingdom. Memphis, you notice, is on the "Father of Waters," where railroads meet, and, as a "a base of supplies," and a point of divergence into the enemy's country, was of great importance. But protected there by our arms, were traitors. They trafficked with the rebel army secretly, and assisted the enemy in every possible way. So the resolute and honorable chief, who often went from Corinth, his headquarters, to Memphis, began to issue orders forbidding such intercourse with the Confederate troops. His course illustrated the old fable of the farmer and the boy stealing his apples: the rogue cared little for words or grass; stones only could bring him down.

The first order required the word PASSED on letters found upon persons going out, from the pen of the provost-marshal, post-commander, or general commanding; and forbidding, on penalty of imprisonment for the first offence, any person to carry arms or ammunition out of, or within the city limits.

But the unprincipled traffic went on. The next order —July 9th, eleven days later—revoked all passes, unless the holders gave the oath of allegiance, or parole of honor; *i. e.*, became loyal by their most sacred pledge, or, with an equally binding promise to conform to the rules of the department, were permitted to be at large.

The artful, treasonable traders were active still. Then came the decisive blow, in the following orders, two days after, showing the rebels what sort of a man they had trifled with too long:

DISTRICT OF WEST TENNESSEE,
OFFICE PROVOST-MARSHAL GENERAL,
MEMPHIS, TENN., July 10, 1862.

The constant communication between the so-called Confederate army and their friends and sympathizers in the city of Memphis, despite the orders heretofore issued, and the efforts to enforce them, induced the issuing of the following order:

The families now residing in the city of Memphis of the following persons, are required to move south beyond the lines within five days of the date hereof:

First. All persons holding commissions in the so-called Confederate army, or who have voluntarily enlisted in said army, or who accompany and are connected with the same.

Second. All persons holding office under or in the employ of the so called Confederate Government.

Third. All persons holding State, county, or municipal offices, who claim allegiance to said so-called Confederate Government, and who have abandoned their families and gone South.

Safe conduct will be given to the parties hereby required to leave, upon application to the Provost-Marshal of Memphis.

By command of   Major-General GRANT.

DISTRICT OF WEST TENNESSEE,
OFFICE OF THE PROVOST-MARSHAL GENERAL,
MEMPHIS, TENN., July 11, 1862.

* * * * * * *

In order that innocent, peaceable, and well-disposed persons may not suffer for the bad conduct of the guilty parties coming within the purview of Special Order No. 14, dated July 10, 1862, they can be relieved from the operation of said order No. 14, by signing the following parole, and producing to the Provost Marshal General, or the Provost-Marshal of Memphis, satisfactory guarantees that they will keep the pledge therein made:

PAROLE.

First. I have not, since the occupation of the city of Memphis by the Federal army, given any aid to the so-called Confederate army, nor given or sent any information of the movements, strength, or position of the Federal army to any one connected with said Confederate army.

Second. I will not, during the occupancy of Memphis by the Federal army and my residing therein, oppose or conspire against the civil or military authority of the United States, and that I will not give aid, comfort, or encouragement to the so-called Confederate army, nor to any person coöperating therewith.

All of which I state and pledge upon my sacred honor.

By command of   Major-General GRANT.

WM. S. HILLYER, Provost-Marshal General.

And, as a warning to the guerrillas who were destroying cotton and plundering, the following order was also issued:

HEADQUARTERS, DISTRICT OF WEST TENNESSEE,
MEMPHIS, TENN., July 3, 1862.

The system of guerilla warfare now being prosecuted by some troops organized under authority of the so-called Southern Confederacy, and others without such authority, being so pernicious to the welfare of the community where it is carried on, and it being within the power of the community to suppress this system, it is ordered that, wherever loss is sustained by the Government, collections shall be made, by seizure of a sufficient amount of personal property, from persons in the immediate neighborhood sympathizing with the rebellion, to remunerate the Government for all loss and expense of the same.

Persons acting as guerillas without organization, and without uniform to distinguish them from private citizens, are not entitled to the treatment of prisoners of war when caught, and will not receive such treatment.

By order of   .   Major-General U. S. GRANT.
JOHN A. RAWLINS, A. A. G.

The disloyal editors and speculators in conspiracy with the enemy at large, took their turn, as will appear in the annexed spicy correspondence. It is *paper* warfare, in part, but, in General Grant's hands, made the traitors wince, and act like honest men:

HEADQUARTERS, DISTRICT OF WEST TENNESSEE,
OFFICE PROVOST-MARSHAL GENERAL,
MEMPHIS, TENN., July 1, 1862.

Messrs. WILLS, BINGHAM & Co., Proprietors of the Memphis *Avalanche:*

You will suspend the further publication of your paper. The

spirit with which it is conducted is regarded as both incendiary ant treasonable, and its issue cannot longer be tolerated.

This order will be strictly observed from the time of its reception

By command of   Major-General U. S. GRANT.

WM. S. HILLYER, Provost-Marshal General.

MEMPHIS, July 1, 1862.

The Avalanche can continue by the withdrawal of the author of the obnoxious article under the caption of "Mischief Makers," and the editorial allusion to the same.

U. S. GRANT, Major-General.

TO OUR PATRONS.—For reasons apparent from the foregoing order, I withdraw from the editorial management of *The Avalanche.* Self-respect, and the spirit of true journalism, forbid any longer attempt to edit a paper. I approved and endorsed the articles in question. Prudence forbids my saying more, and duty less, to the public.   JEPTHA FOWLKES.

U. S. MILITARY TELEGRAPH, CORINTH, July 26, 1862.

To Brigadier-General J. T. QUIMBY, Columbus, Ky.:

GENERAL: Examine the baggage of all speculators coming South, and when they have specie, turn them back. If medicine and other contraband articles, arrest them, and confiscate the contraband articles. Jews should receive special attention.

[Signed]   U. S. GRANT, Major-General.

TRENTON, TENN., July 29, 1862.

GENERAL: The man who guided the rebels to the bridge that was burned, was hung to-day. He had taken the oath. The houses of four others who aided have been burned to the ground.

[Signed]   G. M. DODGE, Brigadier-General.

The inflexibly just and loyal commander, to secure from wanton waste, and obtain material aid, rented the deserted buildings whose owners were in rebel service, whether private residences or stores and manufactories, for and under the protection of the Government.

He issued an order in regard to fugitive slaves, giving directions for their employment; neither permitting them to be returned, nor enticed from the plantations. The only fault to be found with these last regulations, was one which God's providence alone could cure, by prolonging the war; *i. e.*, dealing carefully and tenderly for the master, with the whole question of his rights while in rebellion, and thus sustaining the system of oppression which hatched the scorpion-egg of treason.

General Grant also published an order to enroll the "runaways" from the draft in the States to which they belonged, seeking a hiding place in Southern towns within the Union lines. There was very soon a thinning of the ranks of the worthless refugees.

A specimen of a rebel letter will show you how bitter their hate was, and how demoniac their conduct. It is addressed to General Grant, on account of his proclamation respecting the guerillas, threatening to confiscate rebel property in return for their ravages:

SINATORIA, July 16, 1862.

U. S. GRANT:

SIR: We have seen your infamous and fiendish proclamation. It is characteristic of your infernal policy. * * * If you attempt to carry out your threat against the property of citizens, we will make you rue the day you issued your dastardly proclamation. You call us guerillas, which you know is false. We are recognized by our Government; and it was us who attacked your wagons at Morning Sun. We have twenty-three men of yours, and, as soon as you carry out your threat against the citizens of the vicinity of Morning Sun, your Hessians will pay for it. We are ready, and more than willing, to raise the "black flag." There are two thousand partisans who have sworn to retaliate. Henceforth our motto shall be, Blood for blood, and blood for property. We intend, by the help of God, to hang on the outskirts of your rabble, like lightning around the edge of a cloud.   Respectfully,

GEO. R. MERRITT.

CHAPTER XI.

The Position of our Army—The Grand Programme—Armies in Motion—Bragg tries to Deceive Grant—The Advance toward Iuka—The Fight—The Victory—The Stampede—General Grant's Words of Cheer—Despatch from the President—A Curiosity.

HERE we may pause, and see how the combatants stand. The Mississippi is clear to Memphis, and at the mouth; for Butler, who knew so well how to deal with rebels, is at New Orleans.

The forces defeated by Halleck and Grant had gone to Vicksburg, Port Hudson, and Baton Rouge, and other points on the Mississippi, to blockade and hold that great thoroughfare of trade in the valley of the West.

Let us unroll the map again. Although, during the summer months, there was a lull in the wide arena of the Western conflict, neither army was idle. Major-General Buell's forces were east of Memphis, not far from Huntsville in Alabama, with Chattanooga for his coveted prize. For this, he left Corinth in June. Major-General Curt's was west of the Mississippi, at Helena, Arkansas. Brigadier-General Schofield was north of him, in Southwestern

Missouri; while Major-General Grant, with the central army, was on the line of West Tennessee and North Mississippi, between Memphis and Iuka, protecting the railroads south from Columbus, our only channels of supply.

The mighty sweep of these combined armies was around and across a territory six hundred miles in width, from Western Arkansas to the Cumberland Gap, and more than one hundred and fifty miles in the other direction. From this area the enemy had been recently driven. The foe, greatly reënforced by conscription, while we were weakened by losses, had formed magnificent plans of conquest. The grand programme was, to reoccupy the lost ground back to Kentucky, and then roll their tide of invasion, like the Goths and Huns of old, over the borders of Ohio, Indiana, and Illinois. Raids into Maryland and Pennsylvania, with Indian troubles at the West, were to furnish a most auspicious time for the sublimely daring advance through the valley of the West.

General Braxton Bragg, of the rebel army, opened the gigantic enterprise finely. Hastening from Tripoli, Miss., through Alabama and Georgia, he reached Chattanooga, by nature a stronghold, ahead of Buell, who fell back to Nashville, Tenn. Another hostile column had got into Cumberland Gap, and looked menacingly toward Cincinnati. Meanwhile, the President had wisely, and just in season, issued another call for troops. Oh, how wildly the great Northwest echoed back the appeal! Her sons went streaming down like the rivers, in living tides, toward the seat of war. Cincinnati and Louisville were soon fortified.

To get the advantage further, Bragg had published an order, bearing date at Sparta, away in Alabama, when he was safely at Chattanooga. But he was found, and General Buell sent after him with one hundred thousand men.

At Perryville a severe battle was fought, and the enemy routed. Bragg had hoped to swing, by a flank movement, around Grant, to the Ohio River; Corinth lying nearly in a directly westerly line from Chattanooga. It was ascertained that Generals Van Dorn and Price were advancing toward our camp at Jacinto, which was at once removed, to prepare for the greater conflict impending.

September 18th, soon after break of day, in a drenching rain, and through mud, the uncomplaining volunteers moved toward the enemy; Generals Grant and Ord approaching Iuka from the north, and General Rosecrans from the south. The position of the rebel army cut off communication between Generals Grant and Buell, and at any cost it must be routed. Price, finding that the Union lines were likely to close around him, left the town, and fell on Rosecrans with desperate fury, at four o'clock P. M. Till the sun went down, darkened with the "sulphurous canopy," bullets and steel, cannon and shell did their work well. From the long ridge, commanding a large extent of the country around, the rebels rained down destruction, till one third of our troops were killed or wounded. But so deadly had been our fire, that, in the night, the enemy evacuated Iuka, and, when morning lit up the gory scene, General Rosecrans marched into it with flying banners. General Grant, who, with General Ord, had taken the northern route to cut off Price's retreat, but failed because he escaped toward the east, soon after followed the victorious ranks into the deserted works.

A rebel letter, written after the victory, contains a glimpse of the fight from his side :

"We held peaceable possession of Iuka for one day, and, on the next, were alarmed by the booming of cannon, and were called out to spend the evening in battle array in the woods. On the evening of the 19th, when we supposed we were going back to camp to rest awhile, the sharp crack of musketry on the right of our former lines told us that the enemy was much nearer than we imagined. In fact, they had almost penetrated the town itself. How on earth, with the woods full of our cavalry, they could have approached so near our lines, is a mystery. They had planted a battery sufficiently near to shell General Price's headquarters, and were cracking away at the Third Brigade, when the Fourth came up at double quick, and then, for two hours and fifteen minutes, was kept up the most terrific fire of musketry that ever dinned my ears. There was one continuous roar of small arms, while grape and canister how.ed in fearful concert above our heads and through our ranks. General Little was shot dead early in the action. * * * It was a terrible struggle, and we lost heavily. All night could be heard the groans of the wounded and dying, forming a sequel of horror and agony to the deadly struggle, over which night had kindly thrown its mantle. Saddest of all, our dead were left unburied, and many of the wounded on the battle field, to be taken in charge by the enemy."

General Grant was proud of the brave boys who had driven out eighteen thousand rebels, and taken possession of their quarters, and said to them:

"The General commanding takes great pleasure in congratulating the two wings of the army, commanded respectively by Major-General Ord and Major-General Rosecrans, upon the energy, alacrity, and bravery displayed by them. * * * And, while congratulating the noble living, it is meet to offer our condolence to the friends of the heroic dead, who offered their lives a sacrifice in defence of constitutional liberty, and in their fall rendered memorable the field of Iuka."

But this terrible "whipping" did not stop long the advance of Bragg toward the Ohio River—the goal of his hopes and ambition, as before stated, at the beginning of the campaign.

To command the region farther northward, the direction the enemy were going, General Grant took up his headquarters at Jackson, about forty miles northwest of Corinth. The rebels that fled from Iuka, by the skilful management of Price, had succeeded in reaching a point in Tippah County, Miss., where Generals Van Dorn and

Lovell could join him. So here we have united all the Confederate forces in Northern Mississippi; and by October 1st the entire army was advancing toward Corinth, resolved, by taking it, to cut the Union lines, and compel us to retreat. A diagram will show you nearly the position:

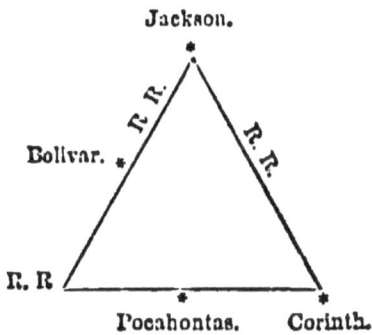

General Grant was at Jackson; General Rosecrans at Corinth; General Ord at Bolivar; and General Hurlbut near Pocahontas, where the main body of the rebel army lay, ready to spring upon either of the Union positions given. The enemy had only the southern line open, not far from which was the Hatchie River.

General Grant, who had been wide awake, and, by sending out scouts in every direction, had learned the enemy's movements, was master of the situation. Of the railways forming the sides of the triangle at whose apex he was intrenched, the rebels had taken possession of the track between Corinth and Jackson, interrupting direct intercourse between the towns Still other lines were clear, and the telegraph working, ready to summon the troops to the position assailed.

October 2d, skirmishing began before Corinth. Brigadier-Generals Hamilton, McKean, Davies, and Stanley, were within its walls with Rosencrans.

The next day, about ten o'clock, the battle opened in earnest. General Grant, with his eye over the triangular field, was directing the whole machinery of the opening struggle. General McPherson, at Jackson, was ordered to join, with a brigade, General Rosecrans; while General Hurlbut, with other forces, was marching to cut off retreat by way of Pocahontas.

Noon came, and thunder, smoke, hissing shot, screaming shell, yelling combatants, and the shouts of command, were the signs of the terrible strife.

The sun sinks toward the west, flinging his golden beams over the rich autumnal landscape, and on the surging columns of the foemen, on both sides equally unyielding. For many miles the heavy roar of the artillery swells with strange distinctness, as the twilight stillness steals upon the bosom of nature. Then, darkness hangs a veil between the fiery eyes of the grappling brethren of a common heritage, and they relax the bloody grasp, and lie down in weariness on their arms to sleep.

The next morning's light kindles upon the uprisen hosts among the dead and wounded, in battle array. Back and forth the swaying masses of armed men move in the darkened atmosphere, till noon. Then the rebel ranks fall back; the die is cast; now, in full retreat, they rush for the Hatchie River.

From the very streets into which some had forced their way, and from the grounds without, strewn with the slain and wounded, they are chased by General Rosecrans to the woods, broken and routed, the fragments of a just now confident and heroic army, leaving nearly a thousand prisoners behind, besides the wounded. He captures also six hundred stand of arms. Our loss in killed, wounded, and missing, is about eight hundred; while theirs is greater, owing to the advantage our troops had in fighting behind intrenchments.

While Rosecrans pushed the flying foe in the direction of Hatchie River, Generals Hurlbut and Ord, who, as before mentioned, had gone to intercept the retreating troops, along narrow roads, through swamps, and over rocky ridges, crossed their path on the banks of the stream.

A furious conflict followed for several hours on the 5th. Nothing could resist the onset, in which General Ord was wounded, and left the command to General Hurlbut; and away the beaten rebels went, like a flock of terrified sheep, over the river, into the wooded heights beyond.

General Grant, in closing his despatch communicating the success, says:

"*I have strained everything to take into the fight an adequate force, and to get them to the right place.*"

His military genius triumphed in the high endeavor

Corinth was lost to the cause of treason, and stood, the great war-clasp, holding unbroken the grand line of the Union army between the traitors and the Ohio River. Peace was restored again to Western Tennessee.

Our sagacious, unpretending hero, possessing preeminently what is termed "pluck," relieved his full heart by an address to his troops, in which are these words:

"It is with heartfelt gratitude the General Commanding congratulates the armies of the West for another great victory won by them on the 3d, 4th, and 5th instants, over the combined armies of Van Dorn, Price, and Lovell.

"The enemy chose his own time and place of attack, and knowing the troops of the West as he does, and with great facilities for knowing their numbers, never would have made the attempt except with a superior force numerically. But for the undaunted bravery of officers and soldiers, who have yet to learn defeat, the efforts of the enemy must have proven successful.

"As in all great battles, so in this, it becomes our fate to mourn the loss of many brave and faithful officers and soldiers, who have given up their lives as a sacrifice for a great principle. The nation mourns for them."

No sooner had the good news reached Washington, than the President sent over the wires the following message:

WASHINGTON, D. C., October 8, 1862.

Major-General GRANT:

I congratulate you and all concerned in your recent battles and victories. How does it all sum up? I especially regret the death of General Hackleman, and am very anxious to know the condition of General Oglesby, who is an intimate personal friend.

A. LINCOLN

This despatch was followed by another, which will be a curious relic in the future archives of the civil war, and of the country. If you live, my young reader, to mature manhood, you will hear it referred to as such. Up to the date of it, and afterward, the Government, and the people generally, supposed we were fighting to get the States back just as they were before the conflict—slavery and all. But God had determined *it should not be so.* Here is the message:

EXECUTIVE MANSION, WASHINGTON, Oct. 21, 1862.

Major-General GRANT, Governor JOHNSON, and all having Military, Naval, and Civil Authority under the United States within the State of Tennessee:

The bearer of this, Thomas R. Smith, a citizen of Tennessee, goes to that State, seeking to have such of the people thereof as desire to avoid the unsatisfactory prospect before them, and to have *peace again upon the old terms under the Constitution* of the United States, to manifest such desire by elections of members to the Congress of the United States particularly, and perhaps a Legislature, State officers, and a United States senator friendly to their object. I shall be glad for you and each of you to aid him, and all others acting for this object, as much as possible. * * * Of course, the men elected should be gentlemen of character, willing to swear support to the *Constitution as of old*, and known to be above reasonable suspicion of duplicity.

Yours, very respectfully,   A. LINCOLN.

Even children smile already at the talk then, of "*peace again upon the old terms under the Constitution.*" The good, honest President had much to learn of the true character of the war, and the will of the King of kings in regard to the struggle then scarcely begun, in its connection with slavery, the bitter cause of the war.

CHAPTER XII.

A larger Field, and bolder Plans—Getting Ready—Skirmishes—Cotton—Negroes—Jews—Speculators—Grant's Sense of Honor—Vicksburg and the Mississippi—Farragut's Fleet—The Bombardment—Failure—A worthless Canal—The Noble Logan—Holly Springs Surrenders to the Rebels—Amusing Scenes.

HOW steady the progress of our hero in military fame! Each success has opened the field for a greater one. Cairo, Forts Henry and Donelson, Shiloh, Corinth, and now "On to Vicksburg!" each attended with a still wider theatre of operations, are the marvellous strides of the conqueror, during a period of less than a year, in the march of destiny. A new and broader department, and more daring designs, open before him. He took command of the Department of Tennessee, which extended into Mississippi as far as Vicksburg, October 25th, 1862. He mapped it out in the following order:

The First Division will constitute the "District of Memphis," Major-General W. T. Sherman commanding; the Second Division, the "District of Jackson," commanded by Major-General S. A. Hurlbut; the Third Division, the "District of Corinth," Brigadier-General C. S. Hamilton commanding; the Fourth Division, the "District of Columbus," commanded by Brigadier-General T. A. Davies.

In every noble and difficult achievement for men or boys, there is first the hard, quiet work of preparation, to do. From the very last of October till late in November, General Grant had just this less exciting and unappreciated toil, before attempting the gigantic enterprise of taking Vicksburg. The vast machinery of a moving army—wagons, tents, stores, hospital shelter—he determined to reduce to the smallest possible amount. Even the officers' baggage must be limited to "blankets, one small valise or carpet bag, and a moderate mess kit," or eating apparatus.

The last of October, Colonel Lee, of General Grant's army, with a body of cavalry, dashed down to Ripley, Miss., took it, held it for a day, captured prisoners, and returned to Grand Junction. This town is east of La Grange, between Corinth and Memphis; to which, two days later, the Commanding General removed his headquarters. The movement deceived the rebels, who went to fortifying near Ripley, because Lee had been there.

This cavalry officer made another grand reconnoissance with two divisions of infantry and artillery, and part of a cavalry division, toward Hudsonville. He met the rebels, fought, conquered, and, besides killing sixteen, took one hundred and thirty-four prisoners, with horses and arms. General Grant was highly gratified, and recommended Colonel Lee earnestly for promotion. He became, afterward, brigadier-general.

By the expedition, he found that General Lovell was at Holly Springs; Price, with twelve thousand men, seven miles below; about twenty miles farther toward the Gulf, thirteen thousand more were encamped.

General Grant was a just and gentlemanly officer. These qualities were visible in all his conduct. He won from friends and foes the homage of true virtue—of honor and integrity above a mean military ambition, or mercenary use of office and its opportunities to get money.

No reasonable complaint was disregarded, though it came from rebels. When the old farmers made bitter charges against the reconnoitring parties, because their fields, larders, and barns were pillaged, he ordered strict watchfulness by officers, and the arrest of offenders.

He overlooked no interest. "King Cotton" had become lawful plunder. If seized south of Jackson, he was directed to be sent there; if seized north, to Columbus, Ky., in care of the quartermasters. Not only so, but the dark-skinned laborers, by whose unrequited toil he flourished, and who had fled from their masters to our lines, were to be cared for; and General Grant was the very man to do it. He established a camp at Grand Junction, under Chaplain Eaton, where food, raiment, medical attendance, and *work* in " picking, ginning, and baling all cotton outstanding in the fields," was to be provided.

He tried an original and pretty sure way of breaking up stealing in a regiment, whose robberies of stores, and of each other, amounted to one thousand two hundred and forty-two dollars. The sum was *charged to the regiment*, and the negligent officers dismissed.

All kinds of speculation were going on. The Jews, that singular, scattered, yet united people, despised, but found everywhere, and always having plenty of money, were the hardest and most troublesome hangers-on of the army. General Grant's ire was a little roused at last, as the tone of the annexed order shows :

HEADQUARTERS, DEPARTMENT OF THE TENNESSEE, }
OXFORD, MISS., December 17, 1862.

The Jews, as a class, violating every regulation of trade established by the Treasury Department, also department orders, are hereby expelled from the department within twenty-four hours from the receipt of this order by post commanders. They will see that all this class of people are furnished with passes and required to leave; and any one returning after such notification will be arrested and held in confinement until an opportunity occurs of sending them out as prisoners, unless furnished with permits from these headquarters. No passes will be given these people to visit headquarters for the purpose of making personal application for trade permits.

By order of   Major-General GRANT.

At the same time, to avoid unnecessary suffering to the conquered inhabitants, he was inclined to allow trade in articles of food and clothing, under proper regulations, with those who took the oath of allegiance. But advantage was taken even of this kind design. The following conversation, if not entirely literal, is a fair illustration of what transpired at headquarters:

"General, I would like to open trade according to your order."

"Have you taken the oath required?"

"I have."

"What do you propose to do?"

"That, with the authority to trade, you name reliable Union men through whom to carry on the business."

"I shall do no such thing. If I did, it would appear, in less than a week, that I was partner with every one of the persons trading under my authority."

It seems incredible, that commanders and provost-marshals should be continually plied by speculators in treason not only, but in the very wants and sufferings of our own soldiers. It is well that we have heroes like Grant, who disdain a bribe, and whose loyalty rings out clear as a bell, when struck by the leprous hand of a traitor, no less than when its metal is tried with the heaviest blows of mortal combat.

All things were now ready for an advance into Mississippi. The majestic river of the same name sweeps along a channel three thousand miles in length, from the beautiful Lake Itasca. Its name is from the Ojibway Indian dialect, and means "Father of Waters." It is of priceless importance to the country, not alone because it is the broad highway of navigation, but on account of its tributaries, spreading like a grand network of water paths for the ceaseless march of commerce over the "empire of the West." The magnificent channel receiving them all had been blockaded at various points, and opened again by the gunboats, whose ponderous hail of shot and bombshell was unendurable by the garrisons.

In January, 1861, the governor of Mississippi commenced the fortifications of Vicksburg—by natural position, with high bluffs, a place of remarkable strength for this purpose. Profiting by the loss of Island No. 10, and the forts above Memphis, no engineering skill and expense were spared to make it impregnable. Fortress was built within fortress; rows of heavy guns rose one over the other in the cliffs, till the stronghold defied ironclads from the river, and armies from the land. Next to Corinth, a railroad and general centre of the conflict in the field, Vicksburg was the object of interest to both armies. During the summer before, the splendid fleet of Farragut, which steamed by the forts guarding New Orleans, in a perfect blaze of the hottest cannonading, arrived before Vicksburg.

June 27th, having reduced Memphis, the bombardment began. For more than four long weeks the awful storm beat, with occasional interludes, upon the walls in vain. Low water then compelled the fleet to drop down to New Orleans. Meanwhile, the ram Arkansas, built up the Yazoo, and run down to the front of Vicksburg to make it more formidable, had been destroyed by our "Essex" and "Queen of the West."

So far, no impression has been made on the bristling giant guarding the mighty current of life to the nation. A new idea is started. At Vicksburg, you have noticed, the Mississippi makes a sharp bend, on whose outer or eastern curve the city stands. Now for a canal across the bend, and lead the river away from the defiant Sebastopol, making it, by isolation, powerless to hinder the navigation. The plan looks well; and July 22d, while General Grant was at Memphis, the canal was finished.

It proved to be a failure. The wrong spot had been chosen, and the waters of the river were too low to flow through the channel. The entire siege was raised, and a shout of exultation went up from the fortress as ships and men departed.

Such was the condition of Vicksburg, when General Grant fixed his eye upon the prize. The brave, Christian General Logan, who said of the war, although relatives opposed it, that he would not return to his home till the rebellion was crushed, and also declared in the National Capitol, that, if not otherwise done, "the men of the Northwest, were they allowed to, would *hew their way* to the Gulf," was placed in command at Cairo. The Western "boys" were ready to carry out the noble assurance of Logan. Additional troops were ordered to General Grant's army; and in all directions, bodies of cavalry were searching for the enemy. The Commanding General moved along the Mississippi Central Railroad from his headquarters at Grand Junction, southward.

All day Saturday and Sunday, November 29th and 30th, the troops poured through the charming streets, lined with foliage, of Holly Springs, until its six thousand inhabitants "began to think the entire North was emptying itself through them."

About the middle of December, General Grant's headquarters were at Oxford, several miles beyond.

On the 20th occurred a sad and memorable affair to delay his onward march. Although he had taken every precaution against surprise, and displayed the highest generalship in the management of the columns covering many miles of the enemy's country, the rebels made a dash at Holly Springs in his rear. He expected it, telegraphed Colonel Murphy, in command, that they were after him, and that reënforcements were on the way, although he was strong enough to defend the place. The troops from Grant were delayed, and on came the rebel cavalry, just as the morning beams fell on the quiet town. Two railroad trains, one loaded with cotton, were soon in a blaze. Then the work of pillage and burning was the order of the day.

Colonel Murphy was a coward, and made almost no resistance. The troops fought without a leader awhile, but in vain. Up and down the streets the raiders went. People in their night clothes rushed out of the houses. One man, whose boots had been carried off, in his fright put on only his coat containing his money, drawers, stockings, and *spurs*, went to the stable, took his horse, and rode away.

Another cotton speculator from Ohio woke up his companion, and exclaimed: "Get up; the town is full of secesh!" Lough jumped up, took a single glance, and replied, excitedly: "King, we're gobbled, by Judas!" King declared he never heard him swear before or since.

Not long after, a member of Van Dorn's staff, who was dealing with the cotton buyers, came to King.

"Where do you live?"

"In Newark, Ohio, sir."

"Are you connected with the army?"

"No, sir."

"What are you doing here, sir?"

Here King tried to evade the question.

"Are you not a cotton buyer, sir?"

"Yes, sir (ahem); have invested all my spare money in cotton, and to-day it has *gone up the spout!*" (That is to say, *lost* by the raid.)

The truth is, King had his money secreted, excepting seventy dollars in greenbacks, and a gold dollar. The officer, returning the wallet, said:

"That little button is worth all the balance."

A Richmond paper contained the following description:

"The breaking streaks of daylight showed the Yankee tents with their undisturbed slumbers. A charge was ordered upon them. To paraphrase 'Belgium's' picture:

> 'Ah, then and there was hurrying to and fro,
>   And running in hot haste,
>   And cheeks all pale and blanched with woe,
>   Exhibiting Yankee cowardice.'"

The last allusion was too true. General Grant was indignant when the news reached him, and issued an order expressing his deep mortification; which, soon after, was followed by another, dismissing Colonel Murphy from the service.

General Grant had to fall back to Holly Springs, get fresh supplies in place of those destroyed, and move again onward.

CHAPTER XIII.

The Grand Plan Deranged—Sherman's Flotilla—His Assault on Vicksburg—Defeat—Fatal Ambition—Disloyalty—President's Proclamation of Freedom and General Grant—Vicksburg again—Canals around the City a Failure—The Copperhead and the Bush.

HOW much evil may result from a single blunder, or, what is far worse, a neglect of duty! A lad, several years ago, by a wilfully careless disregard of his mother's counsels, set fire to the mansion, and consumed everything but the family with it.

The cowardly conduct of the colonel at Holly Springs was not only followed by pillage and burning there, but interfered with General Grant's whole plan respecting Vicksburg.

General Sherman, a gallant officer at Memphis, was intrusted with a grand expedition down the river, to co-operate with the former in the bold attempt to get that key of the Mississippi, which would open its waters to the impatient West.

December 20th, his magnificent flotilla of one hundred

and twenty-seven steamers, besides gunboats, moved down the Mississippi—a sight you, my reader, would like to have witnessed. With streamers flying and bands playing, for miles the Father of Waters presented a rare and stirring scene.

General Sherman did not know of General Grant's detention at Holly Springs. December 27th he arrived at Johnson's Landing, near the mouth of Yazoo River. He immediately prepared to assault Vicksburg from the north.

Sunday, the 27th, the engagement became general. There stood Sherman's "Right Wing of the Army of the Tennessee," amid the sloughs, bayous, and lagoons of the swampy ground between the hills and the city; while the enemy, reënforced by troops which fled before General Grant, rained death on their "rank and file," and the sharpshooters in the woods picked off the officers.

Over ditches in which the horses mired and were left, across bloody rifle pits, through dense woods, and over heaps of fallen timber, the columns struggled, to the sound ringing above all the tumult, "Forward!" It was all in vain. General Sherman was compelled to retire, and reëmbark his troops. In the affair, he did not wait for General Grant, excusing himself by saying, in his order after the battle: "We were on time; unforeseen contingencies must have delayed others."

The costly and fruitless assault looks like the adventurous, ambitious effort to do the work and win the laurels alone. If so, how unlike the patient leader of the advancing host!

After hostilities had ceased, and the slain and wounded were borne away under a flag of truce, the pickets had the following talk:

"How far is it to Vicksburg?"

Rebel picket. "So far you'll never git thar."

Federal picket. "How many men have you got?"

Rebel picket. "Enough to clean you out."

Then another rebel, who seemed to be the stump speaker of the squad, with a flourish, added:

"Banks has been whipped out at Port Hudson, Memphis has been retaken, and you Yankees will not take Vicksburg till hell freezes over."

And so the conversation went on during the four hours of truce. The profane assertion of the rebel was destined to be refuted in the heat of the next midsummer.

Meanwhile, General Grant, having detected disloyalty in the One Hundred and Ninth Illinois Infantry, he immediately put the regiment under arrest, having their arms taken away. A court of inquiry exonerated the troops, excepting the lieutenant-colonel and several subordinate officers, and restored them to their place, "where the Commanding General *hoped* to find them among the pure and patriotic, in their country's defence."

Soon after, General Grant's headquarters again were removed to Memphis, Tenn.

January 1st, 1863! Most memorable New-Year's

day! The PRESIDENT'S PROCLAMATION OF EMANCIPATION went, during all its winter hours, along the network of telegraph wires stretching from the Atlantic to the Pacific. Strong men wept, others shouted, others still could only pray or sing. The chains of millions of slaves had virtually fallen from their limbs.

And what had General Grant to do with it? When Adjutant-General Thomas, clothed with authority to carry out that proclamation, visited the southwestern armies, as he assured me, how he should be received by the officers, many of them Southern men, who hated "abolition," was a serious question. But General Thomas is a lion when roused by resistance or danger. He called the commanders together, and addressed them, declaring that the proclamation would be enforced to the letter. We have our chief's response;

I. Corps, division, and post commanders will afford all facilities for the completion of the negro regiments now organizing in this department. Commissaries will issue supplies, and quartermasters will furnish stores on the same requisitions and returns as are required from other troops.

It is expected that all commanders will especially exert themselves in carrying out the policy of the Administration, not only in organizing colored regiments, and rendering them efficient, but also in removing prejudice against them. * * *

Major-General U. S. GRANT.

Manly and patriotic words!
Early in February, his headquarters are at Young's

Point, in Louisiana, near enough to Vicksburg to observe the enemy's movements, examine their fortifications, and arrange his maturing plans for a fresh advance upon the fortress. For, the school story about "Can't," so perfectly characteristic of the *man*, never had a finer illustration than now. The proud fortress *he must and would take;* *that*, with God's permission, was settled.

Councils of war resulted in the unanimous opinion, in accordance with General Grant's, that the south side was the pregnable side of Vicksburg. But how shall he get there? Port Hudson stands guard below, and Walnut Hills above. The old, abandoned canal, cut by Engineer Williams across the bend on which the city lies, is thought of by General Grant, and its reopening, though it had been filled up by the rebels, commenced, in the hope of getting through with high water in the spring. But the dam gave way at one end; the water overflowed the lands, and the enterprise was abandoned.

Orders, limiting the communications from the army, through negroes and citizens, to the smallest possible number, to preserve the utmost secrecy, were issued. The silent, thoughtful, cautious commander was absorbed in the mighty undertaking in his hands.

A reconnoissance had been made in the neighborhood of Lake Providence, during which Captain Prime, chief of engineers on General Grant's staff, noticed bayous running into the country back of Milliken's Bend, north of Vicksburg. There was another at New Carthage, south of the city.

"Bayous—what are they?" a young reader asks. A bayou is a lake-like expansion, or flow of the river into a curve of the stream, extending often many miles inland. The word means *channel*. "Pass," is a stream from the main current, which returns again at some distance.

A bayou canal had been dug near Island No. 10, and why not around Vicksburg? Captain Prime was sure it could be done, after an examination by himself and Colonel Pride. Lake Providence was only a mile from the river, and was connected by Bayou Baxter with Bayou Macon. The map will give the situation of these waters not only, but make you think the plan a very easy one, to cut a channel from the Mississippi to Lake Providence, which is lower than the current, and was doubtless once a part of it. Commence at this point, and glance along the bayous to Tensas River, then down it to Black River, and to the mouth of this, at Red River, and the course is clear enough to the Mississippi between Port Hudson and Vicksburg.

The work went on till vessels entered Lake Providence. But the falling water of the river, and passable roads, led to the abandonment of the scheme, which General Grant all the while suspected might fail; yet the enterprise was valuable, as a concealment from the enemy of other plots against their stronghold.

Meanwhile, Admiral Porter's fleet of gunboats were acting with General Grant on the Mississippi; Colonel Ellet having run by the batteries at Vicksburg with the

"Queen of the West," near the middle of February, had gone up Red River, and captured transports. The noble ship, with the "Indianola," which followed her, however fell, subsequently, into the hands of the rebels.

And now another and wilder expedition was proposed. It was, to get through the long-neglected Yazoo Pass, leading from the Mississippi to Coldwater and the Tallahatchie Rivers; thus getting a passage for troops by flank movement to Haines's Bluff, a post near the mouth of Yazoo River.

An extract from an officer of the gunboat "Marmora" will afford a vivid view of the adventure:

"The Rubicon is passed. Three and a half days of most tedious, vexatious, bothersome, troublesome, and damaging steamboating has brought this expedition twenty miles on its way, and disclosed to its view the end of the now famous Yazoo Pass. A more execrable place was never known. Should one propose to run a steamboat to the moon, he would be considered equally sane, by those who had seen the Yazoo Pass before this expedition forced its way through it, as the person who proposed this movement.

"I would like to describe the Yazoo Pass. I would like to compare it to something that would be intelligible. But I know of nothing in heaven or on earth, or in the waters under the earth, that will compare with it. Had the immortal bard desired a subject from which to draw a picture of the way that leads to the realms of darkness and despair, he had only to picture the Yazoo Pass. Let me try, in the feeble language I can command, to describe it. Perhaps the reader has passed through the Dismal Swamp of Virginia; or, if not, he has read accounts of travellers who have enjoyed that privilege. Then he has read of the famous jungles of India. He has seen or read of the unbroken silence of the boundless tall forests of the John Brown tract in Western New York. Conceive the ugliest features of these three varieties of territory, and he will be able, by combining them, to form a tolerably correct idea of the region through which the Yazoo Pass runs. Those who have watched the course of a snake as he trails his way along the ground, winding this way and that, hither and yonder, going in all directions at the same time, and yet maintaining something of a regular course in the average, will, by exaggerating the picture in their own minds, understand something of the tortuous course of the Yazoo Pass. I have passed through it from one end to the other, and I assert candidly, that there is not throughout its entire length a piece two hundred feet long of perfectly straight river."

The rebels found out the project, and sent from Vicksburg a force to the mouth of Tallahatchie River, erected Fort Pemberton, and put an end to the enterprise.

The last expedition of the kind was undertaken by Admiral Porter and General Grant, at the suggestion of the former, up Steel's Bayou, through Black Bayou to Duck Creek, Deer Creek, Rolling Fork, and Sunflower

River, into the Yazoo. The country was unexplored, delays were inevitable, and the enemy had time to obstruct the way; and, when near the completion of the difficult, romantic passage, it was reluctantly given up.

One of the party thus graphically describes the Black Bayou:

"Black Bayou, a narrow stream, heretofore only navigated by dug-outs, was made of the width of our steamers, with great labor of felling trees and sawing stumps below the surface. Every foot of our way was cut and torn through a dense forest, never before traversed by steamers. I never witnessed a more exciting and picturesque scene than the transportation, on the last day, of the Third Brigade, by General Stuart. Crowded with men, the steamers, at the highest possible speed, pushed through overhanging trees and around short curves. Sometimes wedged fast between trees, then sailing along smoothly, a huge cypress would reach out an arm and sweep the whole length of the boats, tearing guards and chimneys from the decks. The last trip through the Black Bayou was in a night pitchy dark and rainy.

"While the adventure was of uncertain success— when the result seemed almost accomplished, and when our gunboats were surrounded with an enemy confident of victory, and their extrication seemed almost an impossibility—officers and men worked with equal alacrity, whether in building bridges or making forced marches, both by day and in the night. The whole time was used in labor, constant and severe. It seems almost a miracle that the boats were saved. If Generals Sherman and Stuart, by their utmost exertions and labor, had forwarded their troops a single half day later, if the second forced march under General Sherman had been retarded a single hour, in all human probability the whole force would have been lost."

At different points severe encounters were had, often several thousand rebels appearing from ambush, or behind batteries.

This, like the similar movements preceding, was highly serviceable in deceiving and bewildering the enemy. But the faultfinders at home were loud in their complaints.

Said an heroic captain, now in Libby Prison, who went to the battle field a pro-slavery politician, while on a furlough at home:

"It is hard to fight an enemy in front and rear at the same time. I hear more complaints and carping here, in the midst of plenty, in a week, than in six months in the army."

This fact is the darkest page in the history of the war; no matter whether slavery, or some other question of policy, be the occasion of opposition.

Because of the silence kept around General Grant's army, suspending correspondence on account of guerillas on every hand, who would glean information, reports had been sent home, and circulated, that the army was dying with disease. This was good news for the disloyal; but, as the surgeon-general's report and General

Grant's despatches proved, was entirely and *meanly false*. While these men, who, when the war opened, were more afraid of "abolition" than of death, were enforcing the proclamation, and threading dismal swamps, with the old flag in their hands, the Arnolds at home were scolding and lying.

In Philadelphia an amusing illustration occurred. Rev. Dr. B—— was present in a gathering of ministers, when Dr. C—— opposed the President's course in regard to the slaves. Said Dr. B——:

"Brethren, when I was a young man, living West, I sometimes went over the prairie, kicking the low bushes to see what I could start. One day, when doing so, *out came a copperhead*. But he was there before I hit the bush. And thus with the proclamation. *It has beaten the bush*, and brought out the Copperheads. But they *were there* before."

One crimson face, and a loud laugh from all others, silenced the disloyal lips.

CHAPTER XIV.

A New Plan—Admiral Farragut's Ship—Porter's Fleet—Hot Work—Thrilling Scene—Grierson's Raid—Ludicrous Scenes—Banks and Grant—Passing Grand Gulf Batteries—The Grand Advance—The Night March—The Night Battle—Port Gibson Taken—Governor Yates and the Victory.

OUR unwearied and undaunted commander must give up his favorite *flanking* movement. He cannot get through passes, bayous, and canals, into the rear of Vicksburg, and there take possession of the railroads to Jackson, the capital of the State. He next proposes to try a land route mainly. This is to be below the city, and behind the bluffs of Warrenton, along the country between the Mississippi and Black Rivers.

Admiral Farragut, the middle of March, in his fine flagship the "Hartford," attended by the "Albatross," steamed past Port Hudson, and, reaching a point near Vicksburg, communicated with General Grant and Admiral Porter.

The last day of March, the great movement of the

army began. Three corps of it were set in motion for the Louisiana shore, to concentrate at New Carthage, nearly opposite Warrenton. "The tug of war" is yet to come. How can the gunboats, and the transports to convey the soldiers over the river, under the command of Admiral Porter, get by the terraces of dark-mouthed cannon overlooking the water at Vicksburg?

April 16th shone serene and cloudless upon the flashing tide of the majestic river of the West. At eleven o'clock that night, eight gunboats and six transports were to try the mettle of the Confederate Gibraltar.

Men are called for, willing to go into the jaws of destruction. The brave fellows rush with a hurrah to the decks. All is ready. The signal bell strikes eleven. Oh that kindly clouds would eclipse the stars, and fling their shadows on the devoted ships! But not a speck obscures the vernal sky. The steamers in sight are thronged to watch the scene; and the suspense is painful among the crowds. "A boat is coming!" are words which send a shudder of apprehension through every heart. Slowly, darkly, steadily it steals along the Louisiana shore, lost in foliage-shadow. Now it steers across to the Mississippi side; and another spectral form floats into view; another, and yet another, emerge from the gloom of night and distance.

Midnight comes, and the procession of fourteen vessels is moving in darkness and silence straight toward Vicksburg, whose battlements loom through the gloom, relieved only by an occasional light. The boats are fireless and lampless. Hopes and fears agitate the hearts and are on the lips of the spectators. Shall those strong ships and brave men go down under the fiery storm of a hundred echoing guns, or ride safely through?

Up shoots a flame, and the thunder of ordnance succeeds it. The enemy have discovered the bold navigators. The rows of fire, followed with the roar, go down from the crest of the fortress to the water's edge, flashing on the path of the undismayed warriors of the waters. Just at this moment, a rising, steady flame above the city lights up the theatre of conflict. High and broad it waves, like a luminous banner against the sky. "Vicksburg is on fire!" is the shout. No; on the heights the foe have kindled a beacon, to show them where to strike the advancing line of boats. The intense glare makes a rope's shadow on the bright deck visible. But too late is the blaze thrown on the track of the leviathans.

The rebels are in a fever of excitement. Porter's fleet *must* not join Farragut, if shot and shell can prevent it. Hiss! whirr! crash! are the music of the death carnival.

The beacon dies, and another flame brightens on the gloom, through volumes of uprolling smoke. "A ship is on fire!" The transport Henry Clay has caught from a burning shell.

Soon the long line of blazing battlements from Vicksburg to Warrenton grows dark and still, and the behold ers retire to wait the morning news. Wonderful are the tidings, that take the lightning's wing with the dawn, and fill many eyes with tears of joy. The fleet is safe, with comparatively small damage—one hero killed, and two others wounded. Excepting the Henry Clay, the ships ride securely between the fortress and New Carthage.

General Grant breathes freely again, as the last and boldest plan of getting Vicksburg begins to wear the appearance of success.

The very next day after the splendid feat on the river, an equally daring and extraordinary one on land was started. General Grant wanted all the railroads cut southeasterly from Vicksburg, before he left his position north of it, to prevent an attack in the rear, should he reach and invest the city. Colonel Grierson, of the First Cavalry Brigade, was selected to do the work; and the dashing trooper with delight entered upon the perilous gallop through the enemy's country.

Other regiments were at Colonel Grierson's command. Away they ride for the railways, and across forests, fields, and swamps; now here, to deceive the enemy in regard to the real design, and then in the opposite direction, tearing up a track, capturing a train, or burning a mill.

Amusing scenes enlivened the raiders' wild career. Some of them, stopping at a wealthy planter's house, who was also a guerilla, passed themselves off as Van Dorn's men; for our soldiers, in these adventures, wore "secesh" uniform, more or less. Finding splendid horses in his barn, they began to change the saddles from their tired steeds to the backs of his.

"Can't spare 'em, gentlemen! can't let these horses go!" protested the planter.

"We *must* have them. You want us to catch the Yankees, and we shall have to hurry to do it," replied the raiders.

"All right, gentlemen. I'll keep your animals till you return. I suppose you'll be back in two or three days at the farthest. When you return, you'll find they have been well cared for."

The guerilla is probably waiting still for his friends and horses.

A young lady thus complains:

"The first thing they did, was to carry off Lizzie's buggy. They broke into the storeroom, and took sister Emily's wine, which they drank, and carried away next morning. As we sat quietly awaiting our fate, still hoping that God—in whose care ma had at the beginning placed us, kneeling with us in earnest prayer—would yet save us, we heard them dancing, whooping, breaking, and plundering away over the house. They stole all my jewelry; they broke all sister Emily's pictures. Nan (a servant) was very much distressed at their taking the blankets."

Poor girl! we smile at and pity her. War is no respecter of persons, nor very particular about the amount of damage done along his path.

East, northwest, and south the forces dash, apparently

without order, and yet according to a well-matured plan. The main body of cavalry presses on, to cut a path through to our lines near New Orleans. Rebel camps are destroyed; and, when hotly pursued, Colonel Grierson dashes on a bridge, and, burning it behind him, gains time to escape.

May 1st, at midday, a courier galloped into Baton Rouge, announcing the arrival of Colonel Grierson through the very heart of the enemy's country, near the city. The tidings seemed incredible. An escort soon met him, and, amid deafening cheers, the heroic raiders entered the town.

In fifteen days, eight hundred miles had been traversed, and for thirty hours the column had ridden eighty miles without rest or food, only as, the last night, nature surrendered to sleep; and the worn, soiled, and half-famished heroes rode forward like statues on horseback, excepting when a rebel's gun startled them a moment.

Four million dollars' worth of property was destroyed, the railroads torn up, and the mortifying, alarming fact forced home on the foe, that fancied security may be the moment of greatest danger.

The news, to General Grant, was another assurance of triumph at hand, in the decisive game of which the raid was a single but brilliant move.

My young reader will not forget, that over the field of army movements, many hundred miles in extent, the erection of batteries, cavalry raids, marches, &c., were planned and executed at the same time, in different parts of the vast area.

General Banks was looking after Baton Rouge, in the neighborhood of New Orleans, and in another department; still, connected with the great design of repossessing the whole valley of the West, to the Gulf of Mexico

General Grant believed in secrecy and promptness. Keep still, get ready, and then despatch the business in hand, was his motto.

There was a point called Hard Times, by the circuitous land route, seventy miles down the Louisiana shore, which was nearer the spot on the Mississippi side where he intended to land his troops. To push forward rapidly, he resolved to build a road through the wild region, for the "boys" the transports could not carry, as they were too few to convey the whole.

During the night of April 28th, the Thirteenth Army Corps got on board transports, which, the next morning, were ordered by General Grant to move toward Grand Gulf, on the enemy's side, while Admiral Porter, with his gunboats, *entertained* the fort with his salutes of shot and shell.

At eight o'clock, "boom! boom!" went the admiral's heavy guns. In a moment the compliment was returned. Then, for five hours, the tempest of iron hail raged. On a steamtug in the river stood Grant, watching with intense interest the effect of our guns, ready to bring forward the forces to storm the fortress when the naval work was done.

The enemy had tried to make the fort impregnable since Farragut came and went past it, and fought with a desperate fury, which the admiral declared he never saw equalled. The gunboat "Benton" was hit forty-seven times with the ponderous balls. On this ship, the "Pittsburg," and "La Fayette," over twenty were killed, and nearly sixty wounded.

The batteries at one time were nearly silenced. It was, however, decided to abandon the attempt to take them, and send the transports by at evening, while Porter engaged the enemy. This was accomplished at six o'clock. Three days later, he returned to renew the fight, and found the works deserted.

The next advance must be over the river, and on the soil of Mississippi. No bolder and more sublime military enterprise was ever undertaken.

The Thirteenth Army Corps, under General McClernand—a splendid body of men—push their columns to the river's margin, extending back in long and bristling lines. With brisk movement they soon are in the transports, and sweep over the tide. The die is cast. The troops land at Bruninsburg, below Grand Gulf, and, according to General Grant's instructions, march forward to the bluffs, three miles distant, reaching these highlands just before they catch the glow of the setting sun. Now, in every part of the commander's host, there is activity and haste, under his inspiring and guiding genius. He sets the example of economy in baggage, that no *luxury* might embarrass their advance. Wrote one in the army:

"Starting on the movement, the General disencumbered himself of everything, setting an example to his officers and men. He took neither a horse nor a servant, overcoat nor blanket, nor tent nor camp chest, nor even a clean shirt. His only baggage consisted of a tooth brush. He always showed his teeth to the rebels. He shared all the hardships of the private soldier, sleeping in the front and in the open air, and eating hard tack and salt pork. He wore no sword, had on a low-crowned citizen's hat, and the only thing about him to mark him as a military man, was his two stars on his undress military coat."

From the Bluffs, the corps press on toward Port Gibson, to surprise the rebels there, and protect the bridges between Grand Gulf and Jackson, the capital of Mississippi. An exciting, romantic night march was that of the pioneer volunteers toward Vicksburg. How grand the spectacle, as the ranks for miles sweep along the road under the levee between them and the river; then, turning from it, go winding over the crests of hills, stretching away like a sea of solid waves of orange and emerald hue! Up the precipitous sides of some bold bluff the rows of glittering steel creep, then pass in spectral indistinctness through a deep ravine; now they sweep between wide fields of waving corn, and again over plains of the most fragrant flowers, and through vernal forests, whose magnolias are in full blossom, flinging, from their cups of alabaster, delicious aroma on the midnight air.

Reader, can you think of a greater earthly contrast

than this, beside the track of war's legions? It is not strange that a "soldier boy" in the magnificent cavalcade should write:

"The harmony of the scene, naturally so suggestive of peace, was sadly marred by the constantly recurring evidences that man was at variance with his fellow."

At length the columns approach Port Gibson; they turn southward, passing a "primitive church," nestled in a grove of blooming magnolias, at one o'clock in the morning. They had marched thirteen miles from Bruninsburg without meeting the enemy. But, "crack! crack!" go the light arms of the rebels, followed by the roar of artillery—the signals of an opposing host eleven thousand strong.

As if by magic, the Union battalions wheel into line, and open fire in return. Soon silence settles upon the hostile batteries, till the dawn of day, when the fight opens in earnest. Around that ancient little church, far and near, the battle rages. Almost under its shadow lay twenty bodies on a space of a few rods. The enemy were thrown across the road to Port Gibson, and, at the centre, on that highway, the artillery fire was terrible.

Between the armies, on our left, was a dense canebrake, filled with skirmishers, where they were secure against our fire, and from which "the deadly missiles came singing through the air, laying many a brave soldier low."

How will the fearful struggle turn? The tide of war, with a pendulum swing, beats back and forth over ridges of the slain. But look! Along the road to Grand Gulf, see the splendid First Brigade of the Thirteenth Army Corps, sweeping like a tornado. Reënforcements are at hand. Long and loud, the shout of welcome rises over the din of battle. The fortunes of the day are decided. A letter written from the field, thus describes the scene:

"The boys fixed bayonets and boldly charged the position. Down upon their hands and knees, they worked their way through the young cane, and mercilessly slaughtered all who did not yield. One hundred and fifty men were taken prisoners in this glorious charge, and scores of rebels were killed and wounded. They gained the other side of the thicket, and picked off the men and horses serving the rebel battery. The Union batteries finished the good work, and the position and guns fell into our hands.

"Beaten at every point, losing one hundred and fifty killed, three hundred wounded, and more than five hundred prisoners, the enemy sullenly and rapidly retreated to Port Gibson, harassed in his flight by volleys of musketry and the most strenuous efforts of our artillery.

"Without difficulty they reached Port Gibson, blowing up, when near the village, a caisson filled with shot, shell, and powder.

"Night was wrapping her sable mantle over hill and valley, and the silver moon shone out clear and bright, casting a flood of beautiful light over friend and foe, when the order was given to cease pursuit. We rested on the battle field, wearied and exhausted, and soon deep silence reigned supreme where Mars so recently held high carnival."

Major-General Grant hastened forward from Bruninsburg, and entered the crimson plain of victory, with the sad joy of another dearly-bought promise of reaching the goal of his hopes.

The foe abandoned the fort in the night, and, when the flame of the rising sun paled the conflagration of the bridge over the Bayou Pierre, he finds in his rear the Stripes and Stars lifted by the breeze over the walls of Port Gibson.

Soon a new bridge receives the advancing feet of the triumphant volunteers, and onward toward Vicksburg Grant's great army rapidly push, losing occasionally a hero-boy by the enemy's fire.

The city is twenty-five miles from Grand Gulf, and eighteen are yet to be traversed before the troops get to its gates. The noble commander, never ostentatious, almost without observation, in the wake of the legions with torn yet flying colors headed toward Vicksburg, changed his base from Bruninsburg to Grand Gulf. He then sent over the electric wires to Washington the cheering news of progress. General Grant's congratulatory order to the "Soldiers of the Army of Tennessee," was a grateful and glowing tribute of praise. He refers to the hardships endured, the stormy weather, and the horrid roads, and closes in these words:

"More difficulties and privations are before us; let us endure them manfully. Other battles are to be fought; let us fight them bravely. A grateful country will rejoice at our success, and history will record it with immortal honor."

Generals Carr, Hovey, Benton, and Colonels Macauley, Spiegel, and others, led on the heroic boys with unrivalled valor.

Naturally enough, Governor Yates, of Illinois, who gave our hero his first commission in the conflict, and who was on the late battle field, sent to his State the following enthusiastic and glowing despatch:

GRAND GULF, MISS., May 4, 1863.

Our arms are gloriously triumphant. We have succeeded in winning a victory which, in its results, must be the most important of the war. The battle of May 1st lasted from eight o'clock in the morning until night, during all which time the enemy was driven back on the right, left, and centre. All day yesterday our army was in pursuit of the rebels, they giving us battle at almost every defensible point, and fighting with desperate valor. Last night a large force of the enemy was driven across Black River, and General McClernand was driving another large force in the direction of Willow Springs. About two o'clock yesterday, I left General Logan, with his division, in pursuit of the enemy, to join General Grant at Grand Gulf, which the enemy had evacuated in the morning, first blowing up their magazines, spiking their cannon, destroying tents, &c. On my way to Grand Gulf, I saw guns scattered all along the road, which the enemy had left in their retreat. The rebels were scattered through the woods in every direction. This army of the rebels was considered, as I now learn, invincible; but it quailed before the irresistible assaults of Northwestern valor.

I consider Vicksburg as ours in a short time, and the Mississippi River as destined to be open from its source to its mouth.

I have been side by side with our boys in battle, and can bear witness to the unfaltering courage and prowess of our brave Illinoisans.

Richard Yates, Governor.

The very day this message was dated, the terrible carnage of Chancellorsville, in Virginia, under Hooker, sent him and his battalions staggering back to the Rappahannock, fulfilling strikingly the proverb of Solomon: "He hath set adversity over against prosperity."

CHAPTER XV.

Sherman—Deceiving the Enemy—General Grant's Wisdom, and humane Care of the Men—Ready to move again—Governor Pettus frightened—Grant's Despatch—A Battle—The Capital taken—News—Crossing the River—The Investment and Assault—The Attack repeated—The Siege—The Messenger deserts—The Prison Fortress—Amusing Incidents.

BUT where was the splendid General Sherman?—for he had few superiors in the field. All this time of advance, General Grant's comprehensive military wisdom was shining in secret warfare. It was no trifling part of the campaign, to keep the rebels at the great centres, Richmond and Chattanooga, and, wherever interference with his plans might appear, in the dark. So Sherman was sent up the Yazoo River to threaten Haines's Bluff, and Colonel Corwyn dashed with his cavalry along the Mobile and Ohio Railroad, menacing the posts in that direction.

There was, at this juncture, some hope that General Banks might ascend the river from Baton Rouge, and, taking Port Hudson, join General Grant with twelve thousand troops. But he was doomed to disappointment, and to wait for Grant.

The grand Army of the West has reached a crisis in affairs again. Leaving Grand Gulf as a base, the columns are to strike for the State capital *en route* to Vicksburg. Our heroic chief seems to lay aside the field command, and, with his plain felt hat, soiled clothes, and bearded face, superintends the work of preparation. For now, the preliminary work of clearing the way being done by light marching, the gigantic work of moving the whole caravan of a great army has come. To see that the troops have shelter, and clothing, and food, is quite as needful to success as arms and ammunition. He therefore, in person, looked after his quartermasters, commissaries, &c., reining each man up to duty. This direct and sincere interest in the comfort of the soldiers has always won their purest respect and regard.

General Grant takes up his headquarters at an advanced position on Black River, called Hawkinson's Ferry. All the machinery of warfare is ready. Like a couchant lion prepared to spring on his prey, he waits a few days for Sherman's corps and the wagon trains to arrive; sending out forces toward other points up the river, making the enemy believe that his plan was to lead his army in that direction.

The game of misleading the rebels succeeded admirably. The terrified Governor Pettus issued a flaming proclamation, in which these words occur:

"Fathers, brothers, Mississippians—while your sons and kindred are bravely fighting your battles on other fields, and shedding new lustre on your name, the burning disgrace of successful invasion of their homes, of insult and injury to their wives, mothers, and sisters, of rapine and ruin, with God's help and by your assistance, shall never be written while a Mississippian lives to feel in his proud heart the scorching degradation."

May 7th, General Grant's order to advance flies along the lines. Tents disappear, and miles of supply trains fall into the wake of the proud battalions, with their front toward Vicksburg. With the centre of the three great columns, and not behind, General Grant marches, guiding and watching their every motion. Soon as he was fairly "out to sea," in the mariner's descriptive phrase—cut loose from doubtful territory, and committed to the alternative of resplendent conquest or darkest defeat, he told the Government so, in the following few words:

IN THE FIELD, May 11, 1863.

To Major-General HALLECK, General-in-Chief:

My force will be, this evening, as far advanced along Fourteen Mile Creek, the left near Black River, and extending in a line nearly east and west, as they can get without bringing on a general engagement.

I shall communicate with Grand Gulf no more, except it becomes necessary to send a train with a heavy escort.

You may not hear from me again for several days.

U. S. GRANT, Major-General.

Northeasterly, between him and Jackson, was Raymond, a rebel position. In the morning of May 12th, having brushed the enemy, disputing the right of way, from their path, the Seventeenth Army Corps reached the place, and, from the thick woods on the banks of Foudron's Creek, the rebels poured their fire. Three hours of desperate encounter routed them, and they fell back on Jackson, many of them throwing down their arms and deserting to our lines. What followed, one of the brave fellows finely describes:

"We encamped at Raymond on Tuesday night, and early Wednesday morning started for Clinton, a small town on the Vicksburg and Jackson Railroad. It was considered indispensably necessary for the success of our movement upon Vicksburg, that we should have possession of the railroad and the city of Jackson. We reached Clinton at nightfall, and went into camp.

"During the night, a regiment under the command of Captain Tresilian, of General Logan's staff, moved out on the railroad east and west of Clinton, and destroyed it, tearing up the rails, and burning every bridge and the timbers across every cattle guard for four miles each side of the village. The telegraph office and the post office were seized, and rifled of their precious contents. From this source most valuable information of the enemy's future movements was obtained. In the express packages left by the train of cars which steamed out of town just as our advance came in sight, several orders from General Johnston were discovered, and a package of Confederate scrip.

"At Clinton, a hundred prisoners were found, occupants of rebel hospitals. These were paroled, and taken in charge by the citizens.

"At daylight Thursday morning, the army was on the road to Jackson, moving in line of battle. A strong advance guard was thrown out, and a heavy line of skirmishers on the right and left flank, and thus we moved in the direction of the city.

"All was quiet for the first five or six miles, until we reached a hill overlooking a broad open field, through the centre of which, and over the crest of the hill beyond which, the road to Jackson passes. On the left of this hill the enemy had posted his artillery, and along the crest his line of battle. From the foot of the acclivity, and not a mile removed, we could see the long line of rebel infantry awaiting in silence our onset. Slowly and cautiously we moved up the hill until we came within range, when all at once, upon the heights to the right, we discovered a puff of white smoke and heard the report of booming cannon, followed by the shrill scream of an exploding shell. One of our batteries was moved to the left of a cotton gin in the open field, midway between the enemy's line of battle and the foot of the hill, and played upon the rebel battery with telling effect. The duel was kept up with great spirit on both sides for nearly an hour, when all at once it ceased by the withdrawal of the enemy's guns. Two brigades were thrown out to the right and left of this battery, supported by another brigade at proper distance. A strong line of skirmishers had been pushed forward and posted in a ravine just in front, which protected them from rebel fire. After a little delay, they were again advanced out of cover, and for several minutes a desultory fire was kept up between both lines of skirmishers, in which, owing to the topographical nature of the ground, the enemy had the advantage.

"At last, General Crocker, who was on the field, and had personally inspected the position, saw that, unless the enemy could be driven from his occupation of the crest of the hill, he would be forced to retire. He therefore ordered a charge along the line. With colors flying, and with a step as measured and unbroken as if on dress parade, the movement was executed. Slowly they advanced, crossed the narrow ravine, and, with fixed bayonets, rose the crest of the hill in easy range of the rebel line. Here they received a tremendous volley, which caused painful gaps in their ranks. They held their fire until they were within a distance of thirty paces, when they delivered the returning volley with fearful effect; and, without waiting to reload their muskets, with a terrific yell they rushed upon the staggered foe.

"Over the fences, through the brushwood, into the inclosure, they worked their way, and slaughtered right and left without mercy. The enemy, astonished at their impetuosity, wavered and fell back, rallied again, and finally broke in wild confusion. The brave Union soldiers gained the crest of the hill, and the rebels fled in utter terror. Our boys reloaded their muskets, and sent the terrible missiles after the fleeing rebels, adding haste to their terrified flight. They cast muskets and blankets to the ground, unslung their knapsacks, and ran like greyhounds, nor stopped to look back until they reached the intrenchments just within the city.

"Meantime, General Sherman, who had left Raymond the day before, and taken the road to the right just beyond the town, came up with the left wing of the enemy's forces, and engaged them with artillery. They made a feeble resistance, and they, too, broke and ran.

"After a delay of half an hour, to enable our wearied soldiers to take breath, our column moved forward again.

"We reached the fort, and found a magnificent battery of six pieces, which the enemy had left behind him, and a hundred new tents, awaiting appropriation.

"The hospital flag was flying from the Deaf and Dumb Institute, and this was crowded with sick and wounded soldiers, who, of course, fell into our hands as prisoners of war. Opposite and all around this building were tents enough to encamp an entire division; and just in front of it, hauled out by the roadside, were two small breech-loading two-pounder rifles, which had been used to pick off officers.

"Farther down the street we found a pile of burning caissons; and on the opposite side of the street, directly in front of the Confederate House, the stores, filled with commissary and quartermaster's supplies, were briskly consuming.

"Directly in front of us, the State House loomed up in ample proportions. Two officers, taking possession of the flag of one of the regiments, galloped rapidly forward, and hoisted it from the flagstaff surmounting its broad dome. The beautiful flag was seen in the distance by the advancing column, and with cheers and congratulations it was greeted.

"We had captured Jackson, the hotbed of the rebellion. Guards were established, a provost marshal appointed, and the city placed under martial law. The citizens, particularly those who sustained official relations to the State and rebel Governments, had left the city the evening before; but there were many soldiers left behind, and a large number in hospital, who fell into our hands.

"The State Treasurer and Governor Pettus were gone, taking the funds and State papers with them. A large amount of Government and military property fell into our hands; but private property was altogether unmolested. The offices of the Memphis *Appeal* and Jackson *Mississippian* were removed the preceding night."

Among the news found in the rebel capital, was the clearest evidence that General Joe Johnston had ordered General Pemberton to leave Vicksburg, and fall on the rear of General Grant's army. Away hurries a large force to Bolton, nearly midway between Jackson and Vicksburg, to meet him, more than willing to go *halfway*. General Grant then removed his headquarters to Clinton, keeping all the while among the troops in motion.

Early on the 16th of May, not far from Bolton, the armies met at Champion's Hill. It was a fearfully bloody fight. Our "boys" charged the flying enemy in the woods, covering the ground with the dead. During the engagement, the Commander-in-chief was on the field, directing the swaying host, as it fell crushingly on the changing front of the foe. The defeated army retreated to Big Black River toward Vicksburg. The Thirteenth and Seventeenth Army Corps were in pursuit.

General Grant is remarkable for "looking ahead"—providing for emergencies. In this case, he had sent on a force, with a pontoon train, which was ready when General Sherman, who had been ordered from Bolton, came up to cross. While he could go over the stream there, with the Fifteenth Army Corps, the passage of the Thirteenth and Seventeenth was disputed, at a railroad bridge across the Big Black; but after a severe combat, in which they burned the bridge, the rebels fled. In a single night the troops made their floating bridges, and got over.

Three miles from Vicksburg! Such was the position of Major-General Grant on May 19th, 1863.

The Fifteenth Army Corps swept round to the Walnut Hills, to communicate with Admiral Porter's fleet in the Yazoo River. The other corps took strong positions; in the words of General Grant, "covering all the ground their strength would admit of," and fairly investing Vicksburg. Not knowing the exact condition of the fortress, he thought the disheartening defeats of the enemy would favor an assault.

It has already been intimated that Admiral Porter was in the Yazoo, near Vicksburg; but how he got there, is the unanswered question. The noble old hero had been watching General Grant's progress, pushing up the Yazoo as fast as he could coöperate, with that harmony of action and patriotic sympathy felt only by noble minds. At Haines's Bluff, instead of a battle, the terrified rebels fled at his approach. Destroying magazines and much other property, he had got within sound of the conqueror's guns thundering around Vicksburg.

The assault was fruitless; the works were not entered, and could not be by storming. But, after two days' rest and preparation, establishing supplies north of the city, General Grant resolved to try again. "Can't," in any case, he hated to hear. Johnston, who retreated when the capital surrendered, might fall on his rear, and the troops were impatient to see the interior of the Gibraltar.

On the 22d of May, with all the generals' watches set with General Grant's, that they might move at the same moment—at ten o'clock—the bugle call to charge rang full and clear on the air of spring. The three army corps, led by McClernand, McPherson, and Sherman, under the eye of General Grant, dashed forward, the long lines of bayonets gleaming in the vernal sun. Gaps had been made by the artillery in the outer walls, and, protected by that fire, over ditch, ridge, and through a shower of bullets, the lines advanced, planting the Stars and Stripes upon the bastions. Still, the massive circles of defence stood between the assailants and the assailed, unshaken, unbroken.

The brave troops, uncomplainingly, and in good order, fell back, to fight again.

In the lull which succeeded these assaults, arose an unhappy dissension in camp. General McClernand issued a congratulatory order to his troops, lavishing eulogy upon them, and intimating that success would have attended their splendid action, if General Grant had sent reënforcements asked for, and promised, if wanted. Jealousies sprang up, and threatening dissension cast a gloom over the besieging ranks. General Grant, though warmly attached to McClernand, who had been with him since he assumed the control at Cairo, when his friend acknowledged the order, and defended it, acted promptly for the good of the army, and relieved him of his command.

The rebels, till these waves of the war tide were beaten back by their fortress, had seen *hard times*, as well as the Army of Tennessee, whose *headquarters* once bore that name. Leaders are liable to suspicion when their enterprises fail; and it was muttered in the garrison that General Pemberton had sold the troops at Champion's Hill and Big Black River Bridges. Once sure that his hiding place would stand the Yankee storming columns, he addressed the men as follows:

"You have heard that I was incompetent and a traitor, and that it was my intention to sell Vicksburg. Follow me, and you will see the cost at which I will sell

Vicksburg. When the last pound of beef, bacon, and flour, the last grain of corn, the last cow, and hog, and horse, and dog, shall have been consumed, and the last man shall have perished in the trenches, then, and only then, will I sell Vicksburg."

These defiant words were answered with a shout of approval; and General Grant prepared to test their truth by slow and patient siege. He was right in supposing that the failure to storm, though it cost him valuable lives, would make the troops more willing to enter on the siege.

Vicksburg was surrounded by General Grant's armies, excepting partial communication on the left of our lines, between General Pemberton and General Johnston, at Canton, Miss. From Arkansas, General Herron was called, to complete the enclosure of the city by troops.

There the fated city stands, in the ring of Union cannon and bayonets, while the unyielding, taciturn, patient commander settles down, the last of May, for a summer residence there. If he can continue his visit to Pemberton longer than the latter wishes him to or can *stay at home*, then he will have to leave his castle, and let his outdoor and unwelcome visitor go in, and help himself to what may remain. Subterranean pathways are dug for the gunners, and other troops, who thus escape the bullets of the sharpshooters.

Around Vicksburg, our men took what rations they could, and then tried to live on the country, which was rather hard fare. At one time their movements were so rapid that there was no time to cook, if they had food. A hardbread or a corn pone would command a dollar at any moment. Some one found a negro with a half peck of meal, and six men with bayonets mounted guard over the fire while the bread was baking for General Grant's luxurious repast. After these privations, one of the officers, who was coming down, brought a basket of ale to the General and his staff. General Grant expressed his thanks, appreciated the kindness, and would just taste it, in acknowledgment; but he drank none, not even ale.

In repeating some anecdote of General Grant which he had heard, a gentleman said:

"Grant's answer was, with an oath, 'I don't believe it. It is one of the rebel lies.' An officer replied: 'No, I do not think he said that. I never heard him utter one profane word.'"

The same officer was speaking of the difference between Rosecrans and Grant, in the matter of generalship. On one occasion, during a fight, Rosecrans was standing in a commanding position, and giving his orders. Suddenly he started, and made toward a regiment to chase back one man who was running, and spent some little time, in the height of the battle, sending him back to his place. Grant, in the midst of fighting, was watching intently, and working earnestly, when he was accosted by a surgeon. He had taken a fine house for a hospital, and had his wounded gathered in and about it, when, in the turn of the fight, shot and shell began to fall among the poor fellows. "General," said he, "what shall I do? Some of my poor men are getting wounded a second time." "Don't come to me," said General Grant, mildly, but earnestly; "I have this battle to fight; that is your business. I can't attend to your wounded, nor think of them now. Don't interrupt me!" waving his hand; "I have this fighting to attend to."

Providential incidents had their important part in the successes of our arms. Among them was this striking one: A young fellow named Douglas, formerly an Illinoisan, who had lived South, and there joined the rebel ranks, was sent to Johnston by Pemberton, presuming he would seize a horse outside the walls, and ride through the pickets to Canton. But, tired of the service of Jeff. Davis, he walked to the guard, and delivered himself up prisoner of war. General Grant got the message intended for Johnston. The substance of it was:

"I have fifteen thousand men at Vicksburg, and rations for thirty days—one meal a day. Come to my aid with thirty thousand men. Attack Grant in the rear If you cannot do it within ten days, you had better retreat. Ammunition is almost exhausted, particularly percussion caps."

A cloud passed over the "Confederacy" with the incredible, astounding fact, that General Grant had completely outwitted the traitors—gone across their soil, and set himself down coolly to watch the boasted Sebastopol, making a fearful prison of his enemy's fortress. How fearful it soon became, you can guess from the thousands of horses and mules turned out of it because they could not be fed. General Grant secured and used many of them.

Singular scenes occur across the lines of the hostile armies. Just after Vicksburg was invested, a sharpshooter, from the works, politely asked of one in ours:

"Can you give a fellow a drink of coffee, if he goes there?"

"Plenty of it."

"Well, comrades," says reb., "shall I go?"

"Yes; go ahead."

The rifleman did go, and, for the first time in a year, drank a cup of coffee.

He lingered, and was evidently in no haste to return.

"Come back!" shouted his friends.

"Think not; this coffee won't let me. Good-by!"

And the soldier of Vicksburg remained where he found "enough and to spare," while his disloyal brethren of a common heritage were "in want."

CHAPTER XVI.

The captured Courier—Grant and the Letters—The Sappers and Miners—How they do their strange Work—All is ready—The Explosion—The Advance—The Flag of Truce—The Message, and General Grant's Answer—The Capitulation—The Fourth of July in Vicksburg—The Glad Tidings—The Loss and Gain—The President and General Grant—Scenes after the Fall of the Fortress—Bill of Fare—The Dead—Hurrah!

HE days wear away. Ball and shell rush through the air at intervals, day and night. The gunboats "boom" away in front, and the batteries of the army in the rear. General Grant had sent troops to watch Joe Johnston, who, it was reported, was near the Big Black River, and advancing with a large force.

It is night. And see that rebel soldier creeping in the darkness stealthily from the solid ramparts, and through the lines of Union pickets. He now feels safe. But there come some wide-awake "Yankee boys," and his career as courier is over. The messenger's secreted letters are demanded. and handed over. They are addressed to home friends, and express discouragement, with the hope that Johnston would come to their relief. Some of them, who may have been Christian men in spite of the horrible secession delusion, declared their resignation to God, and their trust in Him.

General Grant wrote to General Sherman, commanding the forces against Johnston, and, referring to these epistles of the rebels, said:

"They seem to put a great deal of faith in the Lord and Joe Johnston; but *you* must whip Johnston at least fifteen miles from here."

But "Joe" kept out of the way, and the siege of Vicksburg went forward. The hardest work was done by the sappers and miners. Let us take a look at them. You notice those soldiers keeping guard, here and there, in line with and near the frowning walls of the fortress. Go nearer, and you will see Welsh, Scotch, English, and Irish miners digging saps, or trenches, leading toward a common point close to the walls of the fort. By the side of them rise gabions, or something like towers, to defend the workmen. To get to the main sap leading to the mine, which is a large square ditch running under the fortress walls, in which the powder is to be put, the men must go nearly an eighth of a mile right before the enemy's guns. To do this alive, trenches are dug one after the other, in such directions—but all making a general passage way—that the shot and shell cannot reach the workmen and officers, as they go and come.

The guards we alluded to allow none to pass but the miners, and the few chief officers. Sharpshooters lie in the trenches to pick off the rebels who venture to look from their battlements and see what is going on below. Occasionally a battery is put in position to aid in the defence. The heaps of dirt thrown up, also, are a protection. Now, having got a "pass," go into the trenches and wind along the damp pathways, venturing now and then to glance at the bristling walls no more than fifteen feet from you, as you approach that deep, dark opening downward, and under the massive ramparts. A framework of timber around this mine keeps back the crumbling earth which the projectiles have broken away from the works, and gabions and boxes defend the entrance to the magazine of destruction.

Listen, now. "Pick! pick!" go the instruments of delving; then the grinding sound of the shovels is heard. The air is spectral, for most of the work is done in the night.

It is June 25th; the day has faded, and the miners dig with rapid strokes, for a few hours will finish the strange, wild, dark business, which the busy, fertile brain of General Grant has carried forward with his wise secrecy of purpose. Hark! the pickaxes and spades are held in mute alarm. The enemy is at work too, sinking his shaft toward our own. The men rush away, fearing an explosion; but now return again to complete the ruin.

Such is a mere glimpse of the perilous, gloomy, awful preparation to blow into fragments hostile battlements, and with them scores, perhaps hundreds of men, into eternity. Writes an eyewitness:

"Everything was finished. The spark has been applied, and the now harmless flashes went hurrying to the centre. The troops had been withdrawn. The forlorn hope—or troops detailed to rush into the breach—stood out in plain view, boldly awaiting the uncertainties of the precarious office. A chilling sensation ran through the frame as an observer looked down upon this devoted band, about to hurl itself into the breach—perchance into the jaws of death. Thousands of men in arms flashed on every hill. Every one was speechless. Even men of tried valor—veterans insensible to the shouts of contending battalions, or nerved to the shrieks of comrades suffering under the torture of painful agonies—stood motionless as they directed their eyes upon the spot where soon the terror of a buried agency would discover itself in wild concussions and contortions, carrying annihilation to all within the scope of its tremendous power. It was the seeming torpor which precedes the antagonism of powerful bodies. Five minutes had elapsed. It seemed like an existence. Five minutes more, and yet no signs of the expected exhibition. An indescribable sensation of impatience, blended with a still active anticipation, ran through the assembled spectators. A small pall of smoke now discovered itself; every one thought the crisis had come, and almost saw the terrific scene which the mind had depicted. But not yet. Every eye now centred upon the smoke, momentarily growing greater and greater Thus another five minutes wore away, and curiosity was not satisfied. Another few minutes, then the explosion; and upon the horizon could be seen an enormous column of earth, dust, timbers, and projectiles lifted into the air at an altitude of at least eighty feet. One entire face of the fort was disembodied and scattered in particles all over the surrounding surface. The right and left faces were also much damaged; but, fortunately, enough of them remained to afford an excellent protection on our flanks.

"No sooner had the explosion taken place, than the two detachments acting as the forlorn hope ran into the fort and sap, as already mentioned. A brisk musketry fire at once commenced between the two parties, with about equal effect upon either side. No sooner had these detachments become well engaged, than the rest of Leggett's Brigade joined them, and entered into the struggle. The regiments relieving each other at intervals, the contest now grew severe; both sides, determined upon holding their own, were doing their best. Volley after volley was fired, though with less carnage than would be supposed. The Forty-fifth Illinois charged immediately up to the crest of the parapet, and here suffered its heaviest, losing many officers in the assault.

"After a severe contest of half an hour, with varying results, the flag of the Forty-fifth appeared upon the summit of the work. The position was gained. Cheer after cheer broke through the confusion and uproar of the contest, assuring the troops everywhere along the line that the Forty-fifth was still itself. The colonel was now left alone in command of the regiment, and he was himself badly bruised by a flying splinter. The regiment had also suffered severely in the line, and the troops were worn out by excessive heat and hard fighting.

"The explosion of the mine was the signal for the opening of the artillery of the entire line. The left division of General McPherson's Seventeenth, or centre corps, opened first, and discharges were repeated along the left through General Ord's Thirteenth Corps, and Herron's extreme 'left division,' until the sound struck the ear like the mutterings of distant thunder. General Sherman, on the right, also opened his artillery about the same time, and occupied the enemy's attention along his front. Every shell struck the parapet, and, bounding over, exploded in the midst of the enemy's forces beyond. The scene at this time was one of the utmost sublimity. The roar of artillery, rattle of small arms, the cheers of the men, flashes of light, wreaths of pale blue smoke over different parts of the field, the bursting of shell, the fierce whistle of solid shot, the deep 'boom' of the mortars, the broadsides of the ships of war, and, added to all this, the vigorous replies of the enemy, set up a din which beggars all description. The peculiar configuration of the field afforded an opportunity to witness almost every battery and every rifle pit within seeing distance; and it is due to all the troops to say, that every one did his duty.

"After the possession of the fort was no longer in doubt, the pioneer corps mounted the work, with their shovels, and set to throwing up earth vigorously in order to secure space for artillery. A most fortunate peculiarity in the explosion, was the manner in which the earth was thrown out. The appearance of the place was that of a funnel, with heavy sides running up to the very crest of the parapet, affording admirable protection not only for our troops and pioneers, but turned out a ready-made fortification in the rough, which, with a slight application of the shovel and pick, was ready to receive the guns to be used at this point.

"Miraculous as it may seem, amid all the fiery ordeal of this afternoon's engagement, one hundred killed and two hundred wounded is a large estimate of casualties on our side.

"From a lookout on the summit of an eminence near the rebel works, the movements of the enemy could be plainly watched. An individual in the tower, just prior to the explosion of the mine, saw two rebel regiments marching out to the fort. Of a sudden—perhaps upon seeing the smoke of the fuse—the troops turned about and ran toward the town in perfect panic. They were not seen again during the fight; but other regiments were brought up to supply their place." *

Another gives the following brief sketch of the explosion:

"This morning the work was completed; an immense

---

* De R. R. Keim.

quantity of gunpowder was stored in the cavity prepared to receive it, and the fuse train was laid. At noon, the different regiments of the Seventeenth Corps selected to make the assault upon the breach when it should have been effected, were marshalled in long lines upon the near slopes of the hills immediately confronting the doomed rebel fortifications, where, disposed for the attack, they impatiently awaited the *dénoûment*. The rebels seemed to discover that some movement was on foot; for, from the moment our troops came into position until the explosion took place, their sharpshooters kept up an incessant fire from the whole line of their works.

"At length all was in readiness; the fuse train was fired, and it went fizzing and popping through the zigzag line of trenches, until for a moment it vanished. Its disappearance was quickly succeeded by the explosion, and the mine was sprung. So terrible a spectacle is seldom witnessed. Dust, dirt, smoke, gabions, stockades, timber, gun carriages, logs—in fact, everything connected with the fort—rose hundreds of feet into the air, as if vomited forth from a volcano. Some who were close spectators even say that they saw the bodies of the poor wretches who, a moment before, had lined the ramparts of the work."*

"As soon as the explosion had taken place, the greatest activity was manifested along the whole line, under

---

* Fitzpatrick's despatch.

the soul-inspiring orders of General Grant. The following is a specimen of the emphatic style with which that General calls for vigilance on the part of his troops:

June 25, 1863.
General Ord:

McPherson occupies the crater made by the explosion. He will have guns in battery there by morning. He has been hard at work running rifle pits right, and thinks he will hold all gained. Keep Smith's division sleeping under arms to-night, ready for an emergency. Their services may be required particularly about daylight. There should be the greatest vigilance along the whole line.

U. S. Grant, Major-General.

"In the meantime, the gunboat fleet off Warrenton commenced a bombardment of the enemy's forts. This was kept up without intermission until midnight, when it was slackened to desultory shots. The fuses of the shells, as they ascended in the air, were easily distinguishable, and looked in their course like shooting meteors. When they would strike, the shell would explode with a terrific report. Some of the shells exploded in the air, and the flashes which they emitted looked like an immense piece of pyrotechny." *

And now, more rapidly the lines of General Grant approached the fortress. He felt sure of the prize, and was willing to continue the siege, rather than, by bolder

---

* Larkee.

and immediately successful assault, sacrifice many lives, among them the women and children in the city. General Grant is *humane;* he values human life, and never flings it away for glory; a high, and, in its excellence, a Christian quality of character.

The rebels, who a few weeks before were defiant, now crowded closely together, and in dread awaited the hour of doom.

The FOURTH OF JULY was at hand! General Grant had not forgotten it; and there were signs of its celebration by a grand *entrée;* at least, an attempt to keep Independence Day in the city.

July 3d lights up the beleaguered fortress, and from the walls emerge two rebel generals, Bowen and Montgomery, and over them waves a flag of truce. They enter our lines with a sealed message. Away flies a courier to General Grant. The calm, expectant commander, who for several months had in anticipation seen this hour, breaks the seal, and reads a proposition from General Pemberton for an *armistice,* that terms of capitulation may be arranged. That proud officer boasted that he could hold out as long as he pleased, but wished to "save further effusion of blood." Entirely characteristic of the brave, magnanimous man, was the answer of General Grant:

"The effusion of blood you propose stopping by this course, can be ended at any time you may choose, by an unconditional surrender of the city and garrison. Men who have shown so much endurance and courage as those now in Vicksburg, will always challenge the respect of an adversary, and, I can assure you, will be treated with all the respect due them as prisoners of war. I do not favor the proposition of appointing commissioners to arrange terms of capitulation, because I have no other terms than those indicated above."

The next proposal is, to meet General Pemberton at three o'clock P. M., on neutral ground, and consult together. General Grant consents, and sends the blindfold messengers back. Mr. Keim, a New York correspondent of the press, graphically describes what followed:

"At three o'clock precisely, one gun, the prearranged signal, was fired, and immediately replied to by the enemy. General Pemberton then made his appearance on the works in McPherson's front, under a white flag, considerably on the left of what is known as Fort Hill. General Grant rode through our trenches until he came to an outlet leading to a small green space which had not been trod by either army. Here he dismounted, and advanced to meet General Pemberton, with whom he shook hands, and greeted familiarly.

"It was beneath the outspreading branches of a gigantic oak that the conference of the generals took place. Here presented the only space which had not been used for some purpose or other by the contending armies. The ground was covered with a fresh, luxuriant verdure; here and there a shrub or clump of bushes could be seen standing out from the green growth on the surface, while several oaks filled up the scene, and gave it character. Some of the trees, in their tops, exhibited the effects of flying projectiles, by the loss of limbs or torn foliage, and in their trunks the indentations of smaller missiles plainly marked the occurrences to which they had been silent witnesses.

"The party made up to take part in the conference was composed as follows:

"United States officers: Major-General U. S. Grant, Major-General James B. McPherson, Brigadier-General A. J. Smith.

"Rebel officers: Lieutenant-General John C. Pemberton, Major-General Bowen, Colonel Montgomery, A. A.-G. to General Pemberton.

"When Generals Grant and Pemberton met, they shook hands, Colonel Montgomery introducing the party. A short silence ensued, at the expiration of which General Pemberton remarked:

"'General Grant, I meet you in order to arrange terms for the capitulation of the city of Vicksburg and its garrison. What terms do you demand?'

"'*Unconditional surrender*,' replied General Grant.

"'Unconditional surrender!' said Pemberton. 'Never, so long as I have a man left me! I will fight rather.'

"'Then, sir, you can continue the defence,' coolly said General Grant. 'My army has never been in a better condition for the prosecution of the siege.'

"During the passing of these few preliminaries, General Pemberton was greatly agitated, quaking from head to foot; while General Grant experienced all his natural self-possession, and evinced not the least sign of embarrassment.

"After a short conversation standing, by a kind of mutual tendency the two generals wandered off from the rest of the party, and seated themselves on the grass, in a cluster of bushes, where, alone, they talked over the important events then pending. General Grant could be seen, even at that distance, talking coolly, occasionally giving a few puffs at his favorite companion—his black cigar. General McPherson, General A. J. Smith, General Bowen, and Colonel Montgomery, imitating the example of the commanding generals, seated themselves at some distance off, while the respective staffs of the generals formed another and larger group in the rear.

"After a lengthy conversation, the generals separated. General Pemberton did not come to any conclusion on the matter, but stated his intention to submit the matter to a council of general officers of his command; and, in the event of their assent, the surrender of the city should be made in the morning. Until morning was given him to consider, to determine the matter, and send in his final reply."

After a consultation with his officers, he sent to General Pemberton this answer:

HEADQUARTERS, DEPARTMENT OF TENNESSEE,
NEAR VICKSBURG, July 3, 1863.

Lieutenant General J. C. PEMBERTON, commanding Confederate forces, Vicksburg, Miss.:

GENERAL: In conformity with the agreement of this afternoon, I will submit the following proposition for the surrender of the city of Vicksburg, public stores, &c. On your accepting the terms proposed, I will march in one division, as a guard, and take possession at eight o'clock to-morrow morning. As soon as paroles can be made out and signed by the officers and men, you will be allowed to march out of our lines, the officers taking with them their regimental clothing, and staff, field, and cavalry officers one horse each. The rank and file will be allowed all their clothing, but no other property.

If these conditions are accepted, any amount of rations you may deem necessary can be taken from the stores you now have, and also the necessary cooking utensils for preparing them; thirty wagons, also, counting two two-horse or mule teams as one. You will be allowed to transport such articles as cannot be carried along. The same conditions will be allowed to all sick and wounded officers and privates, as fast as they become able to travel. The paroles for these latter must be signed, however, whilst officers are present, authorized to sign the roll of prisoners.

I am, General, very respectfully, your obedient servant,

U. S. GRANT, Major-General.

After further correspondence, in which slight modifications were made at the request of General Pemberton, he sent his note of surrender to General Grant, dated July 4th, 1863.

Since the negotiation began, firing had ceased. Silent

curiosity took possession of the men. They collected in groups, walked, talked, and wondered what next.

The glorious Fourth was bright as the hopes of our chieftain and his braves, whose patient labor and siege was crowned with brilliant success. Like a bow strained to its utmost tension, and then unbent, the comprehensive mind of General Grant, and all hearts, were relieved from a long and wearing interest and anxiety.

But mark the crowning quality, as a commander, of General Grant—perseverance. Amid the very joy of the victory, and the excitement of preparation to enter Vicksburg, he formed and mentioned his plan to pursue and crush, if possible, General Joe Johnston. He was resolved to follow up the conquest, and hasten after the enemy outside the walls over which the national ensign would be waving in a few moments.

Before noon, white flags fluttered in the breeze along the battlements of the fort. Then, regiment after regiment of the rebels marched out, stacking their arms—a privilege General Grant magnanimously granted them, and without the usual attendance of a superintending officer. The truly great never meanly triumph over a prostrate foe. March! march! rattle! rattle! goes the musketry into glittering pyramids for three long hours.

At one o'clock the Union army, with the unruffled, plain, modest Grant at the head of it, began to move into Vicksburg. The brilliant staffs, the bands playing, the banners flying, and the columns of happy troops, made a spectacle rarely seen in the world. They poured into the city in steel-crested, glittering tides, till the old camps were all deserted. Then, from the Court House, how grandly the old flag floated on the sunny air!

Where is Admiral Foote? Look up the broad river, and you will know. He has been watching for the signal, and now he catches a glimpse of the Stars and Stripes, and down the flagship steams, followed by the procession of gunboats, cutting the foam, with pennants flying, and music rising over their wake; and soon all nestle under the *friendly* walls.

The rebel loss in the entire campaign of Vicksburg, in killed, wounded, stragglers, and in hospitals, was estimated at over forty-six thousand; and in arms, large and small, forty-five thousand pieces. The Union loss was only about eight thousand.

The loss of Vicksburg was a stunning blow, in the effect every way upon the enemy; and to us a glorious encouragement. It opened the Mississippi, and cut the rebel territory in two, fatally. The great West was hopelessly gone from the grasp of the foe.

Telegrams never flew faster on lightning wing, than those which carried the tidings of the fall of Vicksburg. The cities and prairies of the West sent up the shout of enthusiastic joy. The loyal East echoed back the gladness. When the despatch reached the honest President, he acknowledged General Grant's genius and splendid strategy, in the following message:

EXECUTIVE MANSION, WASHINGTON, July 13, 1863.

To Major-General GRANT: '

MY DEAR GENERAL: I do not remember that you and I ever met personally. I write this now as a grateful acknowledgment for the almost inestimable service you have done the country. I wish to say a word further. When you first reached the vicinity of Vicksburg, I thought you should do what you finally did—march the troops across the neck, run the batteries with the transports, and thus go below; and I never had any faith, except a general hope that you knew better than I, that the Yazoo Pass expedition, and the like, could succeed. When you got below and took Port Gibson, Grand Gulf, and vicinity, I thought you should go down the river and join General Banks; and when you turned northward east of the Big Black, I feared it was a mistake. I now wish to make a personal acknowledgment that you were right and I was wrong.

Yours, very truly, A. LINCOLN.

Abraham Lincoln was not ashamed to acknowledge that General Grant was "too smart for him." However good the intentions at Washington, we shall never know what *meddling* there with army command has cost the country. The President's letter shows what it *might* have done for General Grant.

Mr. Lincoln is a thorough *temperance* man. But when, after Vicksburg fell, some of the complaining gentlemen called on him, between them and himself an amusing conversation occurred:

"So I understand Grant drinks whiskey to excess?' interrogatively remarked the President.

"Yes," was the reply.

"What whiskey does he drink?" inquired Mr. Lincoln.

"What whiskey?" doubtfully queried his hearers.

"Yes. Is it Bourbon, or Monongahela?"

"Why do you ask, Mr. President?"

"Because, if it makes him win victories like this at Vicksburg, I will send a demijohn of the same kind to every general in the army."

The visitors had no more to say about General Grant's dissipation. It has been stated that he entered Vicksburg with his cherished cigar in his mouth. A writer of doubtful loyalty well said :

"We pardon General Grant's smoking a cigar as he entered the smouldering ruins of the town of Vicksburg. A little stage effect is admissible in great captains, considering that Napoleon at Milan wore the little cocked hat and sword of Marengo, and that snuff was the inevitable concomitant of victory in the great Frederick. General Grant is a noble fellow, and, by the terms of capitulation he accorded to the heroic garrison, showed himself as generous as Napoleon was to Wurmser at the surrender of Mantua. His deed will read well in history, and he has secured to himself a name which posterity will pronounce with veneration and gratitude. There is no general in this country, or in Europe, that has done harder work than General Grant, and none that has better graced his victories by the exercise of humanity and virtue. What we learn of the terms of capitulation, is sufficient to prove General Grant to be a generous soldier and a man. A truly brave man respects bravery in others, and, when the sword is sheathed, considers himself free to follow the dictates of humanity. General Grant is not a general that marks his progress by proclamations to frighten unarmed men, women, and children; he fulminates no arbitrary edicts against the press; he does not make war on newspapers and their correspondents; he flatters no one to get himself puffed; but he is terrible in arms, and magnanimous after the battle. Go on, brave General Grant; pursue the course you have marked out for yourself; and Clio, the pensive muse, as she records your deeds, will rejoice at her manly theme."

An Iowa surgeon found a curious bill of fare in the rebel camp, a part of which is given, to show how near famine the troops were:

HOTEL DE VICKSBURG.

BILL OF FARE FOR JULY, 1863.

SOUP.

Mule tail.

BOILED.

Mule bacon with poke greens.
Mule ham canvassed.

ROAST.

Mule sirloin, &c.

Passing over similar dishes, we come to

DESSERT.

White-oak acorns. Blackberry leaf tea.
Beech nuts. Genuine Confederate coffee.

In a "Card," it is added:

Parties arriving by the river, or Grant's inland route, will find Grape, Canister & Co.'s carriages at the landing, or any depot on the line of intrenchments.

One who was there, wrote:

"Pemberton was, of course, the chief attraction. He is in appearance a tall, lithe-built and stately personage. Black hair, black eyes, full beard, and rather severe if not sinister expression of countenance, as of one who had great trials of the soul to endure."

This general was a Philadelphian, but married a Southern lady, and so became a *secessionist*. The same observer adds:

"The greatest curiosities are the caves hewn into the banks of earth, in which the women and children, and non-combatants, crept during the heat of the bombardment. At night, and sometimes during an entire day, the whole of these people would be confined to their caverns. They are constructed about the height of a man, and three feet wide, a fork V shaped into the bank. There are, perhaps, five hundred of these caves in the city around the works. As many as fifteen have been crowded into one of them."

A highly cultivated and Christian lady, who lived in one of these caves, with no words of bitterness, has given a very interesting account of her captivity. They were dug, at first, with their mouths, or doors, opening toward the rear of the city, and away from the gunboats. And when General Grant so arranged his batteries that the shells came from that side, often they exploded right in the caves. One day, near her, a shell went crushing through the roof of a neighbor's cell, and tore in fragments her sleeping babe. What an awful life of suspense! Even the moonlight evening, bathing rampart, deserted mansion, and cave, with soothing radiance, was no protection. She saw a scene, after Burbridge's charge, which she thought looked, after all, as if the millennium might be near. A wounded Confederate was lying nearer to our troops than his own. He looked and begged for water. The air was full of death's missiles. But a noble Union soldier stepped forward, and, taking his canteen, went to the sufferer, and, while he fanned him, gave him the cooling draught.

Beautiful and touching spectacle! A little of Heaven's pure light athwart the sulphurous gloom of war!

Here, my young reader, is a true picture of *the dead* of Vicksburg:

"They lay in all positions; some with musket grasped, as though still contending; others with cartridge in the fingers, just ready to put the deadly charge where it might meet the foe. All ferocity had gone. A remarkably sweet and youthful face was that of a rebel boy. Scarce eighteen, and as fair as a maiden, with quite small hands, long hair of the pale golden hue that auburn changes to, if much in the sun, and curling at the ends. He had a shirt of coarse white cotton, and brown pants well worn; while upon his feet were a woman's shoes about the size known as 'fours.' His left side was torn by a shell, and his left shoulder shattered. Two men, who had caught at a fig tree to assist them up a steep embankment, lay dead at his feet, slain, in all probability, by an enfilade from their right; the branch at which they caught was still in their grasp. Several were headless, others were armless; but the manner of their death was always plain. The Minie left its large, rather clear hole; the shell its horrid rent; the shrapnel and grape their clear, great gashes, as though one had thrust a giant's spear through the tender quivering flesh. In one trench lay two, grasping the same weapon—friend and foe. Across their hands fell a vine, the end upon the breast of a rebel, where it had fallen with them from an elevation above, the roots still damp with the fresh earth; upon it was a beautiful passion flower in full bloom, and two buds; the buds were stained with blood—the flower as bright as was the day when the morning stars sang together. On the faces of both was the calm that follows sleep—rather pale, perhaps, but seeming like him of old, of whom it is said, 'He is not dead, but sleepeth.' But ah, the crimson! All is not well when the earth is stained with blood. In some places the dead were piled, literally, like sacks of grain upon the shore.

"It is remarkable with what patience the fatally wounded—they who already stood upon the shore—bore their sufferings. Some knew that they could not recover, but bore it manfully. Sometimes a tear, and a low voice would say, 'My sweet wife!' or 'Darling!' 'Mother!' or 'God forgive!'—a quiver—then, all was over."

Notwithstanding such havoc, and the mourning homes, the poet, Alfred B. Street, with many other bards, expressed the national rejoicing, and the grateful admiration of Grant·

    Vicksburg is ours!
    Hurrah!
    Treachery cowers!
    Hurrah!
    Down reels the rebel rag!
    Up shoots the starry flag!
    *   *   *   *   *

    Vicksburg is ours!
    Hurrah!
    Arch the green bowers!
    Hurrah!
    Arch o'er the hero, who
    Nearer and nearer drew,
    Letting wise patience sway,
    Till, from his brave delay,

Swift as the lightning's ray,
Bounded he to the fray,
Full on his fated prey;
 Thundering upon his path,
Swerving not, pausing not,
Darting steel, raining shot,
In his fierce onset, hot
 With his red battle wrath;
Flashing on, thundering on;
Pausing then once again,
Curbing with mighty rein,
All his great heart, as vain
Writhed the fierce foe, the chain
Tighter and tighter round,
Till the reward was found—
Till the dread work was done—
Till the grand wreath was won.
 Triumph is ours!
 Hurrah!

CHAPTER XVII.

The Eastern Army—Port Hudson falls—The "Father of Waters" open—Joe Johnston pursued—Jeff. Davis's Library found—Jackson surrenders—General Grant's care of his Soldiers—His Politics—Anecdotes—Looks after his Department—Mrs. Grant visits him—General Grant goes to Memphis—A splendid Reception.

MEANWHILE, the battle was raging in the East. There, too, the army was covered with glory. Almost the very hour that Vicksburg falls, General Meade, at the head of his battalions, beats back the most threatening tide of secession, under Lee, which had ever overswept the border of the Free States. The terrific and glorious field of Gettysburg, Pa., is won, the national honor saved, and the invader sent, stunned and bleeding, back within his lines. Memorable Fourth of July indeed to the war-scarred land! The country was wild with joy amid showers of tears for the slain. But let us look down the Mississippi again.

The morning sun of July 7th floods the "Father of Waters." Hark! how the naval lions roar on the bright waters! Peal after peal reverberates along the green shores.

The rebel garrison of Port Hudson, whose guns are silent, wonder at the sound, the interludes of which were cheers of wildest rejoicing. They listen all day, and, as the evening approaches, their curiosity could endure the strange demonstration no longer. At one of the points, where the armies were within speaking distance, a rebel officer called out:

"What are you making all that noise about?"

Union officer. "We have taken Vicksburg."

Rebel. "Don't believe it."

Union officer. "What will convince you?"

Rebel. "Nothing but the copy of the despatch, or some reliable authority."

Union officer. "Well, I'll get a copy, and pass it over the parapet."

Rebel. "If you'll do that, and vouch for its genuineness on your honor as a gentleman and a soldier, I'll believe it."

The Union man soon furnished the evidence required, copied in his own hand.

The rebel took it, and read it, saying:

"I am satisfied. It is useless for us to hold out longer."

Meanwhile, General Grant had managed to have a message to General Banks intercepted by the enemy, conveying the same intelligence. General Frank Gardiner sent to the latter to know if it were true that Vicksburg had surrendered. When assured it was, he, too, pulled down the rebel flag, and ours was run up instead. This cleared the Mississippi, from its head waters to the Gulf of Mexico.

But what, meanwhile, has Johnston been doing, whom we left hovering in the distance around Vicksburg, impatient to help the beleaguered army? Foiled in his designs by the sleepless vigilance of General Grant, he had chafed like a caged lion in the toils, quite as thoroughly besieged in the open field as his fellow traitors within the city. And now General Sherman, by General Grant's order, moved toward him, animated by the recent victories. The desperate and startled general expressed his alarm in the following proclamation:

FELLOW SOLDIERS: An insolent foe, flushed with hope by his recent success at Vicksburg, confronts you, threatening the people, whose homes and liberty you are here to protect, with plunder and conquest. Their guns may even now be heard as they advance.

The enemy it is at once the duty and the mission of you, brave men, to chastise and expel from the soil of Mississippi. The commanding general confidently relies on you to sustain his pledge, which he makes in advance, and he will be with you in the good work, even unto the end.

The rebel general reoccupied Jackson, the capital of Mississippi, and waited for Sherman's advance. On, freedom's volunteers swept, till they reached Pearl River, running through the city; and, extending the lines in a broad curve, they nearly encircled the city with walls of armed men.

July 11th, troops detailed to forage in the country near—*i. e.*, seek supplies on the enemy's soil—accidentally found in an old building, carefully packed away, a large library, and various mementos of friendship. A glance revealed the owner. A gold-headed cane bore the inscription, "To Jefferson Davis from Franklin Pierce." Precious plunder! The arch traitor has hidden in the quiet country, and in a place which could awaken no suspicion, his valuable library, correspondence, and articles of cherished regard. The excited troopers soon get into the book pile, and volumes, heaps of letters, and handsome canes, are borne as trophies (a new kind of *forage*) to headquarters. Secession is discussed in many letters, by Northern friends of the treasonable leader, and his right to that proud distinction freely granted.

Added to this capture, the railways on every side of the city were destroyed, and hundreds of cars taken from the Confederacy.

The twilight hour of July 16th brought to a projection of the works rebel bands of music, insulting our troops with "Bonnie Blue Flag," "My Maryland," "Dixie's Land," and other airs perverted to the service of treason. The next morning's dawn gave signs of a retreating foe. The "fighting Joe Johnston" had stolen away, leaving all over Jackson the marks of ruin. The day before—July 15th—the President issued a proclamation for national thanksgiving on the 6th day of August, for the recent victories.

A little affair, about this time, illustrated the honesty and humanity of General Grant. The steamboat companies, like other vultures preying upon every department of the great army, charged the soldiers from fifteen to thirty dollars fare from Cairo to Vicksburg, when from one third to a quarter of the sum would have been a large demand. One day, the steamer "Hope" touched at Vicksburg. The decks were covered with the brave volunteers, homeward bound from the late hard service, on a brief furlough. There were twelve hundred bronzed heroes, of whom nearly a quarter were officers. General Grant was informed that the captain had charged them from ten to twenty-five dollars each. Calling an officer, he said:

"Take a guard, and order that captain to refund to enlisted men the excess of five dollars, and of seven dollars to the officers; or he'll be arrested, and his boat confiscated."

The captain listened, and looked with amazement. The armed guard convinced him it was useless to resist. He put on an air of injured innocence in the extortion, and out with his pocketbook. The money was counted and paid over, amid the shouts of the troops huzzaing for Grant, the soldier's friend.

He remarked to those about him:

"I will teach them, if they need the lesson, that the men who have perilled their lives to open the Mississippi River for their benefit, cannot be imposed upon with impunity."

This considerate, magnanimous regard to the interests of the abused soldiers, is one of the most pleasing, attractive features of General Grant's character. It wins confidence from the humblest volunteer in his command.

The General is no politician, if that word means more than a loyal citizen. Like all conspicuous men, especially in the civil war of our country, in which politics—by which you will understand party success and office-seeking—have been a deadly poison, corrupting and threatening the very life of the nation, he was not unfrequently approached on the subject by the "wire-pullers." A good story or two went abroad from his headquarters at Vicksburg. Professed political friends paid him a visit, and, after a short time spent in compliments, they touched upon the never-ending subject of politics. One of the party was in the midst of a very flowery speech, using all his rhetorical powers to induce the General, if possible, to view matters in the same light as himself, when he was suddenly stopped by General Grant:

"There is no use of talking politics to me. I know nothing about them; and, furthermore, I do not know of any person among my acquaintances who does. But, continued he, "there is one subject with which I am perfectly acquainted; talk of that, and I am your man."

"What is that, General?" asked the politicians, in great surprise.

"Tanning leather," was the reply.

The subject was immediately changed.

On another occasion, an infamous proposal was made by a person to General Grant, while he was staying at his headquarters "in the field." The General, irritated, administered a severe kick to the proposer with the toe of his great cavalry boot; and, after the fellow had been driven from the tent, one of his staff remarked to a companion, that he did not think the General had hurt the rascal.

"Never fear," was the reply; "that boot never fails under such circumstances, for the leather came from Grant's store, in Galena."

General Grant was not ashamed of his *origin*. Many, who have been successful in making money, or getting official position, meanly try to hide the humble beginning of life; even treating with scorn relatives who remain in the obscurity they have left. This is never seen in the truly great, or justly honored. My youthful reader, believe and remember this.

The great centres of rebel army operations in Grant's department had been taken. He was determined to clear it entirely of the enemy. The gallant Admiral Porter entered into the plan with all his heart. An expedition was started to Yazoo City, where the enemy was posted; another to Natchez, where supplies were crossing to the Eastern army. Thousands of heads of cattle were captured, and many prisoners. Like brothers, the land and the naval hero sympathized and fought together for the Republic, and accomplished all they proposed to do.

15

They speak warmly of each other in their reports. Smaller minds would have jarred with jealousy, perhaps defeating important enterprises by discordant counsels.

We have an incident which affords another view of the character of the hero of Vicksburg. He invited a captive major-general, who once was in the same regiment with him, to his tent. There a free conversation was had upon the brighter past, and the tragical present. When General Grant expressed his regret to find him in the Confederate service, his prisoner replied:

"Grant, I tell you I ain't much of a rebel, after all; and when I am paroled, I will let the infernal service go to the mischief."

While General Grant's headquarters were at Vicksburg, several interesting scenes enlivened the interlude of exhausting toil. The President nominated him to the office of Major-General, and the commission was issued, bearing date of July 4th, 1863. The officers who had served under him, with appropriate ceremonies presented him a splendid sword. The blade was of finest steel, the scabbard of solid silver, elegantly finished, the handle richly carved with the figure of a young giant crushing the hydra, rebellion; and the box, on whose lid, inside, was wrought his name with crimson silk, was made of rosewood, bound with ivory, and lined with velvet.

An expensive present, you will say. Yes, it cost several hundred dollars; but was worthily bestowed, and modestly accepted.

But now we turn to a domestic view of the warrior's life. His excellent wife, who had patiently waited in the distance for a victorious pause in his stormy career, embraced the moments of comparative rest, and left her home for his camp. With a devoted wife's just pride, she desired not only to see him, but the stronghold which had immortalized his name.

Reaching St. Louis, it soon became known that she was there. A fine band gathered to the hotel, and serenaded the lady, who sought the public applause no more than her husband. When the music died away, three cheers rang out for General Grant, followed by as many more for her. Leaning on the arm of Brigadier-General Strong, he responded to repeated calls for a speech, as follows:

"GENTLEMEN: I am requested by Mrs. Grant to express her acknowledgments for the honor you have done her on this occasion. I know well that, in tendering her thanks, I express your sentiments, when I say the compliment through her to her noble husband is one merited by a brave and great man, who has made his name forever honored and immortal, in the history of America's illustrious patriots, living or dead. Mrs. Grant does not desire, in the testimony you have offered, that you should forget the brave and gallant officers and soldiers who have so largely assisted in bringing about the glorious result which has recently caused the big heart of our nation to leap with joy. She asks you also to stop and drop a pensive tear over the graves of the noble dead, who have fallen in the struggle, that you and I, and all of us, might enjoy the fruits of their patriotic devotion to a country second to none on the earth. We trust that the Mississippi forever will be under the control of our glorious country. Mrs. Grant is now on the way to join her husband, who, since the commencement of the war, has not asked for one day's absence. He has not found time to be sick. With these remarks she bids you good night, and begs that you accept her thousand thanks."

We cannot enter the seclusion of the home in the conquered city, and hear all the words of devotion and congratulation there, which came in like æolian harmony during the pauses of a tempest, to the experience of the great commander.

Nothing in his department escaped General Grant's careful attention. The speculating traders with the rebels, guerillas and marauders, and especially the emancipated slaves, were objects of decided action. Warmly sustaining the proclamation of liberty, he demanded the acknowledgment of the rights of the negroes under it, and their honorable employment.

Noble man! Never evading a measure of the Executive, nor chasing back a fugitive to his master, he stood forth the protector of the poor and dependent.

He personally inspected the whole field of command, and aimed at *thoroughness* in all his official conduct—a trait of character any one who desires the just respect and confidence of mankind, and substantial success, must possess. The pleasure boat goes with wind and tide; the steamer, with its steadily working engine beam, moves, if necessary, against both, to the "desired haven."

But, occasionally, the enthusiastic people compelled him to have a *part* of a holiday, at least.

Leaving General McPherson in command of Vicksburg, he went to Memphis, Tenn., in his survey of the districts under his control. The citizens met him with spontaneous homage. A committee waited upon him, and obtained his consent to the public honors of a festival on a grand scale. In his letter of acceptance, he said:

> I thank you, too, in the name of the noble army which I have the honor to command. It is composed of men whose loyalty is proved by their deeds of heroism and their willing sacrifices of life and health. They will rejoice with me that the miserable adherents of the rebellion, whom their bayonets have driven from this fair land, are being replaced by men who acknowledge human liberty as the only true foundation of human government. May your efforts to restore your city to the cause of the Union be as successful as have been theirs to reclaim it from the despotic rule of the leaders of the rebellion. I have the honor to be, gentlemen, your very obedient servant,
>
> U. S. GRANT.

At nine o'clock in the evening of August 26th, amid thronging guests, with a national air filling the spacious halls, General Grant entered the reception room. What a rush of men and women with extended hands! An hour of such enthusiastic greeting passed, when, leading the long lines of grateful admirers, the hero marched through the banqueting hall, and, after a glance at the rich and varied abundance in tasteful and elegant order, he took his seat. The repast was followed by the toasts:

"The United States of America—They have one Constitution and Government. May they have one grand destiny while human institutions endure." Responded to by Hon. Chas. Kortrecht.

"The Army and Navy—Their deeds and heroism in this war will be the noble theme of poet and historian in all future time." Responded to by Adjutant-General Lorenzo Thomas.

"General Grant—The guest of the city."

This was the signal for the wildest applause, and it was some minutes before order could be restored. It was expected that General Grant would be brought to his feet by this; but the company were disappointed, upon perceiving that, instead, his place was taken by his staff surgeon, Dr. Hewitt, who remarked:

"I am instructed by General Grant to say, that, as he has never been given to public speaking, you will have to excuse him on this occasion; and, as I am the only member of his staff present, I therefore feel it my duty to thank you for this manifestation of your good will, as also the numerous other kindnesses of which he has been the recipient ever since his arrival among you. General Grant believes that, in all he has done, he has no more than accomplished a duty, and one, too, for which no particular honor is due. But the world, as you do, will accord otherwise."

The Doctor then proposed, at General Grant's request:

"The officers of the different staffs, and the non-commissioned officers and privates of the Army of the Tennessee."

"The Federal Union—It must and will be preserved." Responded to by Major-General S. A. Hurlbut.

"The Old Flag—May its extinguished stars, rekindled by the sacred flame of human liberty, continue to shine forever undiminished in number, and undimmed in splendor." Brigadier-General Veatch.

"The President of the United States—He must be sustained." Colonel J. W. Fuller.

"The Star-spangled Banner" was here sung, the whole party joining in the chorus.

"The Loyal Men of Tennessee—Their devotion to the Union, the cause of republican government and constitutional liberty, is like gold tried seven times by fire." Mr. J. M. Tomeny.

The remainder of the toasts were of a local character, with the exception of the closing one, which was as follows:

"General Grant—Your Grant and my Grant. Having granted us victories, grant us the restoration of the 'Old Flag;' grant us supplies, so that we may grant to our friends the grant to us."

The festivities were kept up until near three o'clock in the morning, when General Grant withdrew from the room.

A poem was also read by Dr. Morris, of which are given the lines referring to General Grant's work on the Mississippi:

> The Mississippi closed—that mighty stream
> Found by De Soto, and by Fulton won!
> One thought to chain him! Ignominious thought!
> But then the grand old monarch shook his locks,
> And burst his fetters like a Samson freed!
> The heights were crowned with ramparts sheltering those
> Whose treason knew no bounds; the frowning forts
> Belched lightnings, and the morning gun
> A thousand miles told mournfully the tale,
> The Mississippi closed.
>
> Not long. From the Lord God of Hosts was sent
> A leader, who with patient vigil planned
> A great deliverance. Height by height was gained,
> Island and hill and woody bank and cliff.
> Month followed month, till, on our natal day,
> The last great barrier fell; and never more
> The sire of waters shall obstruction know!
> Now, with De Soto's name, and Fulton's, see
> The greater name of Grant!
>
> Our children's children, noble Grant, shall sing
> That great deliverance! On the floods of spring
> Thy name shall sparkle; smiling commerce tell
> Thy great achievement, which restores the chain,
> Never again to break, which makes us one.

CHAPTER XVIII.

General Grant at New Orleans—His simplicity in Dress—Reviews the Thirteenth Army Corps—Sad Accident—Recovers from the serious Injuries—He cares for the Soldier in little things—A new and larger Command—Chickamauga and Chattanooga—An amusing Incident—The feelings of the Rebels—General Grant at Chattanooga—Clearing the Track—Jeff. Davis on Lookout.

THE first day of autumn, 1863, General Grant was sailing toward New Orleans—was near the Crescent City, so recently cut off from his distant Vicksburg.

September 3d, the announcement was made that the Father of Waters was opened for trade, limited only by the determination to prevent any traffic that would help the rebels.

The next morning lights up a splendid pageant. From St. Charles Hotel, mark that cavalcade of officers mounted amid the gathering thousands anxious to look on the central object of universal interest. Away the horsemen dash! But which is the hero of the day? Turn your eye from dazzling uniforms, to that man of ordinary aspect, "in undress uniform, without sword, sash, or belt, coat unbuttoned, a low-crowned black felt hat, without any mark upon it of military rank," and you see Major-General Grant. Through streets lined with spectators, they gallop into the country toward Carrollton, to review the Thirteenth Army Corps. While passing back and forth on the field of splendid military display, his strange steed makes a sudden dash, and throws the illustrious rider. Consternation passes over the multitudes. It was no trivial accident. Bruised, and with broken bones, he is borne on a litter to the steamer "Franklin," and carried to New Orleans. A whole month he was in the surgeon's care. It was well that he escaped with no more serious results of the fall, and an occasion for gratitude to the God of our fathers, who spared him to the endangered land they gave us.

While only partially recovered, with the aid of a crutch and cane, he embarked on his voyage up the Mississippi. He, like Washington, was careful in *little things*. Who but himself would have thought it worth the while to regulate the fare from Cairo to New Orleans, to save the soldiers from unjust charges? Not only so, but he ordered that "enlisted men be entitled to travel as cabin passengers, when they desire it, at the same rates." The "boys" were not to be thrust into the hold, or on deck, but must be treated like men. He required the "officers in the inspector-general's department to report any neglect" to pay the soldiers promptly. He went further still. Besides a just and kind jurisdiction established in and around

Vicksburg, he had General McPherson issue a general order, beginning thus:

"In order to encourage and reward the meritorious and faithful officers and men of this corps, a 'Medal of Honor,' with appropriate device, has been prepared, and will be presented by a 'Board of Honor,' of which the Major-General commanding is the advisory member, to all those who, by their gallantry in action and other soldier-like qualities, have most distinguished themselves, or who may hereafter most distinguish themselves during the war."

It was an appropriate expression of his regard for distinguished bravery.

"The design of the medals was a blending of the crescent, a star, and a shield; the base being formed of the crescent, to the two extremities of which was fixed the star, while pendent from its lower point was suspended a shield. Upon the crescent the words, 'Vicksburg, July 4, 1863.' The object in the presentation of these badges was to reward the meritorious members of the Seventeenth Corps for conspicuous valor on the field of battle or endurance in the march. This famous corps, since its organization, had been foremost in duty and deeds of glory throughout the entire campaign against Vicksburg, and no better method could have been adopted to continue in the future the same excellent spirit of emulation for which it has always been celebrated, both on the part of officers and men."

A new and wider command, with gigantic work, now opens before General Grant. Look away from Vicksburg, a long distance northeast, into Southeastern Tennessee, and you will notice, on the Western and Atlantic Railroad, eighteen miles apart, Chickamauga and Chattanooga. The Tennessee River flows near, and railways run among the wild summits which guard glorious valleys, and make some of the finest scenery in the world. Every young person should know something of this interesting country. We find, on a stray sheet, a good description of it:

"Chickamauga comprehends a considerable district extending up and down a creek of that name, which empties into the Tennessee River, near Chattanooga, running a northwest course. Seven miles in a direct line up this creek, or fifteen following its course, was located Brainard, the first missionary station established by the American Board among the Cherokee Indians, in 1817. In this region, this tribe held a territory of twelve thousand square miles, or eight million acres, guaranteed to them by the United States, two thirds of which lay in Georgia. Brainard was situated on the west side of this creek. On the same side is situated the ridge of land now called Missionary Ridge, doubtless from the circumstance that the missionary station was in that neighborhood. This station comprised a farm of forty-five acres, which was cultivated by the mission in order to introduce among the Indians habits of industry and of a civilized life·

Lookout Mountain is seven miles due west from Brainard. From its summit a magnificent landscape is open to view, extending over the surrounding country, and even to the Blue Ridge.

"This was the Cherokee's favorite hunting ground. Over it the State of Georgia extended her laws, and imprisoned the missionaries who refused to take the oath of allegiance to them. The United States also took the eight million acres of land, paying them only five hundred thousand dollars, and removing them beyond the Mississippi. The injustice and suffering attending their removal is little known to the present generation. The missionaries were dragged from their fields of labor by the armed soldiers of the State of Georgia, treated with great indignity, and immured in the penitentiary for a year and four months. In the meantime, the lands of the Cherokees were surveyed and divided into farms of one hundred and forty acres each, and distributed by lottery among the inhabitants of the State. Counties were organized, magistrates appointed, and courts held, and the number of whites who crowded into the territory exceeded that of the Indians. There were men who took every means to draw the Indians into intemperance and debauchery. When the time for removal, by a treaty negotiated by a portion of the chiefs, came, families were taken from their houses and farms, leaving their furniture and flocks, and marched under strong guards to camps selected as starting places; and such were the hardships of the journey to their new homes, that one fourth of the nation died on the way.

"Is it strange that God should visit the iniquities of the fathers upon the children of this very region, where so much injustice and wrong had been inflicted upon a people who had ever been the firm friends of the white man, and who were laying aside the pursuits of the chase, and were fast becoming a civilized and Christian people?"

While General Grant was a suffering invalid, September 19th, General Rosecrans, at the head of the Army of the Cumberland, met General Bragg at Chickamauga, and, after a desperate conflict, was glad to retreat to Chattanooga, unpursued by his successful enemy. General Sherman, from General Grant's department, commenced moving over the Memphis and Charleston Railroad, October 11th, toward that position, to help General Rosecrans. He had a hard fight with hostile troops, but reached Chattanooga.

On the 17th, General Grant met General Halleck, from Washington, according to a telegram from him, at Indianapolis. After the usual salutations, General Halleck handed him a general order, putting him in command of the "Departments of the Ohio, of the Cumberland, and of the Tennessee, constituting the Military Division of the Mississippi."

General Grant now held the most extensive military rule on all the field of civil war. The great belt between the eastern boundaries of Alabama and Tennessee and those of Illinois and Indiana, down to the Department of the Gulf, was under his control. It was a magnificent command, and another stride in his rapid advancement. Around him, as subordinate officers, were to stand Generals Sherman, Thomas—who succeeded Rosecrans—Burnside, and Hooker. General Halleck accompanied General Grant to Louisville.

An amusing scene now transpires. The Galt House is the principal hotel, and there the crowd are gathered. Tall and swarthy Kentuckians, old soldiers of the Union, women and children,stand in every place which affords a glimpse of the hero. Among the gazing countrymen, a stalwart son of Kentucky stares a moment at him, and then exclaims:

"Well, that's Grant! I thought he was a large man. He would be considered a small chance of a fighter if he lived in Kentucky."

The mighty host of General Bragg, under Generals Longstreet and Hill, with Joe Johnston's thirty thousand troops ready to coöperate, thought the Union army was securely locked up at Chattanooga. A newspaper, referring to General Rosecrans's removal, and, in his place, the appointment of Generals Grant and Thomas, stated, the Government had supplanted a hero with *two fools*. The President remarked: "If one fool like Grant can do so much work, and win as profitable victories as he, he had no objection to two of them, as they would be likely to wipe out the rebellion." Hear the loud words of the *Atlanta Rebel:*

"The Yankee Army of the Cumberland holds the door to lower East Tennessee, and this door we must leave open. * * * If we continue to gaze listlessly from the bold knobs of Missionary Ridge upon the comfortable barracks of the Federals below, then may we tremble for the next campaign; for, as sure as there is any surety in the future, the spring of 1864 must see us far from the borders of Georgia, or near to the verge of destruction. Nail it to your doorposts, men of the South, and refuse to be deluded into any other belief! Food and raiment are our needs. We must have them. Kentucky and Middle Tennessee can only supply them. Better give up the seacoast, better give up the Southwest, ay, better to give up Richmond without a struggle, and win these, than lose the golden field, whose grain and wool are our sole hope. The enemy has just one army too many in the field for us. We must crush this overplus; we must gain one signal Stonewall Jackson campaign. Destiny points to the very place. And how? Nothing easier. The bee which has really stung our flank so long, once disposed of, our triumphant legions have a clear road before them. Fed sumptuously through the winter, well shod and clad, they have only to meet a dispirited foe, retake the valley of the Mississippi, secure the election of a Peace Democrat to the Presidency in the fall, and arrange the terms of treaty and independence. These results can be accomplished nowhere else than in this department. The Northwest is our real adversary."

October 23d, General Grant reached Chattanooga. Wrote a Union soldier of the sad condition of things there :

"I confess I do not see any very brilliant prospects for continuing alive in it all this winter, unless something desperate be done. While the army sits here, hungry, chilly, watching the 'key to Tennessee,' the 'good dog' Bragg lies over against us, licking his Chickamauga sores without whine or growl. He will not reply to our occasional shots from Star Fort, Fort Crittenden, or the Moccasin Point batteries across the river; has forbidden the exchange of newspapers and the compliments of the day between pickets; has returned surly answers to flag-of-truce messages; in fact, has cut us dead.

"The mortality among the horses and mules is frightful to contemplate. Their corpses line the road, and taint the air, all along the Bridgeport route. In these days, hereabouts, it is within the scope of the most obtuse to distinguish a quartermaster or staff officer, by a casual glance at the animal he strides. 'He has the fatness of twenty horses upon his ribs,' as Squeers remarked of little Wackford; 'and so he has. 'God help the others.'

"I am assured this state of things will not last long; that hordes of men are energetically at work improving our means of communication, and that we soon shall be benefited by the overflowing plenty of the North. The vigor and good spirits of the army, all this time, are developed in a most astonishing manner.

16

"Major-General Grant, who presides over the destinies of this, among other armies, reached Chattanooga to-day."

That state of things *did not last long.* The great trouble was, to get supplies. The valley route of travel lay under the guns of Lookout Mountain. So the poor horses and mules had to drag the heavy wagons among the mountains, through mud and over Alpine ridges, by slow and exhausting stages.

General Grant, soon after his arrival, was riding with Quartermaster-General Meigs along the highways, bordered with carcasses and skeletons, when they passed the decaying body of a gigantic mule. "Ah, General," said Grant, with affected sadness, "there lies a dead soldier of the Quartermaster's Department." "Yes, General," responded Meigs, with equal gravity; "in him you see 'the ruling passion strong in death' exemplified; for the old veteran has already assumed the *offensive.*"

Thus, like moonlight across black storm-clouds, breaks the humor and wit of great minds upon the grim aspect of war.

Generals Hooker and Smith were sent to cut a way through Lookout Valley to meet an expedition which started at midnight, October 26th, near Bridgeport, Ala. in fifty-six boats. Only a few officers knew the destination. What a sail was that! The moon, over whose face drift occasional clouds, shines down on the Tennessee. The boats move a few miles, and reach the enemy's lines. Then comes old Lookout, its rough sides ablaze with hostile signal torches, and crowned with batteries. To get past and join the other forces, and clear a path for supplies, is the perilous voyage before them. Oars are dropped, and the fourteen hundred men, holding breath in suspense, keep their pontoons close to the banks. Slowly the spectres float under the mountain s deep shadow. No sound but a rebel picket's snatch of song from the summit ready to pour down lightning and iron hail, is heard in the awful solitude. The moments seem hours. And now the silent flotilla emerges into moonbeams, and the brave fellows draw a long breath of relief. The passage is made. Landing, under the gallant Hazen and Geary, they fight their way along, and, making a junction with Hooker and Smith, at the base of Lookout, the Bridgeport route is cleared of rebel rule. The famine is soon relieved, and affairs at Chattanooga wear a brighter aspect.

About this time, Jeff. Davis, it is said, visited the fortress on the lofty summit, which seemed to defy attack. His vulture eye swept the circle of the magnificent view, covering a part of four States. And we may believe, with something like the exultation of Satan when he showed the Messiah the kingdoms of the earth, he remarked to General Pemberton, when his gaze came back to General Grant's army, in the distance, working on the fortifications:

"I have them now in just the trap I set for them."

Pemberton turned to Jeff. Davis, and replied:

"Mr. Davis, you are Commander-in-Chief, and you are here. You think the enemy are in a trap, and can be captured by vigorous assault. I have been blamed for not having ordered a general attack on the enemy when they were drawing around me their lines of circumvallation at Vicksburg. Do you now order an attack upon those troops down there below us, and I will set you my life that not one man of the attacking column will ever come back across that valley, except as a prisoner."

CHAPTER XIX.

Preparations for Battle again—The successful Trap—The brave Advance of General Wood—The Contest opened—The Three Days' Fight—General Hooker above the Clouds—General Grant's Despatch—General Bragg's—General Meigs's Despatch—General Grant at the Coffin of Colonel O'Meara.

HE Chief began in quiet earnest to prepare for an attack on Chattanooga. Drill and parade were frequent in front of our fortifications, and within full view of the enemy. General Grant, not yet perfectly well, was daily seen walking "to and fro up the streets of the town, unattended, many times unobserved, but at all times observing." To stop raids and personal violence, he issued an order to hold secessionists responsible for injury done, imprisoning hostages when our people were injured, and taking property in return for losses in our lines.

In vain General Longstreet tried to swing around the rear of the Union army east of Chattanooga, and move on Knoxville, Tenn., before the noble Burnside was at hand, and ready to set the trap General Grant had made for the rebel commander. General Burnside met Longstreet, and, after some resistance, gave way.

November 14th and 15th, the enemy was beaten back, and then our "boys" retreated, leading him on to Knoxville, across the Little Tennessee River.

On the 19th, General Burnside had got within the defences of the city, and General Longstreet was investing it. The traitor thought he had caught the defenders of the Republic; General Grant knew he had him just where he desired to hold him a while. All the time, the watchful eye of the Commander-in-Chief of the Military Division of the Mississippi was on Missionary Ridge and Lookout Mountain—the vital defences of the enemy.

Weakened by the withdrawal of Longstreet's force, and with the troops left spread along the Ridge, General Grant believed that, by keeping the extremities busy in the fight, he could break through the centre of those lines seven miles long. The generals were posted on the right and left flanks, and at the centre, ready to make the bold attack on the 21st. But General Sherman was delayed in his movements by rains, and the ruin of pontoons, against which the rebels sent down rafts; and two days intervened before the grand trial of strength could be made.

The 23d of November came. It was Monday morning. The previous day, prayer and praise had been heard in camp. The chaplains, and other Christian workers for the spiritual good of the soldiers, had kindly spoken to them of the glorious "Captain of our salvation." The faces of brave men had been wet with tears, as they thought of home and the loved ones there. Many letters had been written with the feeling that they might be the last messages of affection from the field of conflict.

The orders pass from General Grant's headquarters to advance toward the Ridge, alive with vigilant enemies. The preëminent *strategy* of the Leader was apparent in the very method of opening the struggle. The columns marched from their works as if on parade. Banners were borne, and bands played, and the whole aspect of the embattled host was that of ordinary review. The deceived foe looked down with comparative indifference, from heights five hundred feet above. But onward toward the rifle pits, and to an advanced position, our forces pressed, till too late for the enemy to send to their camps for reënforcements.

At half past one o'clock in the afternoon, General Wood leaves Fort Wood with his tried battalions. Watch him, as he goes down the slope to the open plain between him and the forest skirting Missionary Ridge. From the battlements of the fortress, General Grant, with Thomas, Granger, and Howard by his side, is looking on with interest too intense for any other language than that of silence. The heavy guns from those ramparts send to the eminences in the enemy's foreground, and over the brave ranks advancing, the thunder and the messengers of death. The columns reach the plain. The battle storm beats down upon them; but steadily, as though on ordinary march, they move on, under the eye of their fearless commander, and of the chieftains on the walls of the fort. They march like men who mean to gladden the sight of beholders, and the land they love. Now they enter the dark woods. The moments fly, and a blue smoke rises from the sheltering trees, and floats like a banner toward Missionary Ridge. A hum of excitement and delight spreads along the battlements of Fort Wood, and rises from loyal, heroic lips in every part of it. The foes dash into Wood's front, but the shock is well sustained. Then, a charge! Up the slope rushes the steel-pointed surge. "Orchard Knob" is taken, the rifle pits cleared, and the decisive contest fairly opened.

The next gloomy day of drizzling rain brought a renewal of the fight. An observer of the attack ordered by General Sherman, furnishes you with an interesting view of the troops on the eve of battle:

"Soldiers are very different beings under the two different circumstances of receiving and making an attack. In the first case they are seldom or never composed, cool, and quiet. Put men behind breastworks to receive an assault, and the delay in the attack creates anxiety, which develops into mental excitement, which finds vent in noise and a certain restlessness of person. Going to the assault, they are different beings. I watched carefully the columns, as they moved out to the assault on Tuesday, each believing that the next step brought his advance against that of the enemy. The silence was painfully noticeable.

A command given at one end of the corps, could be distinctly heard at the other. The men looked serious, and rather gruff, and were painfully quiet. They conversed with each other but seldom, and then in under tones. All appeared anxious to preserve their weapons from the rain. They moved in perfect order. But though one might fail to notice this, the most casual student of human nature could hardly fail to observe how serious those men were. And he would know, too, that it was not the rain which dampened their spirits. Ever and anon they would glance at the hill which they were approaching, and it was easy to see why they looked serious. Perhaps they compared the hills, in their own minds, to the Walnut Hills of Vicksburg; but I do not think there was one man there who feared to test the question of victory or defeat there and then."

For three days the field of the strife for miles exhibited the varying fortunes and awfully sublime scenes of valor and blood, of warfare unrivalled in the annals of the past. Near Fort Buckner, the Union Brigade, under a rocky ridge which protected them from bullets, met a shower of stones hurled upon them from above.

Notwithstanding General Grant's accident at Carrollton, no better horseman drew the rein in either army. It was a common thing on the bloody field of Chattanooga, to see his steed, touched with the spur, dash off at a pace that left his staff stringing along behind, "like the tail of a kite." He went with the speed of the wind from one part of the hail-swept plain to another.

My youthful reader, would you have liked to stand in some safe spot, and witness the grand and terrible combat?

You can never come nearer to such a view, than by reading the finest account of this, or any other battle. It was written by an eyewitness, B. F. Taylor, for the *Chicago Journal:*

"The iron heart of Sherman's column began to be audible, like the fall of great trees in the depth of the forest, as it beat beyond the woods on the extreme left. Over roads indescribable, and conquering lions of difficulties that met him all the way, he had at length arrived with his command of the Army of the Tennessee. The roar of his guns was like the striking of a great clock, and grew nearer and louder as the morning wore away. Along the centre all was still. Our men lay as they had lain since Tuesday night—motionless, behind the works. Generals Grant, Thomas, Granger, Meigs, Hunter, Reynolds, were grouped at Orchard Knob, here; Bragg, Breckinridge, Hardee, Stevens, Cleburn, Bates, Walker, were waiting on Mission Ridge, yonder. And the Northern clock tolled on! At noon, a pair of steamers, screaming in the river across the town, telling over, in their own wild way, our mountain triumph on the right, pierced the hushed breadth of air between two lines of battle with a note or two of the music of peaceful life.

"At one o'clock the signal flag at Fort Wood was a-flutter. Scanning the horizon, another flag, glancing like a lady's handkerchief, showed white across a field lying high and dry upon the ridge three miles to the northeast, and answered back. The centre and Sherman's corps had spoken. As the hour went by, all semblance to falling tree and tolling clock had vanished; it was a rattling roar; the ring of Sherman's panting artillery, and the fiery gust from the rebel guns on Tunnel Hill, the point of Mission Ridge. The enemy had massed there the corps of Hardee and Buckner, as upon a battlement, utterly inaccessible save by one steep, narrow way, commanded by their guns. A thousand men could hold it against a host. And right in front of this bold abutment of the ridge is a broad, clear field, skirted by woods. Across this tremendous threshold, up to death's door, moved Sherman's column. Twice it advanced, and twice I saw it swept back in bleeding lines before the furnace blast, until that russet field seemed some strange page ruled thick with blue and red. Bright valor was in vain; they lacked the ground to stand on; they wanted, like the giant of old story, a touch of earth to make them strong. It was the devil's own corner. Before them was a lane, whose upper end the rebel cannon swallowed. Moving by the right flank, nature opposed them with precipitous heights. There was nothing for it but straight across the field, swept by an enfilading fire, and up to the lane, down which drove the storm. They could unfold no broad front, and so the losses were less than seven hundred, that must otherwise have swelled to thousands. The musketry fire was delivered with terrible emphasis. Two dwellings, in one of which Federal wounded men were lying, set on fire by the rebels, began to send up tall columns of smoke, streaked red with fire. The grand and the terrible were blended.

* * * * * *

"The brief November afternoon was half gone. It was yet thundering on the left; along the centre all was still. At that very hour a fierce assault was made upon the enemy's left, near Rossville, four miles down toward the old field of Chickamauga. They carried the Ridge— Mission Ridge seems everywhere; they strewed its summit with rebel dead; they *held* it. And thus the tips of the Federal army's widespread wings flapped grandly. But it had not swooped; the gray quarry yet perched upon Mission Ridge. The rebel army was terribly battered at the edges; but there, full in our front, it grimly waited, biding out its time. If the horns of the rebel crescent could not be doubled crushingly together, in a shapeless mass, possibly it might be sundered at its centre, and tumbled in fragments over the other side of Mission Ridge. Sherman was halted upon the left; Hooker was holding hard in Chattanooga Valley; the Fourth Corps, that rounded out our centre, grew impatient of restraint. The day was waning; but little time remained to complete the Commanding General's grand design. Gordon Granger's hour had come; his work was full before him.

"And what a work that was, to make a weak man

falter and a brave man think! One and a half miles to traverse, with narrow fringes of woods, rough valleys, sweeps of open field, rocky acclivities, to the base of the ridge, and no foot in all the breadth withdrawn from rebel sight; no foot that could not be played upon by rebel cannon, like a piano's keys under Thalberg's stormy fingers. The base attained, what then? A heavy rebel work, packed with the enemy, rimming it like a battlement. That work carried, and what then? A hill, struggling up out of the valley four hundred feet, rained on by bullets, swept by shot and shell; another line of works, and then, up like a Gothic roof, rough with rocks, a wreck with fallen trees, four hundred more; another ring of fire and iron, and then the crest, and then the enemy.

"To dream of such a journey would be madness; to devise it, a thing incredible; to do it, a deed impossible. But Grant was guilty of them all, and Granger was equal to the work. The story of the battle of Mission Ridge is struck with immortality already; let the leader of the Fourth Corps bear it company.

"That the centre yet lies along its silent line, is still true; in five minutes it will be the wildest fiction. Let us take that little breath of grace for just one glance at the surroundings, since we shall have neither heart nor eyes for it again. Did ever battle have so vast a cloud of witnesses? The hive-shaped hills have swarmed. Clustered like bees, blackening the housetops, lining the fortifications, over yonder *across* the theatre, in the seats with the Catilines, *everywhere*, are a hundred thousand beholders. Their souls are in their eyes. Not a murmur can you hear. It is the most solemn congregation that ever stood up in the presence of the God of battles. I think of Bunker Hill, as I stand here—of the thousands who witnessed the immortal struggle—and fancy there is a parallel. I think, too, that the chair of every man of them will stand vacant against the wall to-morrow, and that around the fireside they must give thanks without him, if they can.

"At half past three, a group of generals, whose names will need no 'Old Mortality' to chisel them anew, stood upon Orchard Knob. The hero of Vicksburg was there, calm, clear, persistent, far-seeing. Thomas, the sterling and sturdy; Meigs, Hunter, Granger, Reynolds. Clusters of humbler mortals were there, too, but it was anything but a turbulent crowd; the voice naturally fell into a subdued tone, and even young faces took on the gravity of later years. Generals Grant, Thomas, and Granger conferred, an order was given, and in an instant the Knob was cleared like a ship's deck for action. At twenty minutes of four, Granger stood upon the parapet. The bugle swung idle at the bugler's side, the warbling fife and the grumbling drum unheard: there was to be *louder* talk—six guns at intervals of two seconds, the signal to advance. Strong and steady his voice rang out: 'Number one, fire! Number two, fire! Number three, fire!

It seemed to me the tolling of the clock of destiny. And when, at 'Number six, fire!' the roar throbbed out with the flash, you should have seen the dead line that had been .ying behind the works all day, all night, all day again, come to resurrection in the twinkling of an eye, leap like a blade from its scabbard, and sweep with a two-mile stroke toward the ridge. From divisions to brigades, from brigades to regiments, the order ran. A minute, and the skirmishers deploy; a minute, and the first great drops begin to patter along the line; a minute, and the musketry is in full play, like the crackling whips of a hemlock fire. Men go down here and there before your eyes. The wind lifts the smoke, and drifts it away over the top of the Ridge. Everything is too distinct; it is fairly *palpable;* you can touch it with your hand. The divisions of Wood and Sheridan are wading breast deep in the valley of death.

"I never can tell you what it was like. They pushed out, leaving nothing behind them. There was no reservation in that battle. On moves the line of skirmishers, like a heavy frown, and after it, at quick time, the splendid columns. At right of us and left of us and front of us, you can see the bayonets glitter in the sun. You cannot persuade yourself that Bragg was wrong, a day or two ago, when, seeing Hooker moving in, he said, 'Now we shall have a Potomac review;' that this is *not* the parade he prophesied; that it is of a truth the harvest of death to which they go down. And so through the fringe of woods went the line. Now, out into the open ground they burst at the double-quick. Shall I call it a Sabbath-day's journey, or a long one and a half mile? To me that watched, it seemed endless as eternity; and yet they made it in thirty minutes. The tempest that now broke upon their heads was terrible. The enemy's fire burst out of the rifle pits from base to summit of Mission Ridge; five rebel batteries of Parrotts and Napoleons opened along the crest. Grape and canister and shot and shell sowed the ground with rugged iron, and garnished it with the wounded and the dead. But steady and strong our columns moved on.

'By heaven! It was a splendid sight to see,
For one who had no friend, no brother there;

but to all loyal hearts—alas! and thank God—those men were friend and brother, both in one.

"And over their heads, as they went, Forts Wood and Negley struck straight out, like mighty pugilists, right and left, raining their iron blows upon the Ridge from base to crest; Forts Palmer and King took up the quarrel, and Moccasin Point cracked its fiery whips, and lashed the rebel left, till the wolf cowered in its corner with a growl. Bridges's battery, from Orchard Knob below, thrust its ponderous fists in the face of the enemy, and planted blows at will. Our artillery was doing splendid service. It laid its shot and shell wherever it pleased. Had giants carried them by hand, they could hardly have been more accurate. All along the mountain's side, in the rebel rifle pits, on the crest, they fairly dotted the Ridge. General Granger leaped down, sighted a gun, and in a moment, right in front, a great volume of smoke, like 'the cloud by day,' lifted off the summit from among the rebel batteries, and hung motionless, kindling in the sun. The shot had struck a caisson, and that was its dying breath. In five minutes away floated another. A shell went crashing through a building in the cluster that marked Bragg's headquarters; a second killed the skeleton horses of a battery at his elbow; a third scattered a gray mass as if it had been a wasp's nest.

"And all the while our lines were moving on. They had burned through the woods and swept over the rough and rolling ground like a prairie fire. Never halting, never faltering, they charged up to the first rifle pits with a cheer, forked out the rebels with their bayonets, and lay there panting for breath. If the thunder of guns had been terrible, it was now growing sublime; it was like the footfall of God on the ledges of cloud. Our forts and batteries still thrust out their mighty arms across the valley. The rebel guns that lined the arc of the crest full in our front, opened like the fan of Lucifer, and converged their fire down upon Baird and Wood and Sheridan. It was rifles and musketry; it was grape and canister; it was shell and shrapnel. Mission Ridge was volcanic; a thousand torrents of red poured over its brink, and rushed together to its base. And our men were there, halting

17

for breath! And still the sublime diapason rolled on. Echoes that never waked before, roared out from height to height, and called from the far ranges of Waldron's Ridge to Lookout. As for Mission Ridge, it had jarred to such music before; it was the 'sounding board' of Chicka-mauga. It was *behind* us then; it frowns and flashes in our face to-day. The old Army of the Cumberland was there. It breasted the storm till the storm was spent, and left the ground it held. The old Army of the Cumberland is *here!* It shall roll up the Ridge like a surge to its summit, and sweep triumphant down the other side. Believe me, that memory and hope may have made the heart of many a blue-coat beat like a drum. 'Beat,' did I say? The feverish heart of the *battle* beats on; fifty-eight guns a minute, by the watch, is the rate of its terrible throbbing. That hill, if you climb it, will appal you. Furrowed like a summer fallow, bullets as if an oak had shed them; trees clipped and shorn, leaf and limb, as with the knife of some heroic gardener pruning back for richer fruit. How you attain the summit, weary and breathless, I wait to hear; how *they* went up in the teeth of the storm, no man can tell!

"And, all the while, rebel prisoners have been streaming out from the rear of our lines like the tails of a cloud of kites. Captured and disarmed, they needed nobody to set them going. The fire of their own comrades was like spurs in a horse's flanks, and, amid the tempest of their own brewing, they ran for dear life, until they dropped like quails into the Federal rifle pits, and were safe. But our gallant legions are out in the storm; they have carried the works at the base of the Ridge; they have fallen like leaves in winter weather. Blow, dumb bugles!

"Sound the recall! 'Take the rifle pit!' was the order; and it is as empty of rebels as the tomb of the prophets. Shall they turn their backs to the blast? Shall they sit down under the caves of that dripping iron? Or shall they climb to the cloud of death above them, and pluck out its lightnings as they would straws from a sheaf of wheat? But the order was not given. And now the arc of fire on the crest grows fiercer and longer. The reconnoissance of Monday had failed to develop the heavy metal of the enemy. The dull fringe of the hill kindles with the flash of great guns. I count the fleeces of white smoke that dot the Ridge, as battery after battery opens upon our line, until from the ends of the growing arc they sweep down upon it in mighty X's of fire. I count till that devil's girdle numbers thirteen batteries, and my heart cries out, 'Great God, when shall the end be!' There is a poem I learned in childhood, and so did you: it is Campbell's 'Hohenlinden.' One line I never knew the meaning of, until I read it written along that hill! It has lighted up the whole poem for me with the glow of battle forever:

'And louder than the bolts of heaven,
Far flashed the red artillery.'

"At this moment, General Granger's aids are dashing out with an order. They radiate over the field, to left, right, and front. 'Take the Ridge, if you can!' 'Take the Ridge, if you can!' and so it went along the line But the advance had already set forth without it. Stout-hearted Wood, the iron-gray veteran, is rallying on his men; stormy Turchin is delivering brave words in bad English; Sheridan—'Little Phil'—you may easily look down upon him without climbing a tree, and see one of the most gallant leaders of the age, if you do—is riding to and fro along the first line of rifle pits, as calmly as a chess player. An aid rides up with the order. 'Avery, that flask,' said the general. Quietly filling the pewter cup, Sheridan looks up at the battery that frowns above him, by Bragg's headquarters, shakes his cap amid that storm of everything that kills, when you could hardly hold your hand without catching a bullet in it, and, with a 'How are you?' tosses off the cup. The blue battle-flag of the rebels fluttered a response to the cool salute, and the next instant the battery let fly its six guns, showering Sheridan with earth. Alluding to that compliment with anything but a blank cartridge, the general said to me, in his quiet way, 'I thought it —— ungenerous!' The recording angel will drop a tear upon the word for the part he played that day. Wheeling toward the men, he cheered them to the charge, and made at the hill like a bold-riding hunter. They were out of the rifle pits and into the tempest, and struggling up the steep, before you could get breath to tell it; and so they were throughout the inspired line.

"And now you have before you one of the most startling episodes of the war. I cannot render it in words; dictionaries are beggarly things. But I *may* tell you they did not storm that mountain as you would think. They dash out a little way, and then slacken; they creep up, hand over hand, loading and firing, and wavering and halting, from the first line of works to the second; they burst into a charge with a cheer, and go over it. Sheets of flame baptize them; plunging shot tear away comrades on left and right; it is no longer shoulder to shoulder; it is God for us all! Under tree trunks, among rocks, stumbling over the dead, struggling with the living, facing the steady fire of eight thousand infantry poured down upon their heads as if it were the old historic curse from heaven, they wrestle with the Ridge. Ten, fifteen, twenty minutes go by, like a reluctant century. The batteries roll like a drum. Between the second and last lines of rebel works is the torrid zone of the battle. The hill sways up like a wall before them at an angle of forty-five degrees, but our brave mountaineers are clambering steadily on—up—upward still! You may think it strange, but I would not have recalled them if I could. They would have lifted you, as they did me, in full view of the heroic grandeur. They seemed to be spurning the dull earth under their feet, and going up to do Homeric battle with the greater gods.

"And what do those men follow? If you look, you shall see that the thirteen thousand are not a rushing herd of human creatures; that, along the Gothic roof of the Ridge, a row of inverted V's is slowly moving up almost in line, a mighty lettering on the hill's broad side. At the angles of those V's is something that glitters like a wing. Your heart gives a great bound when you think what it is—*the regimental flag*—and, glancing along the front, count fifteen of those colors, that were borne at **Pea Ridge**, waved at **Shiloh**, glorified at **Stone River**, riddled at **Chickamauga**. Nobler than Cæsar's rent mantle are they all! And up move the banners, now fluttering like a wounded bird, now faltering, now sinking out of sight. Three times the flag of one regiment goes down. And you know why. Three dead color sergeants lie just there. But the *flag* is immortal, thank God! and up it comes again, and the V's move on. At the left of Wood, three regiments of Baird—Turchin, the Russian thunderbolt, is there—hurl themselves against a bold point strong with rebel works. For a long quarter of an hour three flags are perched and motionless on a plateau under the frown of the hill. Will they linger forever? I give a look at the sun behind me; it is not more than a hand's breadth from the edge of the mountain; its level rays bridge the valley from Chattanooga to the Ridge with beams of gold; it shines in the rebel faces; it brings out the Federal blue; it touches up the flags. Oh, for the voice that could bid that sun stand still! I turn to the battle again; those three flags have taken flight! They are upward bound.

"The race of the flags is growing every moment more terrible. There, at the right, a strange thing catches the eye; one of the inverted V's is turning right side up. The men struggling along the converging lines to overtake the flag, have distanced it, and there the colors are, sinking down in the centre between the rising flanks. The line wavers like a great billow, and up comes the banner again, as if heaved on a surge's shoulder. The iron sledges beat on. Hearts loyal and brave are on the anvil, all the way from base to summit of Mission Ridge, but those dreadful hammers never intermit. Swarms of bullets sweep the hill; you can count twenty-eight balls in one little tree. Things are growing desperate up aloft. The rebels tumble rocks upon the rising line; they light the fuses and roll shells down the steep; they load the guns with handfuls of cartridges in their haste; and, as if there were powder in the word, they shout, 'Chickamauga!' down upon the mountaineers. But it would not all do; and just as the sun, weary of the scene, was sinking out of sight, with magnificent bursts all along the line, exactly as you have seen the crested seas leap up at the breakwater, the advance surged over the crest, and in a minute those flags fluttered along the fringe where fifty rebel guns were kennelled. God bless the flag! God save the Union!

"What colors were first upon the mountain battlement

I dare not try to say; bright honor itself may be proud to bear—nay, proud to follow, the hindmost. Foot by foot they had fought up the steep, slippery with much blood; let them go to glory together. A minute, and they were *all* there, fluttering along the Ridge from left to right. The rebel hordes rolled off to the north, rolled off to the east, like the clouds of a worn-out storm. Bragg, ten minutes before, was putting men back in the rifle pits. His gallant gray was straining a nerve for him now, and the man rode on horseback into Dixie's bosom, who, arrayed in some prophet's discarded mantle, foretold on Monday that the Yankees would leave Chattanooga in five days. They left in three, and by way of Mission Ridge, straight over the mountains as their forefathers went! As Sheridan rode up to the guns, the heels of Breckinridge's horse glittered in the last rays of sunshine. That crest was hardly 'well off with the old love before it was on with the new.'

"But the scene on the narrow plateau can never be painted. As the blue-coats surged over its edge, cheer on cheer rang like bells through the valley of the Chickamauga. Men flung themselves exhausted upon the ground. They laughed and wept, shook hands, and embraced; turned round, and did all four over again. It was as wild as a carnival. Granger was received with a shout. 'Soldiers,' he said, 'you ought to be court martialled, every man of you. I ordered you to take the rifle pits, and you scaled the mountain!' But it was not

Mars' horrid front exactly with which he said it, for his cheeks were wet with tears as honest as the blood that reddened all the route. Wood uttered words that rang like 'Napoleon's;' and Sheridan, the rowels at his horse's flanks, was ready for a dash down the Ridge with a 'view halloo,' for a fox hunt.

"But you must not think this was all there was of the scene on the crest, for fight and frolic were strangely mingled. Not a rebel had dreamed a man of us all would live to reach the summit; and when a little wave of the Federal cheer rolled up and broke over the crest, they defiantly cried, 'Hurrah, and be d——d!' the next minute a Union regiment followed the voice, the rebels delivered their fire, and tumbled down in the rifle pits, their faces distorted with fear. No sooner had the soldiers scrambled to the Ridge and straightened themselves, than up muskets and away they blazed. One of them, fairly beside himself between laughing and crying, seemed puzzled at which end of the piece he should load, and so, abandoning the gun and the problem together, he made a catapult of himself, and fell to hurling stones after the enemy. And he said, as he threw——well, you know our 'army swore terribly in Flanders.' Bayonets glinted and muskets rattled. General Sheridan's horse was killed under him. Richard was not in his role, and so he leaped upon a rebel gun for want of another. Rebel artillerists are driven from their batteries at the edge of the sword and the point of the bayonet. Two rebel guns are swung around upon their old masters. But there is nobody to load them. Light and heavy artillery do not belong to the winged kingdom. Two infantry men, claiming to be old artillerists, volunteer. Granger turns captain of the guns, and—'right about wheel!'—in a moment they are growling after the flying enemy. I say 'flying,' but that is figurative. The many run like Spanish merinos, but the few fight like gray wolves at bay; they load and fire as they retreat; they are fairly scorched out of position.

"A sharpshooter, fancying Granger to be worth the powder, coolly tries his hand at him. The general hears the *zip* of a ball at one ear, but doesn't mind it. In a minute, away it sings at the other. He takes the hint, sweeps with his glass the direction whence the couple came, and brings up the marksman, just drawing a bead upon him again. At that instant a Federal argument persuades the cool hunter, and down he goes. That long-range gun of his was captured, weighed twenty-four pounds, was telescope-mounted, a sort of mongrel howitzer.

"A colonel is slashing away with his sabre in a ring of rebels. Down goes his horse under him. They have him on the hip. One of them is taking deliberate aim, when up rushes a lieutenant, claps a pistol to one ear, and roars in at the other, 'Who the h—l are you shooting at?' The fellow drops his piece, gasps out, 'I surrender!' and the next instant the gallant lieutenant falls sharply wounded. He is a 'roll of honor' officer, straight up from the tanks, and he honors the roll.

"A little German in Wood's division is pierced like the lid of a pepper box, but he is neither dead nor wounded. 'See here,' he says, rushing up to a comrade; 'a pullet hit te preach of mine gun, a pullet in mine pocketbook, a pullet in mine coat tail; dey shoots me tree, five time, and I gives dem h—l yet!'

"But I can render you no idea of the battle caldron that boiled on the plateau. An incident here and there I have given you, and you must fill out the picture for yourself. Dead rebels lay thick around Bragg's headquarters and along the Ridge. Scabbards, broken arms, artillery horses, wrecks of gun carriages, and bloody garments strewed the scene. And, tread lightly, oh, loyal-hearted! the boys in blue are lying there. No more the sounding charge; no more the brave, wild cheer; and never for them, sweet as the breath of the new-mown hay in the old home fields, 'The Soldier's Return from the War.' A little waif of a drummer boy, somehow drifted up the mountain in the surge, lies there; his pale face upward, a blue spot on his breast. Muffle his drum for the poor child and his mother.

"Our troops met one loyal welcome on the height. How the old Tennesseean that gave it managed to get there, nobody knows; but there he was, grasping a colonel's hand, and saying, while the tears ran down his face, 'God be thanked! I *knew* the Yankees would fight!' With the receding flight and swift pursuit the battle died away in murmurs, far down the valley of the

Chickamauga. Sheridan was again in the saddle, and, with his command, spurring on after the enemy. Tall columns of smoke were rising at the left. The rebels were burning a train of stores a mile long. In the exploding rebel caissons we had 'the cloud by day,' and now we are having 'the pillar of fire by night.' The sun, the golden disc of the scales that balance day and night, had hardly gone down, when up, beyond Mission Ridge, rose the *silver* side, for that night it was full moon. The troubled day was gone. A Federal general sat in the seat of the man who, on the very Saturday before the battle, had sent a flag to the Federal lines with the words:

"'Humanity would dictate the removal of all non-combatants from Chattanooga, as I am about to shell the city!'

"Our loss in killed, wounded, and missing, is reported at about four thousand. We captured over six thousand prisoners, besides the wounded left in our hands, forty pieces of artillery, five or six thousand small arms, and a large train. The enemy's loss in killed and wounded is not known."

A new record of sacrifice, of mourning, and of resplendent victory! General Grant, under God's guidance, has redeemed the mighty Southwest!

When our victorious troops had fairly routed the astonished Bragg on Missionary Ridge, a lady, whose residence was within his lines, in alarm said to him: "What are you going to do with me, general?" Replied the *bragging* rebel: "Lord, madam! the Yankees will never dare to come up here."

Relating the incident to our "boys," she added, with a blubber: "And it was not fifteen minutes before you were all around here."

The sweep of General Hooker's column around the spur of Lookout, surprising the enemy, till he reached the dizzy heights and fought *above the clouds* of the misty day, was a deed of heroism which alone would have made the struggle and his name immortal.

You have here the brief despatches of the opposing generals:

CHATTANOOGA, November 25, 1863—7 15 P. M.

Major-General H. W. HALLECK, General-in-Chief:

Although the battle lasted from early dawn till dark this evening, I believe I am not premature in announcing a complete victory over Bragg.

Lookout Mountain top, all the rifle pits in Chattanooga Valley, and Missionary Ridge entire, have been carried, and are now held by us.

U. S. GRANT, Major-General.

CHICKAMAUGA, November 25, 1863.

General S. COOPER, Adjutant and Inspector-General:

After several unsuccessful assaults on our lines to-day, the enemy carried the left centre about four o'clock. The whole left soon gave way in considerable disorder. The right maintained its ground, and repelled every attack. I am withdrawing all to this point.

BRAXTON BRAGG.

Wrote Quartermaster-General Meigs to Secretary Stanton:

"Bragg's remaining troops left early in the night, and the battle of Chattanooga, after days of manœuvring and fighting, was won. The strength of the rebellion in the centre is broken. Burnside is relieved from danger in East Tennessee. Kentucky and Tennessee are rescued. Georgia and the Southeast are threatened in the rear, and another victory is added to the chapter of 'Unconditional Surrender Grant.'

"To-night the estimate of captures is several thousand prisoners and thirty pieces of artillery.

"Our loss for so great a victory is not severe.

"Bragg is firing the railroad as he retreats toward Dalton. Sherman is in hot pursuit.

"To-day I viewed the battle field, which extends for six miles along Missionary Ridge, and for several miles on Lookout Mountain.

"Probably not so well-directed, so well-ordered a battle, has taken place during the war. But one assault was repulsed; but that assault, by calling to that point the rebel reserves, prevented them repulsing any of the others.

"A few days since, Bragg sent to General Grant a flag of truce, advising him that it would be prudent to remove any non-combatants who might be still in Chattanooga. No reply has been returned; but the combatants having removed from the vicinity, it is probable that non-combatants can remain without imprudence."

It is related of General Scott, the old veteran and hero of the last war with England (which, we fear, will not long be the *last*), that, in conversation with a gentleman in office at Washington, about the victories, he expressed his surprise at General Grant's success. He remarked:

"General Grant has shown more military skill than any other general on our side. And I am the more surprised, as I can only remember him in the Mexican war as a young lieutenant of undoubted courage, but giving no promise whatever of anything beyond ordinary abilities."

Among the heroes who fell at Chattanooga, was Colonel O'Meara, of the Irish Legion. When General Grant heard that the body was coffined for its homeward journey, he hastened to the spot where it lay. Standing beside it, he said:

"Lift the coffin lid, that I may take a last look at the gallant colonel of the Irish Legion."

Writes Larkee:

"He was touched at the sight of one whom he had honored and publicly thanked before he had been two months in the Army of the Tennessee. O'Meara's defence of the trestlework, a few miles north of Holly Springs, Miss., when Van Dorn made a raid there in December, 1862, and which saved Grant's army from starvation, was never forgotten by the General. The spectators were moved at the sad and touching farewell of the Commander of the Department of the Mississippi from the corpse of a young Irish soldier, who had forfeited his life to the belief that 'the highest and best duty of all, native or foreign born, was to stand by the flag which is the hope of the exile, the emblem of philanthropy, and the ensign of the American people.'"

CHAPTER XX.

General Sherman at Knoxville—The President and the Victories—Major-General Grant's Congratulations—Colonel Ely, the Indian Sachem's Tribute—Excitement in Washington—A Medal—Other Honors—Hon. Mr. Washburn's Speech—Grant's untiring Activity—Visits a sick Child—He is invited to a Banquet—Accepts the Honor—The brilliant Festival.

GENERAL LONGSTREET has learned the reason why he was allowed to besiege Knoxville. The news of Hooker's mountain climbing, and of Yankee flags on Missionary Ridge, dispelled his dream of success. The proud rebel is exasperated, and determined to save his name from sharing the disgrace of Chattanooga. So, November 29th, he dashed against Fort Saunders, but only got sorely bruised himself. Then, pursuing columns in the track of the defeated foe beyond Ringgold, Ga., wheeled, and marched on Longstreet. Finding himself hard pressed, like Joe Johnston at Jackson, he deemed "prudence the better part of valor," and made his escape in the night of December 4th.

This completed the great work of General Grant in his new Department; and President Lincoln, upon receiving the glad tidings, issued two brief messages. One of them was addressed to the people; the other, a day later, to General Grant:

EXECUTIVE MANSION, WASHINGTON, D. C., December 7, 1863.

Reliable information being received that the insurgent force is retreating from East Tennessee, under circumstances rendering it probable that the Union forces cannot hereafter be dislodged from that important position; and esteeming this to be of high national consequence, I recommend that all loyal people do, on receipt of this information, assemble at their places of worship, and render special homage and gratitude to Almighty God for this great advancement of the National cause.

A. LINCOLN.

WASHINGTON, December 8.

Major-General GRANT:

Understanding that your lodgment at Chattanooga and Knoxville is now secure, I wish to tender you, and all under your command, my more than thanks—my profoundest gratitude for the skill, courage, and perseverance with which you and they, over so great difficulties, have effected that important object. God bless you all!

A. LINCOLN.

Major-General Grant's congratulations to his magnificent army, two days after, is a noble tribute from an unassuming, magnanimous heart. His acknowledgment of God's help is evidently earnest and sincere:

'HEADQUARTERS MILITARY DIVISION OF THE MISSISSIPPI,
IN THE FIELD, CHATTANOOGA, TENN., Dec. 10, 1863.

The General Commanding takes this opportunity of returning his sincere thanks and congratulations to the brave armies of the Cumberland, the Ohio, the Tennessee, and their comrades from the Potomac, for the recent splendid and decisive successes achieved over the enemy. In a short time you have recovered from him the control of the Tennessee River from Bridgeport to Knoxville. You dislodged him from his great stronghold upon Lookout Mountain, drove him from Chattanooga Valley, wrested from his determined grasp the possession of Missionary Ridge, repelled with heavy loss to him his repeated assaults upon Knoxville, forcing him to raise the siege there, driving him at all points, utterly routed and discomfited, beyond the limits of the State. By your noble heroism and determined courage, you have most effectually defeated the plans of the enemy for regaining possession of the States of Kentucky and Tennessee. You have secured positions from which no rebellious power can drive or dislodge you. For all this the General Commanding thanks you collectively and individually. The loyal people of the United States thank and bless you. Their hopes and prayers for your success against this unholy rebellion are with you daily. Their faith in you will not be in vain. Their hopes will not be blasted. Their prayers to Almighty God will be answered. You will yet go to other fields of strife; and, with the invincible bravery and unflinching loyalty to justice and right which have characterized you in the past, you will prove that no enemy can withstand you, and that no defences, however formidable, can check your onward march.

By order of   Major-General U. S. GRANT.

General Bragg lost his command, in losing Chattanooga. General Hardee took his place; of whom General Grant, who knew these men, said: "He is *my choice.*"

Colonel Ely, Indian Sachem, and Chief of the Tonawandas and Seneca Nation, who was on the staff, tells you what he saw and thinks of the Commander of three grand armies:

"I need not describe to you the recent battle of Chattanooga. The papers have given every possible detail concerning it. I may only say that I saw it all, and was in the five days' fight. Of General Grant's staff, only one was wounded—a Lieutenant Towner, Assistant Chief of Artillery, whose parents formerly lived at Batavia, N. Y., but now of Chicago. It has been a matter of universal wonder in this army that General Grant himself was not killed, and that no more accidents occurred to his staff; for the General was always in the front (his staff with him, of course), and perfectly heedless of the storm of hissing bullets and screaming shell flying around him. His apparent want of sensibility does not arise from heedlessness, heartlessness, or vain military affectation, but from a sense of the responsibility resting upon him when in battle. When at Ringgold, we rode for half a mile in the face of the enemy, under an incessant fire of cannon and musketry; nor did we ride fast, but upon an ordinary trot, and not once, do I believe, did it enter the General's mind that he was in danger. I was by his side, and watched him closely. In riding that distance, we were going to the front, and I could see that he was study ing the positions of the two armies, and, of course, planning how to defeat the enemy, who was here making a most desperate stand, and was slaughtering our men fearfully. After defeating and driving the enemy here, we returned to Chattanooga.

"Another feature in General Grant's personal movements is, that he requires no escort beyond his staff, so regardless of danger is he. Roads are almost useless to him, for he takes short cuts through fields and woods, and will swim his horse through almost any stream that obstructs his way. Nor does it make any difference to him whether he has daylight for his movements; for he will ride from breakfast until two o'clock in the morning, and that, too, without eating. The next day he will repeat the dose, until he finishes the work. Now, such things come hard upon the staff, but they have learned how to bear it."

The excitement in the nation's capital over the success of our arms under General Grant, was scarcely less than when the lightning conveyed the news of Vicksburg's evacuation. Congress assembled the very day the thrilling intelligence spread through the city. Soon as the business could properly come before the House, Hon. Mr. Washburn, of Galena, where General Grant had his leather store, rose, and gave the usual notice that he should introduce two bills: one, "to revive the grade of lieutenant-general of the army;" the other, "to provide that a medal be struck for General Grant, and that a vote of thanks be given him, and the officers of the army."

Ten days later, the annexed act of Congress received the President's signature:

LAWS OF THE UNITED STATES

Passed at the First Session of the Thirty-eighth Congress.

[PUBLIC RESOLUTION No. 1.]

JOINT RESOLUTION of Thanks to Major-General Ulysses S. Grant, and the officers and soldiers who have fought under his command during this Rebellion; and providing that the President of the United States shall cause a medal to be struck, to be presented to Major-General Grant in the name of the people of the United States of America.

Be it resolved by the Senate and House of Representatives of the United States of America in Congress assembled, That the thanks of Congress be and they hereby are presented to Major-General Ulysses S. Grant, and through him to the officers and soldiers who have fought under his command during this Rebellion, for their gallantry and good conduct in the battles in which they have been engaged; and that the President of the United States be requested to cause a gold medal to be struck, with suitable emblems, devices, and inscriptions, to be presented to Major-General Grant.

SEC. 2. *And be it further resolved,* That, when the said medal shall have been struck, the President shall cause a copy of this joint resolution to be engrossed on parchment, and shall transmit the same, together with the said medal, to Major-General Grant, to be presented to him in the name of the people of the United States of America.

SEC. 3. *And be it further resolved,* That a sufficient sum of money to carry this resolution into effect is hereby appropriated out of any money in the Treasury not otherwise appropriated.

SCHUYLER COLFAX,
Speaker of the House of Representatives.
H. HAMLIN,
Vice-President of the United States and
President of the Senate.

Approved December 17, 1863.

ABRAHAM LINCOLN.

The token of a grateful nation's regard was designed by the artist Leutze. The picture on one side of the medal was to consist of a profile likeness of the hero, surrounded by a wreath of laurels; his name and the year of his victories inscribed upon it, and the whole surrounded by a galaxy of stars. The design for the reverse was original, appropriate, and beautiful. It was the figure of Fame seated in a graceful attitude on the American eagle, which, with outspread wings, seems preparing for flight. In her right hand she held the symbolical trump, and in her left a scroll on which were inscribed the names of the gallant chief's various battles, viz.: Corinth, Vicksburg, Mississippi River, and Chattanooga. On her head was a helmet, ornamented, in Indian fashion, with featlers radiating from it. In front of the eagle, its breast resting against it, was the emblematical shield of the United States. Just underneath this group, their stems crossing each other, were single sprigs of the pine and the palm, typical of the North and South. Above the figure of Fame, in a curved line, the motto, "Proclaim Liberty throughout the Land." The edge was surrounded, like the obverse, with a circle of stars of a style peculiar to the Byzantine period, and rarely seen except in illuminated manuscripts of that age. These stars were more in number than the existing States—of course, including those of the South—thereby suggesting further additions in the future to the Union.

Honors came from the Executive mansion, Halls of Congress, and, not the least, from the high places of religious sentiment and enterprise in the land. The Cincinnati Conference of the Methodist Church, at the anniversary of its Missionary Society, elected him an Honorary Member. Nearly the same time, he received a note from Morristown, N. J., informing him that he had been elected Life Director of that Society, by a contribution to it of one hundred and fifty dollars. The replies of the General are characteristically brief, and yet expressive :

CHATTANOOGA, December 7, 1863

Rev. F. MARLAY, Secretary Society:

DEAR SIR: Through you, permit me to express my thanks to the Society of which you are the honored Secretary, for the compliment they have seen fit to pay me by electing me one of its members.

I accept the election as a token of earnest support, by members of the Methodist Missionary Society of the Cincinnati Conference, to the cause of our country in this hour of trial.

I have the honor to be, very truly, your obedient servant,

U. S. GRANT, Major-General U. S. A.

HEADQUARTERS, MILITARY DIST. OF THE MISSISSIPPI,
CHATTANOOGA, TENN., December 16, 1863.

To the Rev. LEWIS R. DUNN, Pastor of M. E. Church, Morristown, N. J.

SIR: In reply to your letter of December 19th, to Major-General U. S. Grant, he directs me to express his gratitude to the Christian people of Morristown for their prayerful remembrance of him before the throne of the Most High, and to thank them, through you, for the honor conferred upon him. Be good enough to send his Certificate of Membership to Mrs. U. S. Grant, Louisville, Ky.

Very respectfully, your obedient servant,

J. H. WILSON, Brigadier-General.

A few days later, the Legislature of New York passed the following resolution, similar to one by the similar body in Ohio:

"*Resolved*, That the thanks of the people of this State be tendered to General Grant, and his army, for their glorious victories in the valley of the Mississippi, and the still more glorious victory at Mission Ridge and Lookout Mountain, and that a certified copy of this resolution be forwarded to General Grant."

From Colonel Colt's magnificent manufactory of pistols—since burned to the ground—was ordered, by friends, a pair of revolvers of the richest style. They were inlaid with gold, and the cartridge boxes and other appendages of solid silver.

Early in February, 1864, the debate arose on the lieutenant-generalship—an office held only, in our history, by Washington and General Scott. It gives the honored officer active control of the entire army of the United States, and makes him second in command only to the President, who stands at the head of the troops. Mr. Washburn, in his speech on the question, said:

"Look at what this man has done for his country, for humanity and civilization—this modest and unpretending general, whom gentlemen appear to be so much afraid of. He has fought more battles and won more victories than any man living; he has captured more prisoners and taken more guns than any general of modern times. To us in the great valley of the West, he has rendered a service in opening our great channel of communication to the ocean, so that the great 'Father of Waters' now goes 'unvexed to the sea,' which endears him to all our hearts. Sir, when his blue legions crowned the crest of Vicksburg, and the hosts of rebeldom laid their arms at the feet of this great conqueror, the rebel Confederacy was cut in twain, and the backbone of the Rebellion broken.

"At that moment was seen in General Grant that greatest of all gifts of a military man—the gift of deciding instantly amid the pressure of the greatest emergencies. I was with him when Porter reported his inability to reduce the batteries; and in an instant he made his new dispositions, and gave his orders. They were, to debark all his troops, and march them down three miles below Grand Gulf; 'and,' said he, 'after nightfall I will run every transport I have below their batteries, and not one shall be injured.' And, sure enough, when it became dark, Porter again attacked the batteries with his fleet, and, amid the din and clatter of the attack, the transports all safely passed Grand Gulf.

"And that which must ever be regarded by the historian as the most extraordinary feature of this campaign, is the astounding fact, that, when General Grant landed in the State of Mississippi, and made his campaign in the enemy's country, he had a smaller force than the enemy. There he was, in the enemy's country, cut off, in a measure, from his supplies, with a great river in his rear, and in one of the most defensible of countries, through which he had to pass. To his indomitable courage and energy, to his unparalleled celerity of movement, striking the enemy in detail, and beating him on every field, is the country indebted for those wonderful successes of that campaign, which have not only challenged the gratitude and admiration of our own countrymen, but the admiration of the best military men of all nations. My colleague [Mr. Farnsworth] has well said, that General Grant is no 'carpet knight.' If gentlemen could know him as I know him, and as his soldiers know him, they would not be so reluctant about conferring this honor. If they could have seen him as I saw him on that expedition; if they could have witnessed his terrible earnestness, his devotion to his duty, his care, his vigilance, and his unchallenged courage, I think their opposition to this bill would give way.

"But gentlemen say, Wait, and confer this rank when

the war is over. Sir, I want it conferred now, because it is my most solemn and earnest conviction that General Grant is the man upon whom we must depend to fight out this rebellion in the field, and bring this war to a speedy and triumphant close."

The bill passed; there being only nineteen votes against it.

General Grant improved the cessation of field operations, in planning greater things for the future; in issuing orders to protect deserters from the rebel ranks, cutting off army traders, giving security to the property of loyal citizens, and in providing for the comfort of the soldiers.

When he left Chattanooga on a tour of inspection to the outposts of his department, accompanied by General Sherman, there was much regret among the brave fellows, who had learned to love him. They had seen him walking with a cane about the streets, slowly, and bowed with suffering and care. They had also seen him "riding on the battle's edge," its guiding genius, all forgetful of his weakness. More and better still than this to them, the "boys" could say: "Then, Grant is so easy to approach." He invited their confidence, and never repelled them.

"General Grant will have no one between him and his army but his adjutant, Brigadier-General Rawlings, who is a hearty, jovial, plain-spoken, hard-working staff officer, just such as is indispensable to an energetic chief like 'Old Vicksburg.'"

The victor sailed in the steamer "Point Rock" for

Nashville, thence to Knoxville, Tenn. It was now midwinter, but the indomitable leader determined to see for himself the route for supplies through Cumberland Gap. Down the mountain sides drifts the snow. For thirty years no such winter storms had howled and beaten around the mountain spurs. See the yet physically unsound man, in the simplest attire, walking over the difficult paths, with his officers, all driving the horses before them. He would take nothing second hand, and therefore rarely made blunders.

At Knoxville the excited people called for a speech; but he refused. Then they shouted: "Up in a chair, that we may see him."

"Half pushed by General Leslie Coombs, General Grant mounted the improvised rostrum. General Coombs then introduced him in a neat little speech, in which he said that 'General Grant had told him in confidence—and he would not repeat it—that he never had made a speech, knew nothing about speech-making, and had no disposition to learn.' After satisfying the curiosity of the people, but without ever having opened his mouth, General Grant dismounted from his chair and retired, amid the cheers of the assemblage.

"His arrival at the Galt House was not generally known; and few, who had not looked at the books, suspected that the little man in faded blue overcoat, with heavy red whiskers, and keen, bright eyes, the hero of the two rebel Gibraltars of Vicksburg and Chattanooga, stood before them. This people have been so used to and surfeited with brilliantly dressed and cleanly shaven staff officers, with every pretence star or double star that has flitted across this horizon, that they never dreamed of recognizing in the blue-overcoated men who figured in the scene with him, the admirable and hard-working staff officers who have aided in no little degree to General Grant's success."

Having opened the railway from Nashville to Chattanooga, to the joy of the troops, whose fare had been meagre enough because the supplies could not be obtained, he returned to the latter place January 13th.

The last days of this month saw our hero on a new and touching journey. A child lay sick at St. Louis, and the warrior was lost in the *father*. His family attracted the interest of his manly heart, and his steps.

Arriving at the hotel, he entered his name "U. S. Grant, Chattanooga." The invalid was soon better; and he answered a long and highly flattering letter of invitation to a public dinner, in a few appropriate words. He said :

"GENTLEMEN : Your highly complimentary invitation 'to meet old acquaintances and make new ones,' at a dinner to be given by citizens of St. Louis, is just received.

"I will state that I have only visited St. Louis on this occasion to see a sick child. Finding, however, that he has passed the crisis of his disease, and is pronounced out of danger by his physicians, I accept the invitation."

After visiting the University, and other places of interest, Friday evening, January 29th, 1864, the banquet was spread, and he sat down to it amid the cheers of an enthusiastic multitude.

My reader, let us look in upon the festival, at six and a half o'clock in the evening.

The three long tables are richly laden with all the variety the markets afford. At the centre of one sits Judge Treat, the president. At his right, you notice a man of medium height, with sandy hair and whiskers, both short; his face without any striking expression, excepting the compressed lips—always a mark of decision and firmness; his blue eye mildly and modestly glancing along the lines of enthusiastic guests, and a flush of embarrassment on his bronzed cheeks: *that* is General Grant. On the left, below Generals Rosecrans and Osterhaus, sits a silver-haired, hale, and attractive old gentleman approaching seventy; this happy guest is Mr. Dent, the father-in-law of General Grant. Officers and "honorables" are scattered among the two hundred guests; while that parlor opening out of the hall is radiant with female beauty and enthusiasm, concentrating the light of beaming eyes upon the plainest, most quiet and silent partaker of the festivities. Over the splendid display of social enjoyment and patriotic hero-worship, national banners are hung in tasteful drapings against the elegant walls. The honor of "the distinguished guest, Major-General Grant," is proposed, and "Hail to the chief" breaks in stirring strains from the polished instruments of the band. Now its echoes die away, and General Grant, who could do no less, rises. "Hurrah! hurrah!" fairly rocks the spacious saloons, and each feature of every guest speaks the intense emotions of the citizens of the great Southwest.

Never did a man, great or small, make a briefer speech than did "Unconditional Surrender Grant," when a lull in the cheering made it possible. He said:

"GENTLEMEN: In response, it will be impossible for me to do more than to thank you."

In connection with the toast to St. Louis, was read a letter of the City Council, testifying "their great esteem, regard, and indebtedness due his modest, unswerving energies, swayed neither by the mighty successes which have crowned his genius and efforts in behalf of the Government, nor the machinations of politics—evidences of the true patriot and soldier."

A punning sentiment was also given:

"Major-General Grant—He is emphatically U. S. Grant, for he has given US and the U. S. an earnest of those victories which will finally rescue this nation from the Rebellion and its cause—American slavery."

When, a little later, the people gathered in the street, serenaded the honored chief, and called repeatedly for a speech, he only said, from the balcony:

"GENTLEMEN: I thank you for this honor. I cannot make a speech. It is something I have never done, and never intend to do, and I beg you will excuse me."

Then the "welkin rang again" with cheers; while the object of them, apparently unmoved, took a cigar, lit it, and seemed more interested in the flashing rockets rising gracefully and exploding overhead, than in the crowd below.

Again went up the startling cry to him, "Speech! speech!" "Puff—puff," answered the Havana. No speech followed the wreath of smoke.

Judge Lord, considerably excited, touched with his hand General Grant's shoulder, saying:

"Tell them you can fight for them, but can't talk to them. Do tell them that!"

Coolly replied General Grant: "I must get some one else to say that for me."

But, "Speech! speech!" continued to rend the night air, till he was compelled to add:

"GENTLEMEN: Making speeches is not my business. I never did it in my life, and never will. I thank you, however, for your attendance here."

The surging throng sent up once more the shouts of applause, as General Grant withdrew to seek repose.

Besieged by the ladies of the Sanitary Fair soon to be held in St. Louis, he consented to remain. A few days after, he wrote them a letter much longer than any speech he ever made, expressing grateful appreciation of the benevolent work in their hands, but declining attendance personally, on account of pressing official business.

Thus closed a spontaneous, hearty expression of admiration and respect for the victorious son of the West.

Politicians were getting more anxious about his politics, as he rose in the popular regard. A relative said to him, on one occasion:

"General, I have been inquired of, to-day, about your politics."

"Did you give the parties any information?" was the quiet query.

"I did not," was the answer, "for I don't know what your politics are."

Knocking the ashes from his cigar, the General continued:

"When I resided at the South, I had the opinions and prejudices of Southern people against the Republican party. I brought those opinions and prejudices with me when I came to Illinois. Had I taken active part in politics, I should have been with the party opposed to the Republicans. I watched Mr. Lincoln's course, and was satisfied with his patriotism. But these are not the times for parties. Indeed, in this crisis there can be but two parties—those for the country, those for its foes. I belong to the party of the Union. Those who are the most earnest in carrying on the war and putting down the Rebellion, have my support. As a soldier, I obey the laws and execute the orders of all my superiors. I expect every man under me to do the same."

CHAPTER XXI.

The Spring Campaign—General Grant at Washington—Scenes in the Hotel—The Levee—The Presentation of the Commission of Lieutenant-Generalship—General Grant's Reply—The summit of Honor—He visits the Potomac Army—The Fancy Soldier—The Crisis.

IT is now February. Thoughts of the spring campaign fill the minds of President, Cabinet, and generals. No brain is more busy than General Grant's. Expeditions are sent out to ascertain the position and force of the enemy; but no definite, decisive movement is arranged, when General Grant is called to Washington. Taking his little son with him, early in March he set out for the capital.

Soon after his arrival at "Willard's Hotel," he was recognized; and, as he took his seat at the table, the several hundred guests arose, and loudly, warmly cheered him. The ladies waved the white handkerchiefs. Hands were extended, and a scene similar to that at Memphis and St. Louis transpired. Such has always been the homage of the people to their successful leaders—to the men who wielded victoriously great armies, or power of any kind. And it is a signal fact, that, with all the horrors of war, military heroes awaken the loudest plaudits, and win the greenest laurels.

At evening occurred the President's *levee*. The word *levee* means *the time of rising*. It was applied to a morning assemblage waiting on a prince. In this country it is used to designate the gatherings at the Executive mansion at night. Whoever wishes to go, is welcome there. The President stands in one of the elegant rooms, to shake hands with the throng passing him, as they march through the halls and apartments. The band plays, and the whole scene is a brilliant exhibition of our republican country and government. At one moment, the Chief Magistrate takes the delicate palm of an aristocratic lady; the next, perhaps, that of a poor neighbor whom she never deigns to notice.

General Grant, on this occasion, fairly eclipsed the President. He was borne along by the human tide, and lifted to a sofa, where he could be seen by them all. Thus, as the moon controls the waters, did the embarrassed General, without effort to do so, attract and govern the strong currents of feeling, sweeping in whatever direction he moved.

Such display was not to his taste. When he left the gay scene, he said to a friend:

"I hope to get away from Washington soon, for I am tired of this 'show business.'"

The day following—March 9th—he was summoned to

a more quiet meeting at the "White House." President Lincoln was there, his Cabinet, General Halleck, and other officials.

General Grant came in, and the President, rising, held in his hand a document creating him Lieutenant-General, and said :

"GENERAL GRANT: The nation's approbation of what you have already done, and its reliance on you for what remains to do in the existing great struggle, is now presented with this commission, constituting you *Lieutenant-General of the Army of the United States.*

"With this high honor devolves on you a corresponding responsibility. As the country herein trusts you, so, under God, it will sustain you.

"I scarcely need add, that, with what I here speak for the country, goes my own hearty personal concurrence."

General Grant received the commission from the President, and made the following modest answer :

"MR. PRESIDENT: I accept this commission with gratitude for the high honor conferred. With the aid of the noble armies who have fought on so many battle fields for our common country, it will be my earnest endeavor not to disappoint your expectations. I feel the full weight of the responsibility now devolving on me. I know that, if it is properly met, it will be due to these armies; and, above all, to the favor of that Providence which leads both nations and men."

The hero-boy has now reached the summit of military honor and power in this country. Less than three years before, he was made colonel of an Illinois regiment; his command has rapidly widened, till it covers the entire field of conflict. And it is well for the youth of our land that the renown was earned by an honest, earnest, upright, and unassuming devotion to his country. He was no "favorite of fortune" beyond that of a favoring Providence blessing a faithful performance of duty.

A few days before—February 22d, the anniversary of Washington's birthday—near General Warren's headquarters, an immense ballroom, erected at no small expense, had been thronged with dancers. I am sure I shall not soon lose the impression the unfinished building made on my mind, when, a few weeks before, I saw it. A *ballroom* on a battle field! But the ladies from a distance were delighted with the soldierly frolic, and approached General Grant on the subject, expressing the hope there would be another in the Army of the Potomac.

He coolly listened, and then assured them that, if another were attempted, he should stop it by special order. It was no time or place for music and dancing, excepting the martial airs and firm step of the warriors, many of whom were soon to fall in the strife.

The same day the ball came off, the President had issued an order for preparations in every department of the army for an early advance. For this grand action General Grant was ready. It suited his ideas of carrying on the war. He soon revealed his purpose to move on Richmond. It was not the capital mainly he wanted, but to crush, or fatally cripple, the well-disciplined, formidable army under the splendid leadership of General Lee, was the serious work he resolved to undertake. Notwithstanding the repeated failures before, the losses and retreats of the noble Army of the Potomac, the victor of the West was willing to try his strength against the accomplished commander of "the flower of Southern chivalry" in the East. But one condition was demanded by him, and granted— the entire control of the army for one hundred days. That is, for that period the campaign should be his own; he would assume the high responsibility of its success, with no interference from Washington, however well or wisely intended. This arrangement gave unity of plan and harmony in action. He soon visited the able and gallant General Meade, the hero of Gettysburg, at his headquarters, and inspired new confidence and hope in officers and troops. Strict discipline was enforced. The speculators and hangers-on in the field began to disappear. *Fancy* soldiering was made contemptible, as it ought to be. A pleasant story related of General Grant illustrates his course in regard to it:

While he was looking over his new field, near Culpepper Court House, his headquarters, in a drizzling rain, attended only by his orderly, a carriage approached him. It was drawn by a pair of fine horses, and attendants escorted it. When near him, the driver reined up, the door was opened, and out sprang a dashing officer. He inquired if that dripping, unostentatious man was General Grant. The latter replied in the affirmative. The officer added, that he wished to see the General on business.

"Come, walk with me," answered General Grant.

There was no other way to do. Into the mud went the polished boots; and unprotected from the rain, the gay uniform was worn, till, like a peacock after a tempest has beaten down its plumage and besprinkled it with dirt, the officer stole back to the carriage with soaked, saturated apparel, and drooping feather. The parting counsel of his commander to set an example of a more becoming style of living, was thus enforced by a baptism into the new order of things he was not likely to forget.

The nation, inspirited by the grand successes of the Lieutenant-General, held breath in view of the great and decisive crisis reached. Three years of bloody war, which it was supposed *three months* would close, had left their mournful record. The strain to supply "the sinews of war" had been increasing every year. Men and money had been given lavishly. Great victories had been won. Still, the army which we first confronted on the "sacred soil of Virginia," and the capital of the growingly desperate "Confederacy," were apparently stronger than ever. It was no vainglorious nor ordinary act, to step forth into such a condition of affairs, the master-spirit of the vast and momentous issue.

But the time of renewed and costly activity has come.

God's finger has, it seems, designated the man for the hour and the work.

We find another good story, which sounds like the General. A visitor to the army called upon him, one morning, and found the General sitting in his tent, smoking, and talking to one of his staff officers. The stranger approached the chieftain, and inquired of him as follows:

"General, if you flank Lee, and get between him and Richmond, will you not uncover Washington, and leave it a prey to the enemy?"

General Grant, discharging a cloud of smoke from his mouth, indifferently replied: "Yes, I reckon so."

The stranger, encouraged by a reply, propounded question No. 2: "General, do you not think Lee can detach sufficient force from his army to reënforce Beauregard and overwhelm Butler?"

"Not a doubt of it," replied the General.

Becoming fortified by his success, the stranger propounded question No. 3, as follows: "General, is there not danger that General Johnston may come up and reënforce Lee, so that the latter will swing round and cut off your communications, and seize your supplies?"

"Very likely," was the cool reply of the General, and he knocked the ashes from the end of his cigar.

The stranger, horrified at the awful fate about to befall General Grant and his army, made his exit, and hastened to Washington to communicate the news.

A Galena neighbor, who visited New York about this time, seemed utterly confounded with the sudden growth of his neighbor, the tanner. He couldn't account for it, for he was not a marked man in his home, and nobody supposed him a great man. He seldom talked, asked no advice, gave none to any one, but always did what he agreed to, and at the time.

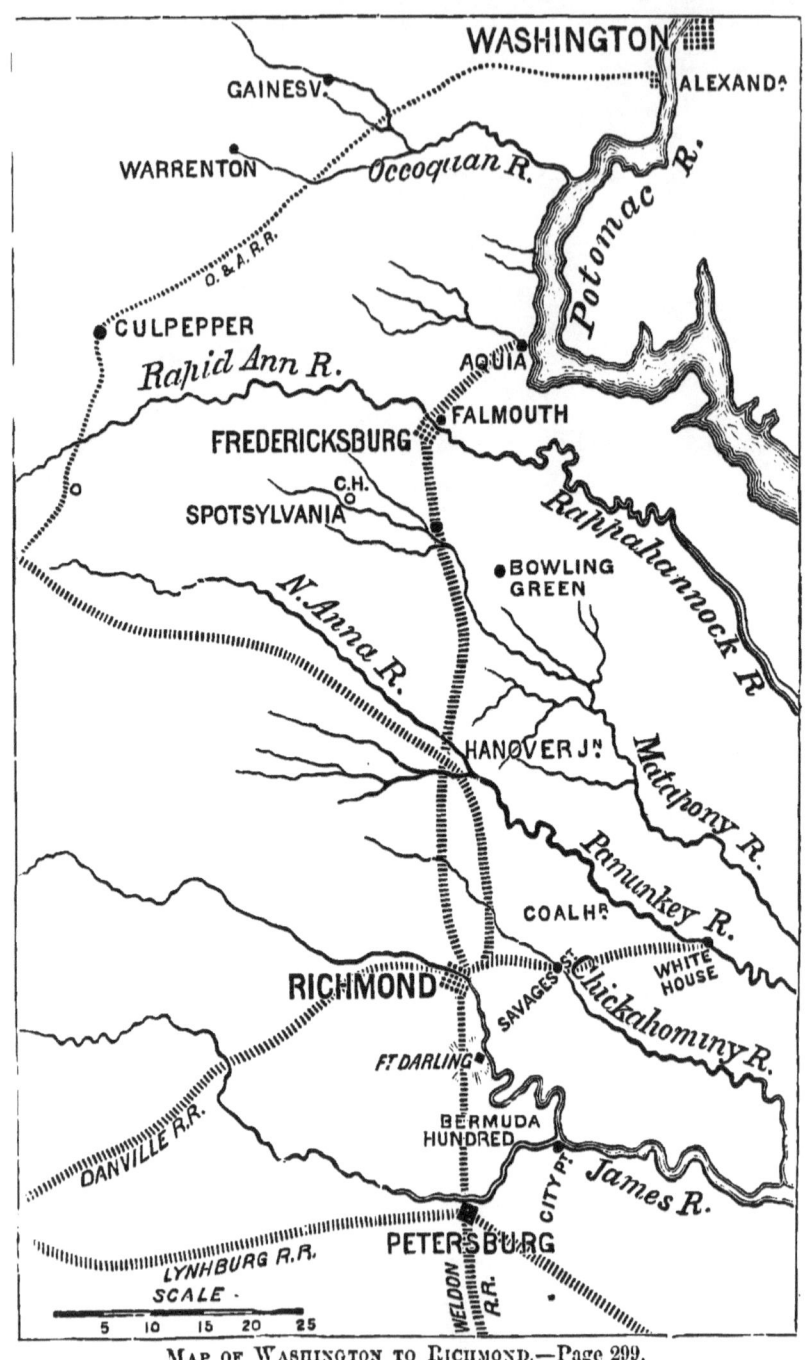

MAP OF WASHINGTON TO RICHMOND.—Page 299.

CHAPTER XXII.

The Advance—Richmond—The path to the Rebel Capital—The "Wilderness"—The opening of Battle—The Days of Carnage—The Death of Sedgwick—Of General Rice—General Grant's Strategy—General Butler—Sheridan—Sherman—The grand Flanking March to North Anna—Chickahominy—James River—What the Rebels think.

GLANCE over the prospective track of the grand army, reënforced by several corps from the Western field. A hundred and seventeen miles from Washington lies Richmond, the capital of the "Old Dominion," and of the new Confederacy of slaveholders. Its population, ordinarily, did not exceed sixty thousand. The situation is pleasant, on the James River. As a war centre, it has become a great hospital and Sodom. The sick and wounded in body, and the corrupt in heart, are the ruling majority in the high place of treason, second only to Charleston in this distinction. Under the accomplished engineer, Beauregard, who, since the first year of the conflict, has multiplied defences, exhausting his skill and resources, it presents circles and angles of fortifications, perhaps unsurpassed by any city in the world. Below Richmond is Fort Darling; and on the same side, to guard an approach, is Petersburg, also strongly fortified and garrisoned. Between the National capital and Richmond lies Lee's veteran army, waiting for Generals Grant and Meade to move. The former has the general direction of the grand campaign, while General Meade is commander of the Potomac Army. Culpepper Court House, ten miles north of the Rapidan, between it and the Rappahannock, and about seventy-five miles from Washington, is the headquarters of General Grant. Ten miles on the other, or south side of the river, at Orange Court House, is the Confederate host. The two vast armies are, therefore, twenty miles apart. Their pickets come to the banks of the stream, and sometimes joke across it, and pass papers and tobacco to each other.

General Lee has for several months been anticipating another attempt to cut a way to Richmond, whose Libby Prison—worse than death to our captive heroes—had awakened the strongest indignation at the North.

May 3d, 1864, the order is issued by General Grant to march. The myriad tents disappear in the night like frostwork before the sun; the knapsacks are packed, the rations secured, and the arms seized. Horses stand by thousands in the darkness, prancing for the fray, or harnessed to the heavy wagons.

The next day dawns upon a sadly magnificent array. Freedom's battalions, two hundred thousand strong, covering miles of scarred and desolate ground, are pressing forward to the bugle's blast, into the bloodiest contest of the war.

General Grant's military capacity and strategy appear in this greatest campaign of the age. It extends over a vast field of movements, from Mobile, which he intends General Banks to look after, to Richmond, including Sigel's and Sherman's expeditions. Failure anywhere must affect, more or less, the success of the whole. Trusting his generals and Providence in the stupendous plan, the time for action has come.

He does not hurl his battalions against those of Lee, protected by the strongest intrenchments, but moves round to the eastward. His plan is, to get past the right wing, and between the enemy and Richmond. Then, Lee must come out of his war den, and try to stop his adversary, or fall back on his capital.

Right across General Grant's path lies the "Wilderness." This is a tract of land a dozen miles or more long, and about five in width, in Spottsylvania County, Va. It runs nearly along the bank of the Rapidan. Oh, what a place for an advancing army! See the tangled scrub-oak bushes, deep, ragged gullies, ravines with steep sides, and, scattered on every hand, patches of swamp. No roads invite the steps of the martial host. A few narrow paths, called roads, cross the sterile woods; and an occasional clearing, with a tavern and a few rough habitations, relieve the desolation. On the skirt of this forest is Chancellorsville, where Hooker fought his disastrous battle.

May 4th, the Union columns cross the Rapidan with pontoon bridges. The youthful Warren leads the Fifth Corps, the lion-hearted Sedgwick the Sixth—both crossing at the Germania Ford. The Second Corps, under the gallant, splendid Hancock, makes the passage at Ely's Ford; the Ninth, under the noble Burnside, remaining as reserve on the north bank of the river. Wednesday night the troops sleep on the quiet shore toward the foe.

May 5th pours its light over the uprisen, marshalled ranks of the Union. Forward into the "Wilderness" they are led by their bravely confident chief.

May 5th, just as they are turning to sweep along and around the enemy's lines, aids from General Sheridan's horsemen, who had been pushing southeastward, come back with despatches. General Meade, a tall, thin man, a little stooping in the shoulders, breaks the seal, and reads. The next moment he turns to General Grant, remarking:

"They say that Lee intends to fight us here."

"Very well," coolly replies General Grant.

Then they step aside, and talk. The Lieutenant-General smokes, and whittles in musing mood while he converses. He now changes the direction of the *cutting* from him, and with quicker motion. He has matured his plan. Action will swiftly follow.

Like the collision of rushing engines will be the shock. Lee is determined to crush through, and break the equally resolute ranks of our unshrinking "boys." Again and again Ewell's and Hills's corps dash upon the columns of

ONWARD TO RICHMOND.- Page 302.

Warren and Hancock, concentrating on the centre, which is now the weakest point.

You know, to cut the army in two, anywhere, makes sad work—often ending in shameful defeat.

The sun sets in smoke, and its beams are reflected from pools of blood. The battle thunders on! The darkness creeps over the forest plain of death, and still, like angry phantoms, the warriors move to and fro. Hancock seems inspired with the awful enthusiasm of unearthly power, and mows down the foe, while his own ranks sink before the scythe of the destroying angel.

After a brief respite, on Friday, the 6th, Longstreet, having come to the aid of Lee, the same desperate game to break our lines is tried with renewed energy. Back and forth in the dense thickets, among ravines and in swamps, the swaying masses of armed men rush, shout, and fight. Many, alas! fall, to rise no more.

As night comes down, away upon the extreme right swing with terrible force the columns of the enemy. Like chaff before the tempest are hurried Seymour's and Shaler's brigades, and the generals taken prisoners. A little farther success, and the wedge is fairly driven through, cutting off the army from its supplies on the other side of the river, with which they were connected. It is well for us the darkness wraps the scene, and hides the greatness of the disaster to us from our foe.

Lee retires. Even General Grant—who, as one that fought then said to me, "*wouldn't* know when he was whipped "—breathed more freely. When told, you recollect, that our lines were giving way, and the men flying, he calmly replied, "I don't believe it!" This confidence in his cause and his men has ever been a source of great strength, reassuring his troops, if apparently overborne for a moment.

The third sanguinary day has closed, and no eye can see the end of the fearful struggle—whether to the Republic it shall be victory or defeat. So far it resembles, more than any part of the civil war, the fighting of the Indian tribes which once roamed unmolested there; madly closing in the combat, here and there, sending the missiles of death from thicket and behind trees, and piling the dead in every possible shape, sometimes in rows like the cradled grain.

I know a young soldier, who, in the darkness, was seized by a stout rebel, and his gun taken. He was a prisoner, and already seemed to see Libby Prison, when a shell came between him and his captor, laying him on the ground, while the "Union boy" made quick step toward our troops.

Saturday, the 9th, has dawned, and again there is the rattle of musketry and the roar of artillery from our troops. But no reply is made by the foe. He was falling back deliberately, ready to pause and grapple again with Grant whenever necessary.

On, the long lines of hostile troops, with all the dread machinery of war, move toward Spottsylvania Court

House, both anxious to secure the position. The Confederate troops first reach it, and make a stand, protected by fortifications.

The Sabbath brings only a partial cessation of the conflict. Over the vast field, at intervals, is the deadly meeting of the combatants. There are tents of prayer, and Christian words are spoken to listening ears. Men are thoughtful out of the bloody strife, at such a time of constant peril.

Monday finds the rations low. The caravan of supply wagons arrives at the moment of need. The hours fly, and an onset is made upon divisions of our forces, with no result besides death. Look off to that conspicuous spot in the line of conflict. There, among the artillery of his corps, stands the cool, intrepid, accomplished Sedgwick. He is directing the gun mounting. The bullets of the sharpshooters whistle around him. The artillerymen involuntarily dodge. General Sedgwick smiles, and says: "Don't duck, men. They couldn't hit an elephant that distance." The words scarcely escape his lips, before a well-directed ball pierces his head. He falls into the arms of his adjutant; the bloody foam wreathes those lips; a smile follows, and all is over. One of the bravest and noblest of the army, after three years of successful service, has yielded up his manly life.

Now, with advancing night, several divisions of Grant's troops cross the branches of the Mattapony, and the struggle is renewed. Every step of progress is stained with blood. Like a half moon, see the white tents and the battle array of the rebel ranks around Spottsylvania Court House. Over against them, with broader curve, lies the Union army. Both are waiting, and preparing, too, for another general clash of arms.

Tuesday opens a terrific contest. The contending columns meet, and shout in the delirium of wildest war. Men and horses go down in ridges. The wounded are borne on every side from their ghastly bed.

General Grant sends his first despatch to Washington. It reveals at once his consciousness of fatal havoc, and yet unyielding courage and hope:

"We have now ended the sixth day of very heavy fighting. The result, to this time, is very much in our favor. Our losses have been heavy, as well as those of the enemy. I think the loss of the enemy must be greater. We have taken over five thousand prisoners in battle, while he has taken from us but few stragglers. *I propose to fight it out on this line, if it takes all summer.*"

Among the killed was the Christian hero, Brigadier-General Rice. He sent to his wife, before he fell, the patriotic words, "I have been true to my country." And, after the fatal wound was received, he desired to have his face turned to the enemy while life ebbed away. But what is better, when asked, by a delegate of the Christian Commission, how Christ, the Captain of our salvation, appeared then—"Oh, Jesus is very near!"

Such are the battle scenes of this tremendous war.

The next message of General Grant, dated the 12th, was as follows:

"The eighth day of battle closes, leaving between three and four thousand prisoners in our hands for the day's work, including two general officers, and over thirty pieces of artillery. The enemy are obstinate, and seem to have found the last ditch. We have lost no organization, not even a company, while we have destroyed and captured one division, one brigade, and one regiment entire of the enemy."

A storm now sets in. The rain drenches the wounded, and compels a respite to the sanguinary and protracted contest. Richmond is yet fifty miles distant.

The awful loss of troops, and the strength of Lee's army, leaves but small prospect of getting to Richmond on this side. General Grant, with a comprehensive and daring strategy, is determined to swing his whole army around on the south side of the capital, and make James River the base of supplies. In that part of the grand field of operations, there had been bold movements. General Butler had sent an expedition up York River to West Point, to make the enemy believe he was going across the peninsula to Richmond. The map will make this plain. Butler, however, dropped down again, and up James River, landing at City Point, fifteen miles from Richmond. His object was, to cut the railroads, and prevent Beauregard from helping Lee, and take Fort Darling also. But the enemy came out of the fort, and beat him back again to his intrenchments.

General Sheridan, meanwhile, with the cavalry, had swept around the right flank of the enemy, and, crossing the North Anna River, went into the outer defences of Richmond, destroying railways, &c. General Sigel, in Western Virginia, had been defeated. The able and gallant Sherman was advancing from Chattanooga against General Joe Johnston, toward Atlanta.

At daybreak on Thursday, the Second Corps are moving, not, indeed, in the grand flanking curves from point to point around the enemy, but with fixed bayonets down upon his works. Still and resolute, through the forest they go, over ravines. Now, nearing the rebel lines, with a wild shout and run, they are upon the foe. In five minutes, Major-General Johnson, Brigadier-General Stewart, and three thousand prisoners are captured, with eighteen cannon and twenty-two standards. All day the swaying lines fill the heavens with the rattle of musketry. Lee at length is compelled to fall back again toward Richmond. General Grant hurries after to the North Anna River. Combats follow.

Sunday comes once more, and the cavalry ride upon each other's front with desperate heroism. The sacred hours pass over the wild and terrific conflict. At Coal Harbor is a deadly meeting by our Sixth and Eighteenth Corps, with Longstreet and Breckinridge.

Several of the army surgeons were afraid to come to

the field of duty to the wounded. General Grant heard of it. To use the words of a wounded soldier, who admires the Chief:

"Old Grant sent word, that, if they did not report at once, he would have them arrested. And they were on hand in a hurry, I tell you."

The army is now on the Chickahominy, ten miles from Richmond. General Grant sees that his only hopeful movement is the daring push across to the James River, on the south of Richmond.

Some of the greatest work of war is the least noisy. The grandest results in nature and in life are secured in silence. General Grant's safe removal, almost in the enemy's face, of his vast army, across rivers, and an enemy's country, to James River, was one of these rare and splendid achievements. It astonished General Lee, and came near costing him the great stronghold lying between the new base and Richmond. But reënforcements reaching the city, our troops were forced to yield in the struggle for the prize.

A gentleman of high editorial position called on Mrs. Grant, when she was in New York—"a plain, sensible, quiet woman, who takes the world as a matter of course." He alluded to the high position of her husband, and appealed to her ambition to see how much vanity lurked under the unassuming surface. She listened; then, with no perceptible change in manner, replied:

"Mr. Grant" (so she always calls him) "had succeeded below, and, when he was called to this position, he thought it was *his duty* to try what he could do."

"We then expressed a hope that he would succeed, and that he would take Richmond.

"'Well, I don't know. I think he may. Mr. Grant always was a very obstinate man.'"

It is further said that the following conversation occurred:

"If General Grant succeeds, he may want to be President."

"But he is Lieutenant-General."

"Yes; but when a man can be elected President, it must be a strong temptation."

"I don't know. There have never been but two lieutenant-generals of the United States—General Washington and General Scott. There have been a number of Presidents; for instance, such men as Frank Pierce and James Buchanan!"

No, it would hardly be ambition which would lead a lieutenant-general to wish to be President.

Truly, "Mrs. Grant, you are a sensible woman, and Mr. Grant is an 'obstinate man.'"

Here is a touching story about a soldier boy found on the Virginia battle field:

"He lay severely wounded. He had fallen the day before, and had remained unmolested within the rebel lines. They had not removed him, and he was almost alone with the dead when I rode up. The poor fellow was crawling about gathering violets. Faint with the loss of blood, unable to stand, he could not resist the tempting flowers, and had already made a beautiful bouquet. Having caused a stretcher to be sent for, I saw him taken up tenderly and borne away, wearing a brave, sweet, touching smile."

Brave boy! Lover of nature, too. Between the hours of musing over visions of home, he plucked the modest, fragrant blossoms from the hostile soil stained with his own blood, and made a bouquet; such an one, perhaps, as a sister, whose eye of love is blue as the violet, or the sky above his bed of earth, had arranged for him in the yard or garden which was pressed by his tender feet.

An incident related of General Grant, while besieging Richmond, is certainly characteristic. He was walking around the docks at City Point, when he stopped to see some negroes roll a barrel of bacon on board of a boat. The negroes were unable to move it, when a crusty lieutenant, who stood near, dressed in his fine blue clothes, shouted: "You niggers, push harder, or go get another man to help you!" Without saying a word, General Grant pulled up his sleeves, and helped the negroes roll the barrel on the boat; then he drew his silk handkerchief from his pocket, and wiped his hands, and moved quickly away. You may imagine how that *second* lieutenant felt, when he was told that the stevedore was no less than the Commander-in-Chief of the United States armies. The General was dressed in coarse homespun, with his hat drawn over his eyes, and one of the most unpretending-looking personages one could imagine.

As if to cheer us in the quiet of our armies at home, June 14th, 1864, occurred a naval engagement, which sent a thrill of wild exultation over the land. The famous and victorious pirate "Alabama," which had been ordered by the French Government to leave the port of Cherbourg, met the United States steamer "Kearsarge," about seven miles from the harbor. The noble vessel was named after a lordly summit among the White Hills—one of the *body guards* of Mount Washington. It is pronounced there as if it were spelled *Keer-sarge*.

The combat was terrible. Balls and shell flew until the thunder of the ordnance shook the ships, and the smoke of the conflict hung darkly over the sea.

After an hour of lightning and hail from ship toward ship, the dark, bloody leviathan of treason began to reel before the blows of the "Kearsarge."

A few moments later, and the waters closed over the pipes from which the breath of the monster's fiery heart had escaped.

The captain—the guilty Semmes—and his crew were saved from a watery grave by the English yacht "Deerhound," commanded by Captain Lancaster. Another evidence of English sympathy with the rebels, which has been mainly felt by the aristocratic classes there, and elsewhere in Europe.

Week after week passes with no important change in

the aspect of the impending struggle. A rebel view of this suspense will interest you. The *Constitutionalist*, of Augusta, Ga., frankly writes of General Grant's strong position, in an amusing way. It is an estimate of General Grant and prophecy of the result of his siege :

"The second danger is of the siege of Richmond. Some of our cotemporaries, and the most of our correspondents, laugh at this; and yet Grant has it in his power to besiege the capital, or force an attack on himself, or force an evacuation of Richmond. Not that he has his choice of these three things, but can force that choice upon us. In Grant's moving upon the south of Richmond, and threatening James River near the city, General Lee has choice of two evils. If he keeps ahead of Grant, and holds the Petersburg line inviolate, that flanker necessarily gets between him and Richmond, and walks into the city at his leisure. If Lee keeps between Richmond and Grant, the latter, of course, gets between him and the Southern States' communication, and cuts off the only source of supplies now left, as the valley of Virginia is in the hands of the enemy. If Lee wants to save Petersburg and Richmond both, he will have to attack Grant in one of his craw-fish movements, and will have to attack the position and intrenchments which the grand spade-and-pick army never exists an hour without.

"In our judgment, the plan of the campaign is at last developed. Western Virginia, the valley and its resources, is, by the movement on Staunton and Lexington, to be rendered unavailable for provisions. Grant is to throw his army into fortifications across the railroads from Richmond south, and so cut off our army supplies. Thus the starvation of a siege will be as effectually secured, as if an army could be found large enough to surround the legions of Lee, as Grant did General Pemberton; provided, of course, that the Danville Road shares the fate that the Weldon Road probably will. If General Lee chooses to stop the game by a fight, he has to put his finger on the slippery Grant, and stop his flea-like flankings; and, having found him and stopped him for a fight, will have to charge the hills Grant will occupy and the trenches Grant will dig. We lose Richmond if we hold the Weldon and Danville Railroads; we lose the railroads if we save Richmond; or we attack Grant in his mighty trenches if we try to save both. It is true that General Beauregard could still keep south of Grant, and prevent raids into South Carolina, but could not keep him from stopping the roads south, unless he has enough men to attack Grant in reverse, and place him between two fires. We hope Grant thinks he has. This is a game with no possible hindrance, perfectly plain to even such unmilitary comprehension as our own, and we respectfully submit that there is no fun in it."

To General Lee it was plain enough that something must be done to frighten, and, if possible, weaken General Grant.

A force of twenty thousand, or more, was sent toward

Washington to threaten it. General Grant informed the War Department, it is affirmed, that troops had gone into the Shenandoah Valley, under General Early. Whether this be true or not, we were unprepared for the raid. Onward the rebels swept toward Maryland, burning and pillaging as they went. This was early in July.

On the 3d, the President issued a call for three months' troops to repel invasion.

On the 8th, the rebels attacked Hagerstown, Md., and sacked the city.

On Saturday, the 9th, a battle took place between the forces under General Wallace and the rebels at Monocacy, commencing at nine o'clock in the morning, and continuing until five in the afternoon, when, overpowered by the superior numbers of the enemy, our forces were obliged to retreat in disorder, with severe loss. The fighting on both sides was desperate, much of it being hand to hand in an open field. The enemy advanced in three lines of battle, covered by their batteries, but were for hours kept at bay by our artillery. Our loss was probably one thousand in killed, wounded, and missing. General Tyler was captured, and several officers were killed. No guns or flags were lost. The strength of the enemy was some fifteen thousand, while that of General Wallace was only five thousand.

The intelligence of General Wallace's defeat occasioned the greatest excitement in Baltimore. The bells were rung, the citizens mustered for service in the defences, and every possible precaution taken for the protection of the city. At midnight on Saturday, Governor Bradford and Mayor Chadman issued a proclamation, declaring the city to be in imminent danger, and calling on every loyal citizen to prepare at once to avert the peril. During the whole of Sunday the city was under arms, and the work of erecting additional defences went vigorously forward. At one time a report reached the city that the rebels were but seven miles distant; but later accounts do not seem to confirm the statement. A proclamation was also issued on Sunday by Governor Curtin, of Pennsylvania, appealing to the people to come forward for the defence of their State.

On Sunday morning, a force of four or five hundred rebel cavalry dashed into Rockville, Md., sixteen miles from Washington, and, after plundering the stores and stealing all the cattle and horses they could find, left in the direction of Frederick; but, before they left, they sent to the Virginia side all their plunder. Persons who came from the upper fords reported that the rebels were conveying large numbers of cattle, horses, hogs, and sheep, stolen from the farmers along the river, across into Virginia, and that every ford was held by small rebel cavalry forces and sections of batteries. They carried off several thousand head of cattle, and from eight hundred to one thousand valuable horses.

The Northern Central Railroad—running from Baltimore to Harrisburg—was cut near Cockeysville, twelve miles north of Baltimore.

On Monday the rebels made rapid progress toward Baltimore and Washington, being within seven miles of the former city, and six miles of the capital. They cut the telegraph communication between Philadelphia and Washington, at Magnolia stat.on, where they intercepted a large number of despatches, among them one from Secretary Stanton to General Cadwallader. Here they captured a passenger train from Baltimore, and robbed the conductor and passengers. General Franklin and another general, name not known, were taken prisoners, together with all the soldiers in the train. The station was then burned down.

The telegraph wires that cross the Susquehanna River at Port Deposit, Md., were also cut. Communication between Harrisburg and Washington was destroyed. It is understood that at least eight bridges were destroyed on the Northern Central Railroad, between Moncton and Cockeysville.

The enemy, on their approach to Baltimore, burned the residence of Governor Bradford, three miles from Baltimore, completely to the ground, stating that they had orders to do so from General Bradley Johnson, in retaliation for the destruction of Governor Letcher's house in Virgina by General Hunter.

Telegraphic communication between Washington and Baltimore was cut, leaving the States north in awful suspense respecting the result of the bold invasion.

On the evening of July 12th, a charge was made upon

the enemy in front of Fort Stevens, and our line was advanced beyond the house of F. P. Blair, Sr., thus driving the rebels from their position. In this charge we had three hundred killed and wounded, and the rebel loss exceeded ours.

The arrival of (General Burnside's) veteran troops at the capital was timely; and the enemy retired across the Potomac during the night.

The only success of their invasion of Maryland was the acquisition of supplies of all kinds, which they took off in large quantities. While in the possession of Frederick, the rebels levied a fine of two hundred thousand dollars, which was paid to save the city from destruction. They swept the surrounding country of horses, cattle, sheep, and hogs, driving large herds toward the Potomac.

General Grant held on to his position, "unterrified and unseduced" from his grapple with the foe. The President remarked, one day, during the attack upon Fort Stevens, to a friend who was somewhat alarmed at the tardiness of General Grant in forwarding troops to the capital:

"General Grant has as much at stake as any man in the country in the management of the campaign. He knows very well, if the rebels should capture Washington, that not even the fall of Richmond would compensate for the national calamity and disgrace. He would lose his reputation as a general. He knows it; and 1 shall trust him."

You will be amused with the manner in which General Franklin, who was captured in the cars near Baltimore, escaped. He was taken to a rebel encampment, and put in charge of guards. He lay down, tired with the hard and rapid travel, and feigned sleep. He listened, and took a peep, now and then, to see if *they* slept.

One after another, supposing he was in deep slumber, they gave themselves up to repose.

General Franklin then stole cautiously away, making noise enough to be sure the guards were not *deceiving him*, till he was over a fence not far off; then, he assures us—and we may believe him—he *ran* for his life and liberty. In the daytime he hid in the bushes, and could hear the enemy near.

At length hunger and fatigue compelled him to show himself. Soon he saw a man in the woods carrying hay. He walked up boldly, and asked him what he was doing with that hay.

"Oh, I am trying to conceal it from the rebs, who are leaving nothing they can take away."

This answer gave him hope. Making himself known, he was cared for by the Union farmer, and escorted into Baltimore.

July 26th, General Grant made another movement of his army, which displayed the strategy of the great *flanker*. A part of his host were ordered to the north of

James River; pressing thus upon the enemy gradually, but surely, with his anaconda-like coil.

The next day, a line of outer intrenchments, and four cannon, were captured.

The 29th was a dark day for Chambersburg, Pa. A cavalry raid of the rebels laid the beautiful town in ruins. Many of the people who, just before, were in the midst of plenty, had not left a meal or a change of apparel.

July 30th, early in the morning, there was an unusual stir at the headquarters of General Burnside. Unknown to all excepting the engineers and a few officers, General Grant had been successfully mining one of the enemy's main batteries. It was in General Burnside's front. At half past three, the fuse was fired. But it burned slowly in the long, damp entrance. Soon after four o'clock a loud report startled the enemy. Another moment, and the air was filled with earth and timbers, and men. Successive shocks, like those of an earthquake, shook the land. Then opened a terrific cannonading. A hundred guns thundered along the lines, and toward the breach, forty rods in width, rushed our heroic "boys." The Ninth Army Corps made the charge.

You will notice that, wherever the fault of a failure to capture the strongly fortified place may be laid by different writers, it is evident, from their losses in that breach of death, the "slaughter pen" it became, *the negroes were no cowards.*

At five and a half o'clock the charge was made, and

the fort, with part of the line each side, was carried in the most brilliant style.

The Second Division, which was in the centre, advanced and carried the second line, a short distance beyond the fort, and there rested, holding their ground with the utmost determination.

It was at this time the colored division, under command of Brigadier-General White, was pushed forward and ordered to charge and carry the crest of the hill, which would have decided the contest.

The troops advanced in good order as far as the first line, when they received a galling fire which checked them; and, although quite a number kept on advancing, the greater portion seemed to become utterly demoralized, part of them taking refuge in the fort, and the balance running to the rear as fast as possible.

They were rallied and again pushed forward, but without success, the greater part of their officers being killed or wounded.

During this time they seemed to be without any one to manage them, and finally they fell back to the rear, out of the range of the volleys of canister and musketry that were plowing through their ranks.

Their losses are very heavy, particularly in officers, as will be seen by the following figures:

TWENTY-THIRD U. S. COLORED.—Fifteen officers killed and wounded; four hundred men, including the missing.

TWENTY-EIGHTH U. S. COLORED.—Eleven officers, and

about one hundred and fifty men killed, wounded, and missing.

TWENTY-SEVENTH U. S. COLORED.—Six officers and about one hundred and fifty men killed, wounded, and missing.

TWENTY-NINTH U. S. COLORED.—Eight officers, and about two hundred and seventy-five men killed, wounded, and missing.

THIRTY-FIRST U. S. COLORED.—Seven officers, and about two hundred men killed, wounded, and missing.

FORTY-THIRD U. S. COLORED.—Six officers, and a large number of men killed, wounded, and missing.

THIRTY-NINTH U. S. COLORED.—Several officers, and about two hundred and fifty men killed, wounded, and missing.

The loss in the Second Division of the Ninth Corps, General Ledlie commanding, was very severe, and is estimated at from one thousand to twelve hundred, while many make the figure larger.

Among the missing, was the name of General Bartlett. He succeeded in reaching the fort with his command, but, having accidentally broken his cork leg, he was unable to get off the field. He, however, held possession of the ground for several hours, and only surrendered when all hope of escape was gone. Some two hundred men, both black and white, were with him at the time, a few of whom managed to get back to our lines amid a storm of bullets.

The high hope of a great victory which was kindled with the first telegram that flew over the North, was quenched by the next tidings of a repulse.

The rebels had, to some extent, prepared for such an attack. From their works they were able to pour an enfilading fire upon our troops, before which they could not stand.

The golden opportunity that followed the terror of the explosion which laid open the works to our army, was lost. *Why*, is not yet known. But no one suspects General Grant of any blame in this great failure, which prolonged the dreadful war.

Oh, my reader, what a sad sight, after the fruitless slaughter, was presented! Wrote one who was there:

"After the battle of Saturday, General Burnside sent a flag of truce to the enemy with a view to recovering the wounded and burying the dead lying between the lines, and whom it had been impossible to approach owing to the continued firing. After some little signalling, the rebels acknowledged and came forward to meet it. The communication was received and forwarded by them to the authority with whom the power rests. Our officers sought permission to succor the wounded while waiting, and it was granted. Accordingly, the poor fellows, who had been lying on the ground nearly twenty-four hours—a portion of the time in the blazing sun—were given each a drink of brandy and water. The crater of the mined fort was plainly in view; but the rebels refused to allow any approach to it, and the wounded near it were supplied by the rebels themselves. The agonies of the wounded were awful. Unable to move, not daring to make even a signal, lest it would attract an unfriendly bullet, they had lain twenty-four hours without food or water. The two past days had been the warmest, as yet, of this summer, and they were subjected to the merciless rays of a scorching sun. The dead presented a sickening sight. There were both white men and negroes; but now it is difficult to distinguish them apart. Their bodies were swollen and bloated, and their faces blackened by the sun.

"Although the rebels refused a flag of truce on Sunday, to enable us to bury the dead and remove the wounded, from five to nine o'clock on Monday was granted for this purpose. Very few were found alive— not more than a dozen; and but a few of these are expected to recover. The ground in front of the crater was thickly covered with the dead bodies, the colored soldiers being in the proportion of four to one of the white, the colored troops having experienced the heaviest fire at this place. The work of burying the dead was finished about half past ten, and firing was commenced by the rebels ten minutes afterward."

And yet the "boys" uncomplainingly bore it all.

The well men had often hard fare, but were even cheerful and happy. Hear what another says:

"One afternoon, about five o'clock, I found myself seated beside an artilleryman belonging, I believe, to a battery from Rhode Island, who had a long and wearisome march from the front, on one of the hottest of hot days, and afterward had been obliged, with his companions, to strain every muscle to get the guns, caissons, horses, &c., on board the boat in the shortest possible period. The time had come to eat his dinner, which was his supper as well—hard tack, cold coffee, raw pork. Without a single word of complaint, he soaked his hard tack in the coffee, drank up the coffee to the last drop, and picked his pork clean to the rind. 'There,' said he, 'as he finished a meal more frugal than Cato's, and wiped and shut up his knife, 'I have often sat down to a fuller meal with a less appetite, and enjoyed a good supper far less than I have done this!' Fortunately, it was in my power to add something to his pork and hard tack. But oh, what a lesson to the lazy, luxurious, discontented grumblers at home! If they cannot feel the moral of such a story, they are beyond hope."

A week later, General Lee tried the underground work, to see what he could accomplish. General Grant was too wide awake for the wary chieftain. He had sunk a shaft, which our men thought was a *well* for General Warren's corps, which went right into one of the enemy's passages.

This discovery, with a poor engineering which failed to estimate rightly the distance, spoiled the affair.

The cannon suddenly opened—the dust and smoke rose *outside* of our works, and *that was all!*

On the 4th day of August, the following noble order was read to the army:

HEADQUARTERS, ARMY OF THE POTOMAC, August 3, 1864.

To-morrow, the 4th inst., having been set apart by the President of the United States as a day of National fasting, humiliation, and prayer, the Major-General Commanding calls upon his fellow soldiers to observe the day with the solemnities due to the occasion; and he recommends that, wherever practicable, religious services be held in the several camps by the chaplains serving with the army; and he commands that all operations that are not matters of military necessity, be suspended during the day.

By command of   Major-General MEADE.

The very next day, Admiral Farragut, or "Old Salamander," entered Mobile Bay in triumph, having conquered the rebel fleet and silenced the forts at its entrance, after a brilliant engagement.

The 18th brought a decisive change in the movements of the Potomac Army. General Grant threw his troops across the Weldon Railroad—a very important path of supplies toward the South. The enemy fought hard to dislodge our brave fellows, but General Warren beat him back in gallant style.

The chivalrous Hancock, the incarnation of heroism, who was helping destroy the railroad, on the 25th had a terrible battle; but—as he always does—held his ground, and slaughtered the rebels.

During these scenes on the Potomac, the equally brave

LIFE OF GENERAL GRANT. 327

and brilliant Sherman was moving upon and around Atlanta, Ga., another stronghold and very important centre of their army munitions and supplies.

A copy of the record on a sword presented General Grant by the citizens of Jo Daviess County, Ill., gives a "bird's-eye" view of his military career:

Palo Alto, May 8th, 1846.
Resaca de la Palma, May 9th, 1846.
Monterey, September 19th, 20th, 21st, 1846.
Vera Cruz, April 18th, 1847.
Molino del Rey, September 8th, 1847.
City of Mexico, September 14th, 1847.
Belmont, November 7th, 1861.
Fort Henry, February 6th and 7th, 1862.
Fort Donelson, February 13th, 14th, 15th, and 16th, 1862.
Shiloh, April 6th and 7th, 1862.
Corinth siege, April 22d to May 20th, 1862.
Iuka, September 19th, 1862.
Hatchie, October 5th, 1862.
Tallahatchie, December 1st, 1862.
Port Gibson, May 12th, 1863.
Black River Bridge, May 7th, 1863.
Champion Hill, May 14th, 1863.
Black River, May 17th, 1863.
Vicksburg, July 4th, 1863.
Chattanooga, November 23d, 24th, 25th, and 26th, 1863.

Battles for Richmond, May 5th, 6th, 7th, 8th, 9th, 10th, 11th, and 12th, 1864.

General Grant has in one respect been only the boy grown; that is, in his unpretending, uniform, taciturn, yet pleasant bearing. He can converse finely, but is reserved. Seldom laughing or weeping, his aspect is not repulsive, but quite otherwise, wearing ever an expression of a smile ready to spread over his plain, marked features. He uses no "vain repetitions," content to say a thing *once* distinctly.

Brave, true in his motives, speech, and policy, firm and resolute in action, possessing great fortitude, he fears no emergency necessary to success, calmly relying upon Providence for results beyond his control; the crowning glory of character in his splendid career, is the absence, in a word or act, of a *selfish ambition*—that "mountain devil," in the language of Willis, which has often made the gifted general a trifler with life and liberty.

The brave and able General McPherson, killed near Atlanta, Ga., in General Sherman's army, and who knew well both him and the Lieutenant-General, just before his death used the following language to a friend. It is just, and especially interesting because from the gifted and departed McPherson:

"Lieutenant-General U. S. Grant I regard as one of the most remarkable men of our country. Without aspiring to be a genius, or possessing those characteristics which impress one forcibly at first sight, his sterling good sense, calm judgment, and persistency of purpose, more than compensate for those dashing, brilliant qualities which are apt to captivate at a first glance. To know and appreciate General Grant fully, one ought to be a member of his military family.

"Though possessing a remarkable reticence as far as military operations are concerned, he is frank and affable, converses well, and has a peculiarly retentive memory. When not oppressed with the cares of his position, he is very fond of talking, telling anecdotes, &c.

"His purity of character is unimpeachable, and his patriotism of the most exalted kind. He is generous to a fault, humane and true, and a steadfast friend to those whom he deems worthy of his confidence, and can always be relied upon in case of emergency.

"Major-General W. T. Sherman is what might be called a brilliant man, possessing a broad and comprehensive intellect. A rapid thinker and ready writer, fertile in his resources and untiring in his exertions, he possesses those characteristics which forcibly impress you at first sight. He has mingled largely with the world, and has tried various professions; has read and reflected much, and, having a remarkably retentive memory, is well informed on most subjects which come within the scope of human thought. He is of a much more excitable temperament than General Grant, and more apt to be swayed by impulses, though his judgment is not so cool and reliable. In other words, though a more brilliant man, he does not possess that sterling *good common sense* which preëminently distinguishes General Grant.

"He is, however, a most brave and generous man, thoroughly in earnest, and ready to sacrifice everything for the good of his country. He is a true friend, and thoroughly unselfish; and there are no better men—or few, at least—than General Sherman."

How touchingly beautiful, in connection with this high testimony, is the correspondence which follows:

"CLYDE, OHIO, August 3, 1864.

"TO GENERAL GRANT:

"DEAR SIR: I hope you will pardon me for troubling you with the perusal of these few lines from the trembling hand of the aged grandma of our beloved General James B. McPherson, who fell in battle. When it was announced at his funeral, from the public print, that when General Grant heard of his death, he went into his tent and wept like a child, my heart went out in thanks to you for the interest you manifested in him while he was with you. I have watched his progress from infancy up. In childhood he was obedient and kind; in manhood, interesting, noble, and persevering, looking to the wants of others. Since he entered the war, others can appreciate his worth more than I can. When it was announced to us by telegraph that our loved one had fallen, our hearts were almost rent asunder; but when we heard the Commander-in-Chief could weep with us too, we felt, sir, that you have been as a father to him, and this whole nation is mourning his early death. I wish to inform you that his remains were conducted by a kind guard to the very parlor where he spent a cheerful evening in 1861 with his widowed mother, two brothers, an only sister, and his aged grandmother, who is now trying to write. In the morning he took his leave at six o'clock, little dreaming he should fall by a ball from the enemy. His funeral services were attended in his mother's orchard, where his youthful feet had often pressed the soil to gather the falling fruit; and his remains are resting in the silent grave scarce half a mile from the place of his birth. His grave is on an eminence but a few rods from where the funeral services were attended, and near the grave of his father.

"The grave, no doubt, will be marked, so that passers by will often stop and drop a tear over the dear departed. And now, dear friend, a few lines from you would be gratefully received by the afflicted friends. I pray that the God of battles may be with you, and go forth with your arms till rebellion shall cease, the Union be restored, and the old flag wave over our entire land.

"With much respect, I remain your friend,

"LYDIA SLOCUM,
"Aged 87 years and 4 months."

GENERAL GRANT'S REPLY.

"HEADQUARTERS ARMIES OF THE U. S.,
CITY POINT, VA., Aug. 10, 1864.

"MRS. LYDIA SLOCUM:

"MY DEAR MADAM: Your very welcome letter of the 3d instant has reached me. I am glad to know that the relatives of the lamented Major-General McPherson are aware of the more than friendship existing between him and myself. A nation grieves at the loss of one so dear to our nation's cause. It is a selfish grief, because the nation had more to expect from him than from almost any one living. I join in this selfish grief, and add the grief of personal love for the departed. He formed, for some time, one of my military family. I knew him well; to know him was to love. It may be some consolation to you, his aged grandmother, to know that every officer and every soldier who served under your grandson felt the highest reverence for his patriotism, his zeal, his great, almost unequalled ability, his amiability, and all the manly virtues that can adorn a commander. Your bereavement is great, but cannot exceed mine.

"Yours truly, U. S. GRANT."

We pause here, with the tidings most cheering from every part of the vast theatre of war.

The exact posture of affairs is clearly and well expressed in the subjoined letter to the Hon. Mr. Washburn, of Illinois:

"Headquarters Armies of the U S.,
City Point, Va., Aug. 16, 1864.

"Dear Sir: I state to all citizens who visit me, that all we want now to insure an early restoration of the Union, is a determined unity of sentiment North.

"The rebels have now in their ranks their last man. The little boys and old men are guarding prisoners, guarding railroad bridges, and forming a good part of their garrisons or intrenched positions. A man lost by them cannot be replaced. They have robbed the cradle and the grave equally to get their present force. Besides what they lose in frequent skirmishes and battles, they are now losing from desertions and other causes at least one regiment per day. With this drain upon them, the end is not far distant, if we will only be true to ourselves. Their only hope now is in a divided North. This might give them reënforcements from Tennessee, Kentucky, Maryland, and Missouri, while it would weaken us. With the draft quietly enforced, the enemy would become despondent, and would make but little resistance.

"I have no doubt but the enemy are exceedingly anxious to hold out until after the Presidential election. They have many hopes from its effects. They hope a counter revolution. They hope the election of the peace candidate. In fact, like Micawber, they hope for something to 'turn up.' Our peace friends, if they expect peace from separation, are much mistaken. It would be but the beginning of war, with thousands of Northern men joining the South because of our disgrace in allowing separation. To have 'peace on any terms,' the South would demand the restoration of their slaves already freed; they would demand indemnity for losses sustained, and they would demand a treaty which would make the North slave hunters for the South; they would demand pay for or the restoration of every slave escaped to the North.   Yours truly,

"U. S. GRANT."

I am sure you will read with pleasure the evidence of the entire confidence existing between the President and General Grant, the additional letters will afford. They have quietly gone from the White House of the capital, and the headquarters of the Lieutenant-General, since the latter took the Virginia field:

"LIEUTENANT-GENERAL GRANT:

"Not expecting to see you before the spring campaign opens, I wish to express, in this way, my entire satisfaction with what you have done up to this time, so far as I understand it. The particulars of your plans I neither know nor seek to know. You are vigilant and self-reliant; and, pleased with this, I wish not to obtrude any restraints or constraints upon you. While I am very anxious that any great disaster or capture of our men in great numbers shall be avoided, I know that these points are less likely to escape your attention than they would be mine. If there be anything wanting which is within my power to give, do not fail to let me know it. And now, with a brave army and a just cause, may God sustain you.

"Yours, very truly, A. LINCOLN."

"THE PRESIDENT:

"Your very kind letter of yesterday is just received. The confidence you express for the future, and satisfaction for the past, in my military administration, is acknowledged with pride. It shall be my earnest endeavor that you and the country shall not be disappointed. From my first entrance into the volunteer service of the country to the present day, I have never had cause of complaint, have never expressed or implied a complaint against the Administration, or the Secretary of War, for throwing any embarrassment in the way of my vigorously prosecuting what appeared to be my duty. Indeed, since the promotion which placed me in command of all the armies, and in view of the great responsibility and importance of success, I have been astonished at the readiness with which everything asked for has been yielded, without even an explanation being asked.

"Should my success be less than I desire and expect, the least I can say is, the fault is not with you.

"Very truly, your obedient servant,
"U. S. GRANT, Lieut.-General."

Over the immense territory of States which belonged

to the rebels, are scattered forts behind whose walls the enemy have fought us on *their own soil*. And it must not be forgotten, that the South had made, for years, preparation for separation, while we had made none.

Notwithstanding our disadvantages, with treachery at the North and in the army, New Orleans, Forts Henry and Donelson, Corinth, Vicksburg, Port Hudson, Mobile, and Atlanta have fallen; and, as this page is written, the glad tidings of Early's defeat by the gallant Sheridan is flying over the land.

With union and energy, the crest of the hydra Secession will soon be trodden into the dust by the march of Freedom's host, to be lifted no more to the wrath of God and the scorn of the world.

It is not partial, extravagant praise, to say that Lieutenant-General Grant belongs with singular preëminence to the class of military chieftains of Revolutionary memory, at whose head stands the immortal WASHINGTON.

DEFINITION OF MILITARY WORDS.

OFFICERS.

LIEUTENANT-GENERAL.—The highest officer in the United States Army. He has command of the entire force. The President is, by his office, Commander-in-Chief; but the Lieutenant-General is at the head of troops in actual service.

MAJOR-GENERAL.—The next in rank to the former. The commander of a division, or several regiments.

BRIGADIER-GENERAL.—The commander of a brigade, which is an indefinite number of regiments. It is the grade below that of the Major General.

COLONEL.—The commander of a regiment, which comprises, when full, about a thousand men.

LIEUTENANT-COLONEL.—Next to the former, commanding the regiment in his absence.

MAJOR.—The officer next in command.

CAPTAIN.—The officer over a company, the number of which is usually one hundred men.

LIEUTENANT.—The officer next to the captain, and who fills his place in his absence.

AIDE-DE-CAMP.—A general officer's assistant officer.

ADJUTANT.—An officer who aids a superior officer in receiving and giving orders. He places guards, distributes ammunition, &c.

ENSIGN.—The standard bearer; the lowest commissioned officer in the infantry. CORNET is the same in cavalry.

SERGEANT.—A non-commissioned officer, whose duty it is to instruct the soldiers in the ranks, form the ranks, &c.

CORPORAL.—The lowest officer in the infantry, having charge of a few men, relieving sentinels, &c.

ADMIRAL.—The highest officer in the navy. The commander of a fleet. Vice-Admiral commands the second squadron, and is next in rank. Rear-Admiral has command of the third squadron, or last division of the fleet.

COMMODORE.—The commander of a squadron, or portion of a fleet, on some special service. A naval captain, who has two or three ships under his command, is sometimes honored with the title.

OTHER TERMS.

ABATIS.—Piles of trees, or branches sharpened, and laid with their points outward, in front of fortifications, to prevent the approach of the enemy.

AMBULANCE.—A carriage for the sick and wounded.

ARTILLERY.—The soldiers who manage the heavy guns.

BATTALION.—A body of troops less than a regiment.

BATTERY.—Six cannon make a full battery. The term is applied to a smaller number.

BOMB.—A large cast-iron shell, charged with powder, and thrown from a mortar, which ignites a fuse, exploding the bomb where it falls.

BOMBARDMENT.—An attack with bombs; throwing them into a fort, town, or ship.

CAISSON.—An artillery carriage containing ammunition.

CANISTER.—A tin cylinder filled with shot, made to explode when fired from the gun.

CASEMATE.—A vault or covered chamber, of masonry, to protect from shot and shell.

CAVALRY.—Horsemen in the army.

COLUMBIAD.—A large cannon; sometimes ten feet in length.

COLUMN.—A body of troops drawn up in deep files with narrow front.

COUNTERSIGN.—A word given by the highest officer to guards and sentinels, and all who have occasion to pass them; so that no improper person may get by them.

ENFILADE.—To sweep the inside of a fortification, or line of troops, with shot.

FILE.—A row of soldiers one behind the other.

FLANK.—The side of a body of men, or place. To outflank right or left, is to get round on that side.

FUSE.—A tube filled with combustible material, or a cord of similar character, set on fire when the shell is fired; its length in proportion to the distance the shell is designed to go.

GRAPE.—The proper term is *grapeshot:* several small balls in a canvas bag, fitted to the bore of a gun, bursting, and scattering the balls upon the discharge.

GUNBOAT.—A vessel fitted up with cannon. An *ironclad*, is one covered or plated with iron.

INFANTRY.—Soldiers on foot.

MORTAR.—A short, wide-mouthed gun, used for throwing shells.

PICKETS.—The soldiers in front of the army, to watch and report movements of the enemy.

Pontoon.—A boat bridge for crossing streams, which can be carried in wagons.

Reveille.—The first drumbeat in the morning.

Rifle Pits.—Excavations in the ground to protect the riflemen.

Staff.—The group of officers which attend a general.

Tattoo.—The drumbeat at night, giving notice of time for soldiers to retire.

www.ingramcontent.com/pod-product-compliance
Lightning Source LLC
Chambersburg PA
CBHW031425230426
43668CB00007B/434